DOES
MONEY
MATTER?

DOES MONEY MATTER?

The Effect of School Resources on
Student Achievement
and Adult Success

Gary Burtless
Editor

BROOKINGS INSTITUTION PRESS
Washington, D.C.

Copyright © 1996
THE BROOKINGS INSTITUTION
1775 Massachusetts Avenue, N.W., Washington, D.C. 20036

Library of Congress Cataloging-in-Publication data

Does money matter?: the effect of school resources on student achievement and
adult success / Gary Burtless, editor.
    p.   cm.
Includes bibliographical references and index.
ISBN 0-8157-1274-X (cloth: alk. paper). ISBN 0-8157-1275-8 (pbk.: alk. paper)
1. Education—Economic aspects—United States.   2. Education—United
States—Finance.   3. Academic achievement—United States.   4. Wages—
Effect of education on—United States.   I. Burtless, Gary T., 1950–
LC66.D64   1996
338.4'737'0973—dc20   96-10085
                                                                          CIP

9 8 7 6 5 4 3 2 1

The paper used in this publication meets the minimum
requirements of the American National Standard for
Information Sciences—Permanence of Paper for Printed
Library Materials, ANSI Z39-48-1984.

Typeset in Sabon

Composition by Harlowe Typography Inc.
Cottage City, Maryland

Printed by R. R. Donnelley and Sons Co.
Harrisonburg, Virginia

₿ THE BROOKINGS INSTITUTION

The Brookings Institution is an independent organization devoted to nonpartisan research, education, and publication in economics, government, foreign policy, and the social sciences generally. Its principal purposes are to aid in the development of sound public policies and to promote public understanding of issues of national importance.

The Institution was founded on December 8, 1927, to merge the activities of the Institute for Government Research, founded in 1916, the Institute of Economics, founded in 1922, and the Robert Brookings Graduate School of Economics and Government, founded in 1924.

The Board of Trustees is responsible for the general administration of the Institution, while the immediate direction of the policies, program, and staff is vested in the President, assisted by an advisory committee of the officers and staff. The by-laws of the Institution state: "It is the function of the Trustees to make possible the conduct of scientific research, and publication, under the most favorable conditions, and to safeguard the independence of the research staff in the pursuit of their studies and in the publication of the results of such studies. It is not a part of their function to determine, control, or influence the conduct of particular investigations or the conclusions reached."

The President bears final responsibility for the decision to publish a manuscript as a Brookings book. In reaching his judgment on the competence, accuracy, and objectivity of each study, the President is advised by the director of the appropriate research program and weighs the views of a panel of expert outside readers who report to him in confidence on the quality of the work. Publication of a work signifies that it is deemed a competent treatment worthy of public consideration but does not imply endorsement of conclusions or recommendations.

The Institution maintains its position of neutrality on issues of public policy in order to safeguard the intellectual freedom of the staff. Hence interpretations or conclusions in Brookings publications should be understood to be solely those of the authors and should not be attributed to the Institution, to its trustees, officers, or other staff members, or to the organizations that support its research.

Foreword

MOST AMERICANS think their schools are in trouble. Many believe students graduate from U.S. schools knowing less than school graduates knew thirty years ago. Standardized test results certainly suggest that American youngsters learn less about science and mathematics than their counterparts in other industrialized countries. Disadvantaged children in the nation's poorest schools attain abysmal scores on standardized tests of reading and math achievement.

Performance at this low level has been a spur for educational reform. In 1983 the National Commission on Excellence in Education called attention to the poor performance of American schools in its widely cited report *A Nation at Risk*. Since that year a variety of comprehensive reforms have been undertaken, primarily at the state level and often in states with historically underperforming school systems.

In some cases, reform has been combined with higher levels of spending. Policymakers and ordinary voters often assume American schools can only be improved if there is a substantial increase in spending on K–12 education. The question posed in this book is simple: Will additional money actually improve performance in the nation's schools? Does the level of resources affect the achievement or future success of youngsters who graduate from school?

Most economists take it for granted that money matters. When public schools are financed by larger budgets, taxpayers must pay heavier taxes. If the spending has no other effect, it surely reduces the net incomes of taxpayers. Social scientists are less certain that additional spending provides benefits to the youngsters who are supposed to gain from it. Are children better off as a result of larger school budgets?

Researchers hold disparate views on the effectiveness of greater school spending. The disagreement arises in part because analysts focus on different measures of school performance. But disagreement is also apparent among researchers who study the same measures of school performance. Some conclude that greater spending is useful in promoting student progress; others find little evidence that extra spending produces meaningful improvement in student performance.

The studies in this book focus on two measures of educational effectiveness. Half examine the effect of school spending on the academic achievement of youngsters while they are in school. The other half assess the impact of school resources on students' earnings after their formal schooling has ended. Most economists who have studied the effects of school spending on achievement do not find a consistent or powerful effect. Surprisingly, researchers who study the impact of school spending on the earnings of school graduates usually find that extra resources have a beneficial effect. Is it possible that school resources have *no* effect on youngsters' achievement while they are in school but nonetheless have a measurable and beneficial effect on students' earnings after they leave school? This startling inconsistency is a major focus of the book.

The authors propose a variety of kinds of evidence and methods to determine whether additional school spending yields improvements in student outcomes. About half the papers find no persuasive evidence that increased spending produces consistent gains, either in student achievement or in adult earnings. Two sets of authors conclude that added spending improves student outcomes. The last two groups of authors argue that variations in the level of school spending are less important than effective organization of school resources in determining whether spending differences have important consequences for student outcomes. The full range of scientific disagreement on the influence of school spending is thus reflected in the essays in this book.

Early versions of the papers were presented in a conference on school spending that was held at the Brookings Institution on June 3, 1994. The conference was sponsored by the newly formed Brown Center on Education Policy of the Brookings Institution. Major financial support for the Brown Center was provided by the Andrew W. Mellon Foundation and the Brown Foundation, Inc.

Tanjam Jacobson, Caroline Lalire, and Deborah M. Styles edited the manuscript; Gerard E. Trimarco checked it for factual accuracy; Ellen Garshick proofread the pages; and Mary Mortenson prepared the index. Kathleen M. Bucholz and Anita G. Whitlock provided administrative assistance for the conference and for the Brown Center.

The views expressed in this book are those of the individual authors and should not be attributed to the trustees, officers, or staff members of the Brookings Institution.

MICHAEL H. ARMACOST
President

May 1996, Washington, D.C.

Contents

Tables

Figures

Contributors

JULIAN R. BETTS
Department of Economics,
  University of California at
  San Diego

GARY BURTLESS
The Brookings Institution

DAVID CARD
Department of Economics,
  Princeton University

ROB GREENWALD
Department of Education,
  University of Chicago

ERIC A. HANUSHEK
Department of Economics,
  University of Rochester

JAMES HECKMAN
Department of Economics,
  University of Chicago, and
  American Bar Foundation

LARRY V. HEDGES
Department of Education,
  University of Chicago

ALAN B. KRUEGER
Department of Economics,
  Princeton University

ANNE LAYNE-FARRAR
Graduate Student, Department of
  Economics, University of
  Chicago

FRANK LEVY
Department of Urban Studies and
  Planning, Massachusetts
  Institute of Technology

RICHARD J. MURNANE
School of Education,
  Harvard University

PETRA TODD
Department of Economics,
  University of Pennsylvania

CHAPTER 1

Introduction and Summary

Gary Burtless

EDUCATION IS one of the most important—and most costly—activities of American government. Public spending on education totaled $375 billion in 1993, more than 6 percent of national income. Educational expenditures were substantially larger than spending on national defense or social security. In the 1993–94 school year, approximately 43 million youngsters were enrolled in public elementary and secondary schools, and these schools consumed over $250 billion out of public budgets. Federal, state, and local spending on public schools amounted to slightly more than $5,300 per pupil enrolled.[1]

Expenditures on schooling are not equal all across the country, however. In the 1993–94 school year, Alaska and New Jersey spent more than $8,500 per youngster enrolled in public elementary and secondary schools; Oklahoma spent only about $3,900 per student; Mississippi, less than $3,300 (table 1-1). Some of the disparity occurred because of differences in the cost of purchasing educational inputs in different parts of the country. It is more expensive to hire teachers in Alaska or New Jersey than it is to hire people with identical qualifications in Oklahoma or Mississippi. Even when state spending levels are adjusted to reflect differences in regional wages and prices, however, the gap in spending remains large. After price adjustment, New Jersey spent about twice as much as Utah to educate a public school student.[2]

Spending differences across school districts within the same state are also sizable. Assume that the average spending on public schooling in a state is $4,600 per student enrolled (the actual national average in 1989–

1. Wright (1994, p. 241).
2. Barro (1994, p. 6). The adjusted spending data refer to the 1989–90 school year.

Table 1-1. *Spending per Pupil and Average Teacher Salaries in Selected States, 1993–94*

State	Spending per pupil	Spending rank	Average teacher salary
New Jersey	$9,429	1	$45,308
Alaska	8,501	2	46,581
Connecticut	7,991	3	49,500
New York	7,642	4	46,800
Pennsylvania	7,583	5	43,688
Oklahoma	3,889	46	26,749
Alabama	3,815	47	28,705
Arkansas	3,657	48	27,873
Mississippi	3,297	49	25,235
Utah	3,203	50	28,056

Source: Wright (1994), p. 241.

90). If disparities in spending across local school districts in the state are typical of those in the "average" state, about one student in eight would live in a district where spending is $3,800 or less, and one student in eight would live in a district where per pupil spending is $5,400 or more. The gap in spending between school districts in the top and bottom quartiles of the spending distribution would amount to $1,500 per pupil.[3] Some states, such as California, do not allow large spending disparities across school districts. But in other states, including Massachusetts and Missouri, the disparities are significantly wider than the national norm.

When spending disparities across students are this large, it is natural to ask whether the disparities make any difference. Do richly endowed schools produce better results than schools that spend little per student served? This question has practical significance for legislators, who must decide how to divide public spending between education and other functions of government and how to allocate public resources across school district boundaries. It may also have legal implications in states where disparities in spending are particularly glaring. About 46 percent of public spending on elementary and secondary schools is derived from local government budgets. One reason for large disparities in spending across school districts is that districts differ widely in the size of their local tax base. Is it equitable to depend on local sources of funding when the size of the tax base differs sharply from one district to the next? Some state courts might reason that the present financing arrangements are illegal if it could be demonstrated that schools with high spending per pupil

3. Barro (1994, pp. 6–7).

achieve better results than poorly endowed schools. In fact, courts in several states, including California, reached this conclusion years ago.

Do added school resources actually improve student outcomes? If so, is the effect large enough to have a practical significance? The chapters in this book offer conflicting evidence on these questions, with the authors focusing on two important but distinct strands of the research evidence.

The first and better-known type of research asks whether additional school resources can improve the educational achievement of students *while they are in school*. Though this may appear to be a simple question, researchers have yet to agree on a clear answer. One of the most authoritative surveys of the subject was prepared by Eric Hanushek, writing in the September 1986 issue of the *Journal of Economic Literature*. His conclusion was simple and emphatic: "There appears to be no strong or systematic relationship between school expenditures and student performance."[4] Though Hanushek's conclusion has been challenged by many educators, it probably remains the prevailing view among economists who study school resources and educational achievement. It is hotly disputed by researchers from other academic disciplines.

A second line of research considers the effects of school resources on student performance *in the labor market*. Do graduates of resource-rich schools perform better in the labor market than graduates who attended poorly endowed schools? Most of the early economic research on this question concluded that resource-rich schools produce graduates who earn more than graduates from schools where resource endowments are meager. That is, if two adult workers attended school for the same number of years, the worker educated in a richly endowed school is likely to earn more than the worker educated in a less well endowed school. The best known contribution to this literature, by David Card and Alan Krueger, was published comparatively recently, but the conclusion of that study extended and confirmed older findings dating back almost thirty years.[5] Some researchers now dispute Card and Krueger's conclusion, as will become plain in this book.

The literature on school resources and adult earnings is smaller and less widely known than the research on the effect of school resources on academic achievement. Its findings have broader significance, however. The effect of school resources on students' earnings has important im-

4. Hanushek (1986, p. 1162).
5. Card and Krueger (1992a).

plications for the level and distribution of economic well-being in the United States. These implications are much more important than any possible effect of school resources on academic test scores, unless test scores can be shown to influence student success in the labor market.

The best-known findings from the two strands of research seem totally at odds. One set of findings implies that added school resources produce little if any measurable improvement in students' academic performance while youngsters are in school. The other suggests that extra school resources can improve the job market success of school graduates. Researchers and policymakers are left with a puzzle. How is it that principals and teachers can effectively use school resources to produce improvements in labor market outcomes but fail to use extra resources to produce gains in academic achievement? This peculiar combination of findings is so perplexing that many observers believe at least one of the conclusions must be wrong. If both findings are correct, researchers should be scrambling to understand why.

School Differences and Student Achievement

Since publication of *A Nation at Risk* in 1983, Americans have become increasingly concerned about the quality of their schools.[6] Most observers now agree that American schools are in trouble. U.S. high school and junior high school students stand near the back of the class in international rankings of student knowledge and achievement. The mediocre quality of American education is apparent in a wide variety of measures of student performance. None of these measures is perfect, but many of them point in a similar direction. Americans leave school knowing less than U.S. graduates in the 1950s and 1960s and far less than typical secondary school graduates in other industrialized nations.

The publication of *A Nation at Risk* did not occur in a vacuum. Education scholars had long known that by many measures U.S. academic performance was slipping. Standardized test scores offer one barometer of the basic health of schools. The sharp drop-off in average scholastic aptitude test (SAT) scores between 1963 and 1979 gave palpable evidence of a decline in American educational standards. The trend in average scores on tests administered to younger students was not very encouraging either. During the late 1960s and early 1970s, the direction

6. National Commission on Excellence in Education (1983).

of these test scores was negative.[7] The decline in standardized test scores was larger and longer lasting in high school and in tests of higher-order reasoning ability. Performance on the tests has subsequently improved, though, ironically, this improvement began before the appearance of *A Nation at Risk*. At the high school level, average performance continues to lag behind levels achieved during the 1960s, though it has improved modestly since the late 1970s.

The perception that average school quality is slipping, as well as a suspicion that the slippage may help explain disappointing trends in the labor market, has pushed educators and policymakers to ask whether changes in school funding or educational policy can lead to improvements in average achievement. In fact, as just noted, some of the discouraging achievement trends of the late 1960s and early 1970s were reversed by the middle of the 1980s. Average American students nonetheless continue to rank low in international comparisons of student knowledge and ability. In science and mathematics, junior and senior high school students fare dismally on international tests of achievement. American seventeen-year-olds score below average students in nearly all other countries surveyed in tests of mathematics competence.[8]

It is not obvious how academic performance can be improved, however. The simplest suggestion—to spend more money—is attractive to educators but is not guaranteed to yield improved results. If better performance automatically followed higher spending, the deterioration in average achievement would not have occurred in the first place. Calculations by John Chubb and Eric Hanushek show that average U.S. spending per student, controlling for the effect of inflation, rose more than 60 percent between 1966 and 1980, when most of the test score decline occurred.[9] Since 1960 spending per pupil has tripled, the student-teacher ratio has fallen more than a third, and teachers' salaries have risen by half (figures 1-1 and 1-2). Increased spending on school inputs has not led to notable gains in school performance.[10]

It is possible, of course, that past increases in school inputs have helped offset what would have been even larger achievement declines in the absence of higher spending. As Larry Hedges and Rob Greenwald argue in this volume, some background characteristics of U.S. school children

---

7. For an excellent survey, see Koretz (1986).
8. Baily, Burtless, and Litan (1993, pp. 112–13).
9. Chubb and Hanushek (1990, pp. 217–19).
10. Hanushek and Rivkin (1994, table 1).

Figure 1-1. *Spending per Pupil, U.S. Average, 1940–90*

Constant 1990 dollars

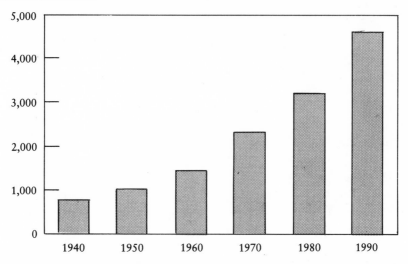

Source: Hanushek and Rivkin (1994, table 1).

have deteriorated over time. In comparison with the 1960s, for example, a larger percentage of children are now raised in single-parent households. A higher proportion of youngsters are members of historically disadvantaged minority groups. Hence aggregate time series trends cannot be used by themselves to draw strong conclusions about the effects of investing in more expensive school inputs.

Evidence from cross-sectional studies is not much more encouraging than the time-series evidence, however. One of the earliest and certainly one of the best-known of the cross-sectional studies was *Equality of Educational Opportunity*, prepared by James Coleman and his collaborators.[11] This 1966 report was based on a massive data collection effort, which assembled information on detailed characteristics of schools, teachers, and students that might help explain individual student performance. An original goal of the study was to document differences in the quality of education available to different groups in the population, especially to racial minorities. (The report was prepared in response to a mandate of the 1964 Civil Rights Act.) The authors went beyond this mission and attempted to show how differences in student performance

11. Coleman and others (1966).

Figure 1-2. *Pupil/Teacher Ratio, U.S. Average, 1940–90*

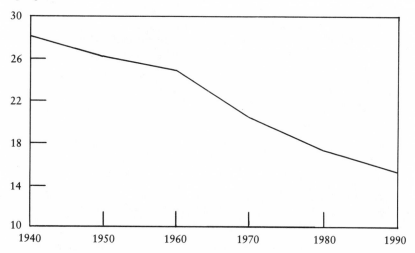

Source: Hanushek and Rivkin (1994, table 1).

on standardized tests were connected to differences in socioeconomic background characteristics and school resources.

The Coleman report reached two surprising conclusions. First, the difference in educational resources available to black and white youngsters was far smaller than commonly supposed. Some differences actually favored black children, who, for example, were more likely to attend schools that offered free text books, a full-time librarian, and free school lunches. Second, the report found very small and uncertain effects of school resources on student achievement. The authors concluded that the measurable characteristics of teachers and schools played only a negligible role in determining student outcomes. Socioeconomic background variables and the composition of the student body played a more important role in determining student success, but most of the variation in student test scores could not be explained by factors measured in the study.

Equality of Educational Opportunity sparked fierce controversy among educators and social scientists. It would be hard to show, however, that the two main conclusions of the study have been convincingly overturned. As Henry Aaron has noted, the strong criticism leveled at Coleman's report had the ironical effect of drawing attention to its conclusions and increasing their influence.[12] It is difficult to believe that a 740-page government report would have earned such a durable place in policymaking or social science without the publicity generated by its passionate critics.

Since 1966 a large number of data sets have been analyzed in an attempt to measure the impact of school inputs and teacher, student, and parental characteristics on measures of student performance, including scores on standardized tests, school attendance, promotion, and graduation. Most analysts agree with Coleman and his collaborators in finding that family background is very important in explaining achievement differences.[13] Children of well-to-do, well-educated parents tend to outperform children who are raised in less-favored families. Also like Coleman, many analysts do not find a consistent or powerful effect of school inputs on student performance.

In surveys of this literature, Eric Hanushek concludes that there is no evidence that teacher-pupil ratios, teacher education, teacher experience, teacher pay, or spending per pupil has a consistent or significant effect in improving school achievement.[14] Hanushek's table 2-3 in this volume shows a tabulation of the findings from 377 statistical relationships, estimated in many separate studies, of the effect of school inputs on student performance. The first column shows the total number of equations that examine a particular input. The second shows the number of estimates implying that the input has the expected positive influence on performance and that the effect is statistically significant. The third shows the number implying that the effect has an unexpected *negative* effect on performance and that the effect is statistically significant. The remaining columns show the number of estimates that imply a factor is insignificant in explaining performance. Where possible, Hanushek has indicated the number of estimates showing that the factor has a positive or negative effect, even when that effect has been determined to be statistically insignificant. (Not all analysts report the sign of a statistically insignificant coefficient.)

In a paper written with John Chubb, Hanushek states his interpretation of these findings even more bluntly. "For more than two decades . . . researchers have tried to identify inputs that are reliably associated

12. Aaron (1978, pp. 75–81).
13. For a detailed survey, see Hanushek (1986).
14. Hanushek (1986); Hanushek (1989).

with student achievement. The bottom line is, they have not found any. Researchers have found no systematic relationship between student achievement and the inputs that reformers (and researchers) always assumed matter."[15]

Hanushek's interpretation of the evidence has not gone unchallenged. Larry Hedges and two coauthors have reexamined the studies analyzed by Hanushek in his landmark synthesis of the previous literature.[16] They reject the "vote counting" method implicitly used in Hanushek's synthesis and argue instead for applying formal statistical procedures (referred to as meta-analysis) to combine the results from the studies included in Hanushek's survey. After applying these procedures, they conclude that the data show "systematic positive relations between resource inputs and school outcomes. Moreover, . . . the median relation (regression coefficient) is large enough to be of practical importance."[17]

Hedges and his coauthors interpret their reanalysis of Hanushek's evidence to suggest that a $500—or roughly 10 percent—increase in average spending per pupil would increase student achievement by 0.7 standard deviations, a meaningful amount. They argue that even a casual examination of the studies summarized in Hanushek's table shows that resource inputs probably have a positive influence on school outcomes. First, if the results in the table were due to chance alone, one would expect that roughly half the coefficients would be positive while half would be negative. For several of the inputs, including expenditures per pupil, substantially more than half of the coefficients that are known are positive. Second, if the results were due solely to chance, only 5 percent of the coefficients would differ from zero by a statistically significant amount. The proportion of coefficients actually found to be statistically different from zero is much greater than 5 percent.

Other researchers reject Hanushek's interpretation of the evidence because they believe that improved data sets and statistical methods have shown that school resources matter. For example, Ronald Ferguson has used unusually rich information about the instructional qualifications of Texas teachers to argue that higher literacy skills among instructors, reductions in class size, and more experienced teaching staffs all lead to improvements in average student scores on standardized tests.[18] More-

15. Chubb and Hanushek (1990, p. 220).
16. Hedges, Laine, and Greenwald (1994).
17. Hedges, Laine, and Greenwald (1994, p. 5).
18. Ferguson (1991).

over, he argues that higher teacher salaries can improve the average qualifications of a school district's teaching staff. His analysis strongly suggests that larger school budgets, holding the number of students constant, can improve average student outcomes.

In one respect, Ferguson's findings are consistent with Hanushek's. Both agree that individual teachers make a difference. Even if *measurable* teacher characteristics have little observable impact on student performance, as Hanushek believes, *un*observed characteristics appear to matter a great deal. To quote Hanushek: "Teachers and schools differ dramatically in their effectiveness."[19] After controlling for the characteristics of students and their parents that affect student achievement, as well as the observable characteristics of schools and teachers, analysts often find that students in particular schools or enrolled in particular teachers' classes consistently perform better than average. Some unobserved characteristic of the skilled teachers causes them consistently to outperform teachers who achieve only mediocre results with their students. In addition, unmeasured characteristics of effective schools cause them to be more productive than other schools in raising student performance. Ferguson differs from Hanushek in finding that *measurable* characteristics of teachers also make a difference to student outcomes. Equally important, he argues that added school resources can improve the likelihood that good teachers will remain on a school's faculty.

Hanushek does not disagree with Hedges or Ferguson that additional resources *can* make a difference to student achievement. But in his surveys he interprets the statistical evidence to show that, on average, additional resources are not effectively used by most schools to produce improved student outcomes. It is a surprising and distressing conclusion.

Several methodological criticisms have been raised against the original Coleman report and many of the individual studies summarized by Hanushek and Hedges. Some of these criticisms are repeated fairly often and are worth mentioning here. A common complaint is that studies that attempt to link school resources to student achievement often do not have good measures of student or teacher background characteristics. Though this criticism is undoubtedly valid, it is not clear why it should cause the studies to be biased against the finding that additional school resources can improve student performance. In the simplest model of missing data, the bias would usually operate in the opposite direction.

19. Hanushek (1986, p. 1159)

Part of the positive effect of students' (unobserved) affluent backgrounds would be attributed to the effect of greater school resources.[20]

Another criticism is that compensatory school financing policies can confound the interpretation of the observed correlation between school resources and average student achievement. If policymakers give additional resources to the most disadvantaged schools, schools with low average achievement might be the ones that devote the most resources to educating each student. This correlation could hardly be used to prove that generous resources cause low student achievement; it would prove only that policymakers have been successful in targeting resources on the poorest schools.[21]

This criticism is less devastating than it may appear. The targeting of resources on the most disadvantaged students is not nearly large enough to eliminate wide spending disparities across U.S. school districts, as should be plain from the statistics mentioned earlier. In addition, compensatory funding schemes are usually aimed at redressing resource inequities caused by the unequal distribution of tax resources or low-income students across school districts. Resources are only rarely targeted on schools or districts where student achievement is lower than would be anticipated given the average level of spending per pupil. Compensatory financing programs reduce the amount of spending differences across school districts. If the poor districts effectively use the compensatory resources provided to them, it is hard to see why the additional school resources would not show up in the long run as improved student performance in the poorest districts. Increases in school resources across school districts should still produce the expected effect: improvements in student outcomes.

Finally, measures of school resources are often criticized because they provide a poor guide to the resources actually available to educate individual children; resources are frequently measured at the district level. Resources at the school or classroom level may be unobserved. Some

20. If the analyst does not possess any information on the socioeconomic status of individual youngsters, a statistical regression of average achievement on school resources would be expected to show a positive effect of resources on achievement. The reason is straightforward. Students with affluent backgrounds are more likely to attend schools with greater resources than average. In the absence of good information about socioeconomic background, the regression will show a positive relationship between school resources and student achievement even if high student achievement is wholly attributable to family affluence rather than to school resources.

21. This criticism is mentioned both by Aaron (1978) and Murnane (1991).

students who receive their schooling in districts with lavish resources in one year may have obtained their schooling in districts with meager resources in earlier years. The potential advantages of lavish resources are diluted because children do not have steady access to these resources over a substantial part of their school careers. If actual school resources are measured with error, the estimated effect of resources on student achievement will probably be biased toward zero.

Each of these problems may tend to reduce the estimated impact of school resources on student outcomes in some statistical studies. The severity of the problems can obviously differ from one study to the next, and in some cases the problems may be negligible. Whether the problems are severe enough to explain the discouraging pattern of results shown in Hanushek's table remains an open question.

Educational Resources and Earnings

Schooling attainment profoundly affects the productivity and earnings of individual workers. It is therefore logical to think that the resources invested in schools might affect the productivity and earnings of school graduates. The powerful relationship between educational attainment and earnings capacity has been recognized and analyzed for a long time. The most popular model to explain the relationship between schooling and earnings rests on the theory that educational investments in human beings are similar to physical investments in plant and equipment. Just as investment in buildings or machines involves an initial expenditure that must be weighed against a future stream of financial benefits, investments in students involve an initial sacrifice of time and money that is eventually offset in the form of higher output or earnings.

Economists have devoted considerable effort to measuring the exact payoff from different forms and levels of schooling. A few have even sought to determine the contribution of educational investments to overall economic growth and productivity improvement. Such studies typically find that increases in the educational attainment of American workers account for as much as a quarter of the growth in output per person employed.[22] If these calculations are valid, the contribution of educa-

22. Denison (1985, p. 30).

tional investment to productivity growth has been greater than the contribution of investment in physical plant and equipment.

Of course, the insight of a rocket scientist is not needed to recognize the positive association between educational attainment and earnings. The significant correlation of education and earned income does not necessarily prove a causal relationship between the two variables, however. Education and income could be affected by an identical set of determinants—race, family background, innate ability, or other factors. Because these variables simultaneously affect both educational attainment and earnings, and affect them in the same direction, the correlation between education and earnings might be spurious. But it seems unlikely that the correlation is wholly spurious. Social scientists investigating the payoff to schooling have typically included statistical controls for the most important social and economic factors that might affect both education and earnings. Thus recent estimates of the benefit from schooling take into account the impact on earnings of observable factors such as race and family background. These estimates generally imply that the rate of return on investment in additional schooling is positive and in the range of 5 to 12 percent.

Of greater relevance to the debate over school resources is research on the influence of school quality on earnings. The inherent quality of schools is of course unobserved and probably unmeasurable. Analysts can, however, measure some observable characteristics of school systems, such as student-teacher ratios, average teacher salaries, length of school year, and the demographic character of the student bodies.

Economists have long suspected that differences in the average quality of schools can help explain differences in the return to schooling enjoyed by members of different races. Finis Welch's tabulations of the age profile of earnings, calculated separately for blacks and whites, revealed that black men in the 1950s obtained far smaller earnings gains as a result of additional schooling than did white men with the same age and work experience. Because most black workers had been educated in segregated and woefully underfinanced schools, a plausible inference was that black workers with high levels of schooling attainment were disadvantaged relative to similar white workers because of the poor quality of their schooling.[23] This inference was apparently confirmed when economists discovered in the 1970s that black-white differences in returns to school-

23. See Welch (1966); Welch (1967).

ing had shrunk for cohorts of men entering the labor force in the 1960s, by which point the average quality of schooling among young blacks—as measured by its cost—approached that among young whites.[24]

Differences in returns to schooling enjoyed by blacks and whites provide strong, though not definitive, evidence that school quality as well as quantity can affect individual earnings. A number of analysts have investigated the effects of statewide or regional differences in schooling resources on the economic payoff from education. Until the 1950s states varied widely in average class size, teacher pay, length of school year, and spending per pupil. (They continue to differ, but disparities were much larger during the 1920s through the 1940s than they are today.) According to a number of studies, workers educated in states or regions spending more on educational inputs derived a higher payoff per year of attendance in school. That is, the earnings gain generated by an additional year of schooling is greater for workers educated in states where per pupil spending is higher.[25]

The most exhaustive and famous research on this topic is a study by labor economists David Card and Alan Krueger.[26] Their analysis is based on individual-level 1980 census data on earnings of men born between 1920 and 1949. After dividing their sample into three large birth cohorts (with birth years between 1920–29, 1930–39, and 1940–49), Card and Krueger essentially estimated separate earnings functions for men classified by the state of their birth and their birth cohort. This procedure yields an estimate of the rate of return to additional schooling for each of the cohorts in each of the states. The authors then statistically estimated the relationship between the return to schooling in a given state and several attributes of the state's educational system, including class size, teacher training, average teacher salary relative the state's mean wage, and length of school year. Using historical data derived from the U.S. Office of Education's *Biennial Survey of Education and Digest of Educational Statistics*, the authors calculated average values of these variables for years in which men in their sample were in school.

Card and Krueger's statistical results suggest there is a significant and

24. Welch (1973a); Welch (1973b).

25. Studies of the impact of U.S. school quality include Morgan and Sirageldin (1968) and Johnson and Stafford (1973). A study based on a similar methodology for the case of Brazil is described in Behrman and Birdsall (1983). All three studies find significant and meaningfully large impacts of school quality—as measured by the cost of school inputs—on adult earnings. For reviews of this literature, see chapters 5 and 6 in this volume.

26. Card and Krueger (1992a).

meaningful relationship between the cost and quality of educational inputs on the one hand, and earnings gains attributable to educational attainment on the other. Increases in length of school year and teacher salaries and reductions in the pupil-teacher ratio lead to statistically significant gains in the measured return to additional schooling. Thus factors under the control of policymakers—teacher pay, time spent in school, and average class size—were found to affect the distribution of lifetime earnings. Card and Krueger suggest, for example, that a decrease in the pupil-teacher ratio of five students is associated with a 0.4 percentage point increase in the rate of return to schooling, and a 10 percent increase in teachers' pay is associated with a 0.1 percentage point increase in the rate of return to schooling. (A student educated in the average state can expect to earn about 5 to 7 percent higher wages for each additional year of schooling.) In addition, the two researchers found some support for the hypothesis that average teacher quality, as measured by teachers' educational attainment, can have a beneficial effect on the returns to schooling. Finally, in a separate analysis they confirmed the earlier finding by Finis Welch that returns to schooling among black workers have converged toward those enjoyed by whites as the average quality of black schooling has improved.[27]

The Card and Krueger research, along with the earlier studies by Welch and Johnson and Stafford, seemed to offer clear evidence that school resources matter.[28] Economists had found a strong correlation between educational attainment and more costly school inputs on the one hand, and lifetime earnings on the other. Improvements in both the quantity *and* the quality of formal schooling appeared to cause measurable differences in the earnings capacity of individual workers.

This hopeful conclusion about the effects of school resources on adult earnings has been challenged in a recent study of school quality and earnings by Julian R. Betts.[29] Betts's analysis is based on the National Longitudinal Survey of Youth (NLSY), a nationally representative longitudinal survey of young men and women who were first interviewed in 1979. Several thousand young people were interviewed in the 1979 survey, when respondents were between fourteen and twenty-two years old. The education and labor market data analyzed by Betts were collected in twelve annual surveys spanning the period from 1979 to 1990. Betts's

27. Card and Krueger (1992b).
28. Welch (1966, 1967, 1973a, and 1973b); Johnson and Stafford (1973).
29. Betts (1995).

analysis focuses on white males for whom labor earnings are actually observed.

The NLSY contains information on characteristics of the high schools attended by respondents. These characteristics include the teacher-pupil ratio, relative teacher salaries, and teachers' educational attainment. Betts finds that none of these school characteristics has a statistically significant or meaningfully large effect on students' earnings, though the standard errors of several of his estimates are relatively large.

The surprising contrast between his findings and those of Card and Krueger led Betts to try a variety of statistical specification tests to determine the source of the difference. In his most interesting test, Betts uses different measures of school resources than the ones available to him in the NLSY data files. Ignoring school resource information about the actual high schools attended by NLSY respondents, Betts instead substitutes information about average school resources in the *state* where respondents resided when they were in high school. Note that this is the information available to Card and Krueger in their analysis of 1980 census files. Since Card and Krueger had no information on the actual schools attended by census respondents, they were forced to use information on statewide average resources available when respondents were growing up.

Curiously, Betts finds that when he uses state-level measures of school resources, the estimated impacts of class size and teacher salaries increase and the statistical significance of his results rises dramatically. In other words, when he uses measures of school quality that are weakly correlated with actual school quality he obtains a "better" statistical fit than when he uses the best measures available to him. Betts points out that "the state-level measures of school quality are capturing some aspect of the state other than the quality of the actual high school which the person attended."[30] This unexpected finding clearly raises the possibility that the statistical association between statewide measures of school resources and statewide returns to a year of schooling does not indicate a causal relationship between the two variables.

Reconciling the Results

The generally gloomy verdict reached by researchers studying the influence of school resources on student achievement stands in marked con-

---

30. Betts (1995, p. 242).

trast to the best-known findings of the human capital literature. While most analysts examining school performance have concluded that observable teacher and school characteristics make little difference, many scholars working in the human capital tradition find that school characteristics have a noticeable impact on the economic benefits workers derive from their schooling. Students educated in more costly schools may obtain a larger earnings gain per year spent in school.

The contradiction between the two sets of findings is deeply puzzling. If both sets of conclusions are accepted at face value, they imply that public spending on more costly school inputs can raise productivity in two or three decades but cannot affect student achievement in the short run. At least two explanations for the apparent contradiction have been offered. Card and Krueger argue that the aspects of schooling that raise labor-market earnings are poorly measured by standardized test scores. Consequently, better schools could succeed in improving students' capacity to earn even though they apparently do not succeed in raising academic achievement.[31]

Hanushek suggests that data limitations have prevented analysts from estimating well-specified models of the effect of school quality on subsequent earnings. Schooling quality, as measured in a typical human capital study, is correlated with unobservable characteristics of family background, which, because they are unmeasured, must be excluded from the analysis. The correlation between measured school quality and unobservable parental inputs leads to a spurious finding that school quality—as measured by school inputs—affects subsequent earnings.[32]

Card and Krueger's argument implies that schools effectively use resources to achieve a goal they cannot measure—post-school economic success. Perversely, however, they are very inefficient in achieving improvements in the only outcomes they seem to care about and can actually observe, namely, those related to the achievement of students in school. Arguably, schools should try to maximize the earnings gains their graduates can obtain as a result of school attendance. As a practical matter, it is very difficult to know how to accomplish this. Few schools even try. Secondary schools do not seem interested in what happens to their graduates after they leave; most do not even know whether school leavers find jobs. By contrast, all schools have a passable idea of the scholastic accomplishments of students in their care. Scholastic achieve-

31. Card and Krueger (1992a).
32. Hanushek (1986, pp. 1153, 1172).

ment is, after all, the main goal most educators set for their students. Yet much of the school performance literature suggests that when given more resources (or better paid teachers, or smaller class sizes, or greater teacher experience), educators cannot reliably organize those resources to improve student achievement. It would be astonishing if they could organize them to improve post-school earnings.

A simple explanation for the paradox may be that variations in U.S. school inputs once made an important difference in terms of both in-school achievement and post-school earnings. Current variations in school inputs, even though fairly sizable, are small enough to make their practical significance for school achievement small and inconsistent. However, the historical variations were quite wide, so the effects of past input differences continue to have observable effects on the personal income distribution.

Most research on the relationship between school inputs and American educational achievement relies on data collected after the early 1960s. Studies of the relationship between school inputs and U.S. labor market performance typically rely on earnings data collected during the past three decades. Many are based, however, on the experiences of people who received their schooling before 1950. Until World War II there were wide differences between states in the resources invested in education. According to Card and Krueger, the student-teacher ratio facing students born between 1920 and 1929 was 34 in South Carolina, 36 in North Carolina, Alabama, and Arkansas, and 38 in Mississippi. It was only 28 in New York, Rhode Island, and Massachusetts. The school year lasted 154 days in Georgia, 150 days in Alabama, and just 139 days in Mississippi. In New York, New Jersey, and several midwestern states, the average school year had already reached 180 or more days. Teachers were paid only 65–70 percent of the average state wage in several southern states; in the mid-Atlantic and southern New England states, teachers were paid substantially more than the average wage.[33]

These differences are quite wide, especially when one considers that they reflect the average conditions in an entire state or region. Many students in the most disadvantaged regions presumably attended schools that had even higher class sizes, even shorter school years, and even lower teacher pay. For black pupils in the south, conditions were especially grim. Finis Welch notes that Georgian black students in school in 1920 faced a student-teacher ratio of 56. In 1930, 38 percent of the teaching

33. Card and Krueger (1992a, pp. 12–13).

staff of black southern schools had not graduated from high school; only 9 percent had obtained four or more years of college.[34] It is easy to believe that a year of schooling received under these conditions would not be worth as much as a year of schooling received in New York or New England.

By the 1950s, however, school inputs grew more nearly equal across the states. Black schooling was significantly improved, even before desegregation occurred in the 1950s. The Coleman report, issued in 1966, concluded that there were no sizable differences between the educational resources available to black and white students. The input statistics tabulated by Card and Krueger show a tremendous equalization in school inputs, even for students born in the thirty-year period between 1920 and 1949. Julian Betts documents the further equalization of state-level teacher salaries and teacher-student ratios over the period 1939–79.[35]

A plausible inference might be that as school resources in the poorest regions approach those in the average region, the payoff to extra investment in school inputs decreases substantially. Unfortunately, this conjecture cannot be confirmed until sometime in the future when lifetime earnings patterns of students educated in the 1960s and 1970s become available. The data assembled by Card and Krueger, though more extensive than those collected by earlier researchers, are probably insufficient to detect nonlinearities in the relationship between school inputs and the rate of return to schooling.[36] Betts's data are limited by the fact that respondents are fairly young. Few of them had reached age thirty by the date of the last NLSY interview, so it is possible that beneficial effects of school resources will not begin to turn up until men reach their peak earnings years, after age thirty-five or forty.[37]

Stephen Childs and Charol Shakeshaft provide some suggestive evidence in their survey of research on the relation between school spending and student achievement.[38] Like Hedges they apply formal meta-analytical methods to combine the research findings from many statistical es-

34. Welch (1973b, pp. 59, 65).

35. Betts (1995, p. 244).

36. It is necessary to test for nonlinear effects in order to determine whether the payoff to additional school resources drops off after some threshold point representing resource adequacy. Card and Krueger (1992a) probably do not have enough degrees of freedom to estimate reliably a nonlinear relationship. The second step of their analysis is based on just 147 observations of birth-decade/birth-state groups of workers.

37. Betts rejects this explanation, however. See his chapter in this volume and Betts (1994).

38. Childs and Shakeshaft (1986).

timates obtained in several dozen separate studies. (They examine 417 correlation coefficients estimated in 45 studies. The studies are not necessarily the same as those analyzed by Hanushek and Hedges.) Childs and Shakeshaft conclude that "the relationship between student achievement and level of educational expenditures is minimal," although the correlation of *instructional* expenditures to student achievement is more powerful.[39] Of greater interest, however, is their finding that the estimated correlation between spending and achievement depends critically on the vintage of the research study. Older studies find a larger and more significant correlation between spending and achievement. The estimated correlation of spending and achievement was 0.25 in studies conducted before 1960, 0.16 in studies conducted during the 1960s, and −0.04 in studies conducted during the 1970s.

One interpretation of this trend, suggested by Childs and Shakeshaft, is that the similarity of spending levels in more recent decades may have eliminated the positive association between expenditures and achievement. The authors argue that threshold effects can be important: "past a certain point, it may well be that the amount of money a school district spends is not so vital as how the money is spent."[40] Another interpretation, of course, is that research methods may have improved (or deteriorated) over time, so that the relationship between spending and achievement found in recent studies cannot be validly compared with the relationship estimated in the distant past.

The Evidence in This Book

Voters and policymakers are left with an important but unsettled question: do school resources matter? Much of the evidence summarized so far implies that additional resources do not have predictable or large effects on student achievement. On the other hand, much of the historical evidence suggests that investments in added school resources can improve the earnings prospects of school graduates. Both these conclusions may be correct, but many will find it hard to understand how both can be true at the same time.

The authors of the chapters in this book try to make sense of the

39. Childs and Shakeshaft (1986, p. 260).
40. Childs and Shakeshaft (1986, p. 261).

voluminous research on school resources and student success. They do not reach a common conclusion about the current state of knowledge. Chapters 2–4 focus on the relationship between school resources and student achievement; chapters 5–7, on the effect of school resources on adult success.

School Resources and Student Performance

In chapter 2 Eric Hanushek offers a broad survey of current evidence on the effectiveness of resource utilization in schools. He distinguishes between two kinds of evidence, neither of them favorable to the hypothesis that additional resources are efficiently used by schools to improve student performance.

Historical data about American public schools show a striking and consistent pattern of increased resource use over time. They do not show a corresponding improvement in average student performance, at least in the period since 1960. In the century after 1890, school spending per student rose about 3½ percent a year after adjusting for price inflation. Part of the increase was attributable to rising salaries and fringe benefits for teachers and principals, but a large part was due to the growing intensity of use of instructional and noninstructional staff. Much of the rapid growth in school spending, especially after 1960, occurred because schools pursued policies often advocated by educators: they reduced the pupil-teacher ratio and increased teacher compensation.

Information about student performance over the past century is more elusive. Reliable data became available only after World War II, and consistent data on a broadly representative group of students did not begin until 1970. College admission test scores, such as those achieved on the SAT, fell sharply from the middle 1960s through the end of the 1970s but then staged a modest rebound in the first half of the 1980s. The National Assessment of Educational Performance (NAEP) evaluates the performance of a nationally representative sample of test takers, and hence is subject to fewer criticisms than the SAT. In science and mathematics, the performance of seventeen-year-olds shows a pattern that broadly conforms to the trend in SAT scores, with declines in performance through the 1970s and early 1980s and small improvements thereafter. Among minority test takers, recent improvements have been more impressive. On the whole, Hanushek sees little indication in the aggregate data that student performance has improved in line with school spending.

An alternative source of information about the effectiveness of resource use comes from studies of cross-sections of students, individual schools, or states. Most studies rely on immediate measures of school "outputs," including student performance on cognitive tests, students' promotion to higher grades, and school completion rates. A smaller number of studies examine later outcomes, such as students' earnings as adults in the job market.

No matter which measure of performance is selected, all studies confront formidable analytical problems. One of the most serious is the absence or low quality of information about school inputs and other factors that affect student outcomes. Hanushek highlights three particular problems that have challenged past researchers: poor information about students' innate ability, absence of data about family background, and ignorance about school inputs received by students before the period covered by the study. Each of these problems can seriously compromise the reliability of a study.

As mentioned, Hanushek summarizes the findings from 377 studies in table 2-3, updating his 1986 and 1989 surveys. As in his earlier surveys, he finds little evidence that increases in the ratio of teachers to pupils or increases in teacher education have improved student performance. The vast majority of studies find that the relationship between these two factors and student performance is insignificant. Among studies that find a statistically significant relationship, almost as many show that increases in the factor cause *reductions* in student performance as show the reverse.

Hanushek also finds no strong or systematic relationship between spending per pupil and student performance. He does not interpret this to mean that added school resources could *never* be effectively used to improve performance. He acknowledges that in some cases researchers have convincingly shown that additional resources were used effectively to obtain better results. But the statistical evidence he summarizes suggests that this result is not automatic. Given the current organization of schools, policymakers might boost spending on schools but could not be assured that the extra spending would generate superior outcomes. Nor could they be assured that spending money on higher teacher salaries, smaller class size, or better teacher preparation would yield improved student performance.

Most of the outcome measures included in Hanushek's survey relate to student performance on cognitive tests. These tests may provide an inappropriate or incomplete measure of performance. Should we be concerned that additional school resources do not consistently produce improvements in students' cognitive abilities? Hanushek sees at least two reasons for concern. First, recent evidence suggests that cognitive ability plays a significant role in determining worker productivity and job market success. Thus the failure of schools to boost cognitive ability when they are given added resources represents a serious waste of investment funds. Improvements in cognitive ability are also known to increase the likelihood that students will continue in school. Higher educational attainment, in turn, generates increased productivity and earnings, giving policymakers a second reason to place great weight on improving students' cognitive ability. Unfortunately, there is little evidence that added resources will reliably produce improvements in cognitive ability.

Turning to evidence about the effect of school resources on adult earnings, Hanushek sees little reason to be confident in the reliability of most recent research. Almost all the evidence so far has been produced by two types of studies. One kind relies on detailed longitudinal information about young people, the schools they attended, and their early labor-market experience. Most of the information about earnings comes from a period that is relatively early in workers' careers, when schooling differences have less influence on hourly wages.

The second and better-known kind of study attempts to measure the effect of school resources using census data. These studies use information about workers' wages at later stages of a career, but they suffer serious limitations. The precise schooling experiences of workers in the sample are unknown. Instead, researchers must assign school inputs to individual workers based on the assumption that workers received the average amount of resources provided to students in the state where the worker was born. This procedure introduces serious measurement problems. In addition, the census tapes do not contain information about workers' family backgrounds, even though background variables are known to have an important influence on individual success both in school and in the job market.

Hanushek's conclusion is straightforward. Resource-intensive policies to improve school performance will not work, or at least will not work reliably. Increased school spending, increased teacher salaries, reduced class size, and improved teacher qualifications are all policies that have been tried. They have not been shown to improve student performance in a consistent or meaningful way.

The Relation between School Resources and Student Performance

In chapter 3 Larry V. Hedges and Rob Greenwald, commenting on the evidence assembled by Hanushek, draw a different conclusion from the data. They believe the historical trend of student performance is less gloomy than Hanushek claims, while the cross-sectional evidence about school resources and student achievement is much more hopeful. Hedges and Greenwald dismiss out of hand the evidence from college entrance examinations. In their view the trend in SAT scores cannot provide reliable evidence about average student performance, because the population that takes the test is a self-selected sample of American secondary school students. Moreover, changes in the composition of the test-taking population imply that the average score reflects the ability of a changing class of students over time.

Hedges and Greenwald acknowledge that the NAEP provides a more reliable measure of average student performance, but they interpret the test score trends to show a modest gain in performance in the core academic areas of mathematics and reading, with especially large gains for black and Hispanic students. They also argue that these modest gains occurred in an environment in which less "social capital" was available for child rearing than was available in previous decades. The rise in the percentage of mothers who work, the decline in the proportion of children who live with two parents, and the increase in out-of-wedlock births have all combined to reduce the time and quality of parental involvement in child rearing. But other changes in the family environment, not mentioned by Hedges and Greenwald, have tended to improve the quality of family resources. Parental education has increased and the number of children in typical families has shrunk, possibly augmenting the quality and quantity of time that parents can devote to each child. On balance, Hedges and Greenwald interpret the modest gains in NAEP scores in an environment of declining social capital to provide evidence in favor of investing in additional school inputs.

The heart of their argument focuses on a reinterpretation of the studies summarized by Hanushek in his 1989 survey. The authors also assemble additional studies to include in their survey. They first show that their new sample of studies follows the general pattern found in Hanushek's original study. That is, their new sample shows the same basic pattern of positive and negative coefficients and significant and insignificant coefficients as the original Hanushek sample of studies.

The important difference between the way Hedges and Greenwald summarize their studies and Hanushek's original summary follows from the analytical method the authors use in combining statistical results from a variety of research projects. Hanushek emphasizes the large number of statistically insignificant findings and the seemingly erratic pattern of positive and negative coefficients across studies. In contrast, Hedges and Greenwald use a technique known as "combined significance testing," which permits the analyst to combine statistical significance levels from a variety of studies, each of which tests the same conceptual hypothesis. For example, collecting the results from three separate studies, each of which obtained a statistically insignificant result, analysts might find that the combined result from the studies is statistically significant.

The authors test two different hypotheses, using the results from earlier studies. The first hypothesis is that an increase in a particular school input has a *positive* influence on student outcomes. (This hypothesis would be accepted if the combined statistical test led to a rejection of the authors' initial null hypothesis, which is that no positive relation exists between the input and the student outcome.) Their second hypothesis is that an increase in the school input has a *negative* influence on student outcomes. (The null hypothesis in this case is that no negative influences could be detected in the data.) If the authors statistically rejected their first null hypothesis while failing to reject their second null hypothesis, they would interpret the combined studies to provide powerful confirmation that added school inputs lead to improvements in student outcomes.

Hedges and Greenwald perform several statistical tests. They examine the influence of three school inputs—the teacher-pupil ratio, teacher education, and teacher experience—using two different samples of studies. Unfortunately, they are forced to exclude from their analysis studies in which the sign and significance level of the estimated coefficient are unknown. This leads to the exclusion of many studies in which statistically insignificant coefficients were obtained. One of their samples includes the studies originally summarized by Hanushek in which the coefficient and statistical significance level of the coefficient are known. The other sample includes, in addition, further studies not originally used in Hanushek's survey. Finally, the authors test the robustness of their findings by excluding studies that obtained extremely low and extremely high coefficient estimates.

Although the results of these statistical tests are not always clear, Hedges and Greenwald interpret them to show that reductions in class size and additions to teacher experience result in improvements in student outcomes. The results for added teacher education are more ambiguous. The authors conclude that school resources are systematically related to student achievement and that the statistical relationship is large enough to be educationally important. Their chapter does not precisely describe the size of the expected gain from additional resources, however. Hanushek notes that Hedges, Laine, and Greenwald's 1994 meta-analysis yielded an estimate that a 10 percent increase in school expenditure produces an improvement in student performance of approximately 0.7 standard deviations, which is equivalent to more than one grade of schooling on many achievement tests. The findings of the chapter in this volume are somewhat less optimistic, but they still suggest that school expenditures have a statistically significant and positive influence on student achievement. This finding may be hard to square with actual trends in spending and student achievement. Expenditures per pupil nearly doubled between 1970 and 1990, while average student achievement either climbed slightly or declined, depending on the measure of average performance one prefers.

The authors reach at least one conclusion that is consistent with Hanushek's findings. They do not believe their results provide detailed policy implications for educators. Their findings do not show educators or policymakers the most educationally or economically efficient way to invest new or existing resources in the nation's schools. In contrast with Hanushek, however, they believe the statistical evidence is consistent with the view that additional resources have produced meaningful improvements in student achievement.

Evidence from Fifteen Schools in Austin

Hanushek and Hedges-Greenwald attempt to synthesize the findings from a large number of individual studies. In chapter 4 Richard J. Murnane and Frank Levy summarize the results from just one natural experiment. Between 1989 and 1993 fifteen Austin, Texas, schools were given substantial extra resources as a result of a desegregation court case. Two of the fifteen schools used the extra resources effectively. By 1993 students in the two schools showed significant improvement in achievement and attendance. The other thirteen schools enjoyed no comparable gains. Average student achievement and attendance remained stuck at very low levels.

Murnane and Levy point out that this evidence can be interpreted in either of two ways. The fact that students in two schools enjoyed significant gains in attendance and achievement can be interpreted to mean that added resources do make a difference. When considering the performance of all Austin schools, the infusion of extra resources into fifteen of the schools provided tangible educational benefits to some students in the favored schools. The fact that students in thirteen schools enjoyed no achievement gains *in spite of* the availability of extra resources demonstrates that added resources, by themselves, are not enough to yield improved school outcomes.

The correct interpretation of Austin's experience requires a closer look at how extra resources were used in the fifteen schools. What distinguished the two successful schools from the thirteen schools where achievement remained unchanged? Murnane and Levy are skeptical that the studies summarized by Hanushek and Hedges-Greenwald can help us answer this question.

Labor Market Effects of School Quality

The last three chapters consider evidence about the effects of school resources on student success in the job market. David Card, Alan B. Krueger, and Julian R. Betts evaluate the existing statistical literature on this subject; James Heckman, Anne Layne-Farrar, and Petra Todd reanalyze and extend the models estimated in earlier studies.

In chapter 5 Card and Krueger argue that added school resources have a positive and measurable impact on students' earnings as adults. They show that the influence of school resources is produced by two separate effects. First, additional school resources tend to increase the return that students enjoy from remaining an additional year in school. The higher return is evident in the extra earnings students receive from each successive year they remain in school. Students in a well-endowed school system will gain more in future earnings from remaining an additional year in school than they would gain if they were in a poorly endowed system.

The second channel of influence can be just as important. Students in well endowed school systems will be induced to attend school for longer periods. In other words, additional educational resources may encourage higher school attainment. The school attendance effect may be particularly large in the case of more able students. These students already derive

Figure 1-3. *Relationship of School Attainment and Earnings in Two School Systems*

Log of earnings

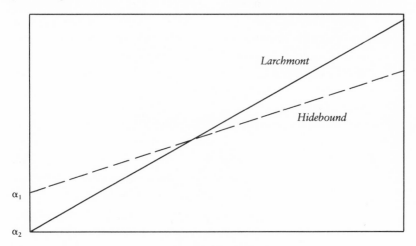

School attainment

better than average gains from school. An improvement in school quality will make their gains even larger, perhaps inducing them to lengthen their school attendance in comparison with less able students.

The combined effects of school quality on adult earnings can be seen in figure 1-3, which compares the adult earnings–school attainment relationship in two kinds of school systems. One system, labeled Larchmont, spends heavily on the students in its schools; the other, labeled Hidebound, spends little per student. Each line traces out the relationship between school attainment and the logarithm of earnings for adults who received their schooling in the two systems. Note that the relationship is more steeply sloped for the students who attended Larchmont schools than it is for the Hidebound students. This reflects the higher return from schooling enjoyed by the Larchmont students, who benefited from greater educational resources during each year they were in school.

At very low levels of school attainment, however, the Larchmont students actually earn less as adults than the Hidebound students. This puzzle is explained by the effect of school resources on school attainment. Because the Larchmont students benefited from greater educational resources, the more able students may have been induced to remain in school longer or to attend college. As a result, the Larchmont students whose education ends at the ninth grade are less able than the Hidebound students whose schooling ends at the same grade. Even though they may have benefited more from each year they spent in the Larchmont schools than did their counterparts in the Hidebound schools, their lower average ability places them at a labor-market disadvantage in comparison with Hidebound students who received the same amount of education. At the level of school attainment where the two lines cross, the extra advantage enjoyed by Larchmont students as a result of higher school quality exactly offsets the lower relative ability of Larchmont students who end their schooling at that level of attainment.

The likely effect of school quality on school attainment makes it difficult to predict whether Larchmont students will earn more or less as adults than Hidebound students who receive the same amount of education. Card and Krueger emphasize that the most convincing evidence of the value of extra school resources will be found among adults who have received above average amounts of schooling. If statisticians attempt to measure the influence of school resources in a sample that excludes college graduates, for example, they will miss the part of the population where the gains from additional resources are likely to be largest.

After describing a general theoretical model that traces out the link between school quality, school attainment, and adult earnings, Card and Krueger review three kinds of evidence about the relationship between education, educational quality, and earnings. They briefly summarize the well-known and voluminous literature showing a positive association between school attainment and adult earnings. They then evaluate the less well-known literature on the link between school resources and earnings. They place the heaviest emphasis on research into the effects of educational spending per pupil and variations in the pupil-teacher ratio. Finally, they consider the much more limited research on the relationship between school quality and schooling attainment.

The most important part of their review treats the relationship between school quality and adult earnings. They distinguish among four classes of statistical models that have been used to estimate this relationship. The earliest studies treated school quality as though it affected the intercept in figure 1-3 without influencing the slope of the school attainment–adult earnings relationship. If school resources can be accurately measured, reliable estimation of this relationship requires the statistician to regress the logarithm of earnings on individuals' school attainment and on the educational resources that were available to individuals when they were in school. A second class of studies is based on the assumption that school resources affect both the intercept *and* the slope of the school attainment–earnings line.

A third class of studies recognizes the potential influence of school quality on the intercept, but does not explicitly estimate this effect. Instead, analysts focus on estimating the differences in slope that can be attributed to school quality effects by comparing earnings differences among adults who reside in one area of the country but who received their education in school systems elsewhere. Finally, a fourth class of studies attempts to estimate the reduced form effects of school quality on earnings. In these studies analysts do not attempt to measure either the slope or intercept of the lines in figure 1-3 but instead try to estimate the overall effect of added school resources on adult earnings independent of workers' school attainment. The reduced form estimate of the earnings gain attributable to added school resources would include both the direct effect on the rate of return to schooling and the indirect effect that occurs because students in well-endowed school systems obtain extra schooling.

Card and Krueger summarize twenty-four estimates of the effect of school spending derived in eleven separate studies. All of these estimates, which are based on the first and second models described above, show a positive effect of spending on adult earnings. Nearly all of them also imply that the effects of added resources are large enough to cause economically significant wage improvements for adults who were educated in well-endowed school systems. The authors also summarize findings from five studies that examine the influence of the pupil-teacher ratio on adult earnings. Most show that a lower pupil-teacher ratio tends to boost adult earnings. Card and Krueger emphasize that two of the studies that show either an insignificant effect or an effect of unexpected sign focus on workers who are comparatively young. Most research shows that the effects of school attainment on earnings are comparatively small among workers just entering the work force, so it should not be surprising if the effects of a low pupil-teacher ratio are also small in a sample of workers who are mostly in their twenties.

When the authors turn to research results based on the third class of theoretical models, including many results reported by Heckman, Layne-Farrar, and Todd in this volume, they see a high degree of consistency across estimates. Researchers typically find that higher levels of spending per pupil and lower pupil-teacher ratios are associated with higher rates of earnings gain per year spent in school. In their brief overview of the literature on the effect of school resources on educational attainment,

Card and Krueger report that most evidence on this issue suggests that there is a statistically significant and positive effect of resources on attainment. They conclude that the available evidence supports the hypothesis that added school resources boost adult earnings through two kinds of influence. Extra resources increase the return from an added year of schooling, and added resources induce students to remain in school longer than they otherwise would.

In the last major section of their paper, Card and Krueger consider fascinating evidence on the impact of school spending on the adult earnings of African Americans educated in segregated schools. Until the Supreme Court declared segregation unconstitutional in 1954, southern states educated black youngsters in school systems that were separate from those available to white youngsters. Black schools in the South received significantly less funding than schools available to whites. In most states the pupil-teacher ratio was significantly higher in black schools than in white schools. Card and Krueger estimate the impact of these resource differences by examining the earnings of workers who attended school in the South but who later moved north to find work. Thus their estimates of the effect of resource differences are based solely on the experiences of men born in the South who earned wages in the North. The results from this kind of comparison reveal that the payoff to education was greater for individuals (of either racial group) who were from states that provided more resources for the education of each child.

Even though all southern states maintained segregated school systems, there were wide differences in the penalty imposed on black children as a result of attending segregated schools. In some states, like Oklahoma, Kentucky, and Missouri, the pupil-teacher ratio in black schools was very similar to the ratio in white schools. States in the Deep South, including Louisiana, Mississippi, and South Carolina, had black school systems with much higher pupil-teacher ratios than comparable ratios in their white school systems. Card and Krueger show that the black-white differences in the rate of return on schooling closely match the black-white differences in the pupil-teacher ratio. For example, the difference between blacks and whites in the rate of return on schooling was comparatively small for youngsters educated in Oklahoma, Kentucky, and Missouri, but it was very large for youngsters educated in Louisiana, Mississippi, and South Carolina. This pattern conforms closely with the pattern of black-white differences in the pupil-teacher ratio.

Card and Krueger acknowledge that their conclusions about the influence of school resources on adult earnings stand in marked contrast to most authors' findings about the influence of resources on student achievement. They note that student achievement as measured on standardized tests is not a strong predictor of students' later success in the job market. Thus the contrast between the results of the two kinds of study does not prove that results from either are necessarily wrong. In addition, they question the conclusion that school resources have no influence on test scores. They point to a randomized trial in which students assigned to smaller classes achieved higher test scores on standardized tests. The authors' basic confidence in their findings rests, however, upon the large number and variety of studies which find that increases in school resources are powerfully linked to increases in students' earnings as adults.

Is There a Link between School Inputs and Earnings?

In chapter 6 Julian Betts reaches a very different conclusion from his reading of the evidence. He identifies twenty-three studies that have examined the relationship between school inputs and students' later job-market success. Betts points out, however, that many of these studies cannot be treated as independent. Nine of the studies measure school inputs using an identical source of information, the *Biennial Survey of Education*. Measurement errors in this data source will produce similar problems for drawing reliable conclusions in all nine of the studies that rely on it. Six of the studies follow the labor market fortunes of young men surveyed in the National Longitudinal Survey of Youth.

Betts summarizes the findings from these studies somewhat differently from either Hanushek or Hedges and Greenwald. He calculates the percentage of reported statistical findings from each study which show that school resources have the expected effect on student earnings and which are statistically significant. (An estimate with the expected sign would show that increases in a school input cause improvements in students' later earnings.) Betts's summary shows how student earnings are affected by school expenditures per pupil and by six inputs that are thought to influence student outcomes, including the teacher-pupil ratio, teacher education and experience, and teacher salary.

His summary reveals some striking patterns. First, an overwhelming majority of studies based on state-level average inputs suggest that increases in school spending lead to improvements in student earnings. A slight majority of the studies that rely on school-district averages show the same thing. However, no study that measures school resources by assessing the exact inputs available in local schools was able to duplicate this finding. If the school resources available to students are measured using school-level data, school expenditures apparently have no statistically significant effect on later earnings. If inputs are measured using statewide or districtwide averages, there is a better chance that the study will find a statistically significant effect of school expenditures.

This general pattern is repeated for most other school inputs. If inputs are measured using school-level data, the study is less likely to find a statistically significant effect; if inputs are measured using state-level or district-level averages, a statistically significant effect is more likely to be found. Betts asserts that "inputs that appear effective when measured at the state level prove to be insignificantly related to earnings when the input is measured for the actual school attended."

A second pattern is also evident in Betts's summary. Studies that examine students who received a grade school education before 1960 are more likely to find that added school resources produce significant gains in adult earnings. Studies that examine students who received a grade school education after 1960 almost invariably find little evidence that additional school resources are linked to higher adult earnings. Unfortunately, this pattern of results is confounded with another pattern. Studies that measure earnings when students are aged thirty-two or younger seldom find statistically significant effects of school resources on earnings. Nearly all the studies that find a significant link between resources and earnings rely on earnings data covering workers who are more than thirty years old.

To determine the overall effect of school resources on adult earnings, Betts calculates the average estimated effect of spending per pupil obtained in the studies in his sample. In performing this calculation, he ignores the findings from studies that use local school data. He is also forced to exclude the findings from some studies that do not contain enough information for him to calculate the percent gain in earnings that would occur as a result of a 10 percent increase in a school input. These exclusions tend to eliminate studies that show that school spending has a small or even a negative effect on earnings. Consequently, Betts has calculated upper-bound estimates of the effect of school resources, given the results obtained in the twenty-three studies.

Using this information, Betts estimates the rate of return from increased school spending on selected educational inputs. These estimates require several debatable assumptions. The first is an assumption about the cost of increasing a particular school input, such as the teacher-pupil ratio. The second is an assumption about the social benefits that result from increased spending. Betts focuses on only a single benefit—higher lifetime earnings—but there may be other social benefits. Moreover, Betts assumes that the only earnings gain that occurs as a result of higher spending is the earnings difference between students educated in resource-rich and resource-poor schools. Some might question this assumption. If students educated in resource-rich schools produce innovations or productivity gains that are widely shared by students educated in resource-poor schools, some of the social benefits of greater school inputs will be missed. Nonetheless, Betts has attempted to be evenhanded in his assessment and to duplicate as closely as possible the assumptions typically used when estimating the return from investing in an additional year of schooling.

Betts's estimates, shown in tables 6-7 and 6-8 of his paper, suggest that added investments in school "quality" have a very modest payoff, even using assumptions that he considers optimistic. The return on investment may be positive, in the sense that the sum of future earnings gains exceeds the sum of additional costs. The case for extra investment in school inputs is weak, however, if one takes account of the time pattern of the payoff. To achieve earnings gains, investments must be made when students are young. But the benefits do not materialize for years or even decades in the future. If society must borrow money to make these investments, the interest rate would have to be extremely low to make the investment appear worthwhile. Betts estimates that the internal rate of return on investing in smaller class size, even using favorable assumptions about the value of this investment, is only 2.35 percent. If government must pay an interest rate of more than 2.35 percent on money it borrows to pay for additional teachers, smaller class size will not seem a sound investment. In contrast, most studies of the value of an additional year of schooling suggest that the internal rate of return on an extra year of school attainment is in the range of 5 to 12 percent. Borrowing money to finance extra schooling is much more attractive in this case.

Betts considers several hypotheses to explain the pattern of findings in the literature. One hypothesis is that the payoff to investing in extra school resources has declined over time because of fundamental changes in the link between resources and earnings. This may have occurred because the marginal payoff declines when the average level of school inputs rises. Though Betts finds some evidence to support this interpretation, the evidence is not powerful. That is, the variation in the data is not large enough to reliably detect a nonlinear effect of school resources on earnings. It is also possible that specific changes in the organization of schools, such as increased bureaucratization or teacher unionization, have made it more difficult to translate extra school resources into improved student outcomes.

Betts finds mixed evidence for the hypothesis that school resources produce earnings gains only for workers once they reach their thirties or forties. He strongly rejects one explanation for the pattern of statistical results. According to one hypothesis, recent students have received their schooling in an environment in which resource differences across schools (or districts or states) are comparatively small. Because resource differences are small, it is more difficult to reliably estimate the effects of resources on earnings. Although this description of the trend in school differences is generally accurate, it is incorrect to infer that recent studies lack statistical power. For at least two school inputs—teacher education and teacher-pupil ratios—differences across schools and school districts are still large enough to produce statistically significant findings if the input is actually linked to student outcomes. For other school inputs, including term length, the variation across schools is now small, which makes it much more difficult to detect a genuine effect.

Betts is critical of the studies that rely on state-level measures of school resources. Many of his criticisms are similar to the ones raised by Hanushek and by Heckman, Layne-Farrar, and Todd, however, and will not be described further here.

In the last main section of the chapter, Betts considers evidence on the effects of school resources on educational attainment. Even if additional resources do not affect earnings, holding constant a worker's schooling attainment, added resources might still be worthwhile if they encouraged students to remain in school. Few researchers seem to have investigated this possibility in a systematic way. Betts finds a clear dichotomy in the research findings reported in this literature. Studies that measure school inputs using state-level averages find that additional school resources are linked to higher school attainment. In contrast, studies using school input data from the actual school attended almost never find significant effects of school resources on educational attainment. Betts's summary of the literature on schooling attainment thus conforms to his summary of the literature on school resources and earnings. The most persuasive evidence that school resources have

Figure 1-4. *Relationship of School Attainment, School Quality, and Earnings*

Log of earnings

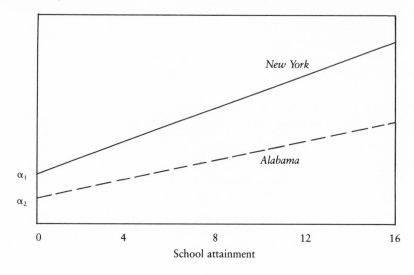

School attainment

an effect is derived in research using school input data that do not come from the school actually attended by students in the study. Betts is skeptical of the value of that kind of evidence.

Does Measured School Quality Really Matter?

In chapter 7 James Heckman, Anne Layne-Farrar, and Petra Todd present the only study in this volume that directly examines microeconomic data on the link between school resources and student outcomes. They develop a statistical framework to evaluate school quality that is broad enough to encompass several of the previous models evaluating this question. That is, they lay out a statistical model general enough to include important models that have been estimated in the past. The past models can then be viewed as special cases of the more general models of school quality and earnings determination that are estimated in their chapter.

The advantage of this procedure is that it permits the authors to rigorously test some of the modeling assumptions used by previous analysts. A simple illustration might make the authors' procedure clearer. Figure 1-4 shows the possible relationship between earnings and school attainment among forty-year-old men who were educated in two states, Alabama and New York. Alabama spends less to educate its pupils than New York, so it is conceivable that men educated in Alabama earn less than men educated in New York at every level of school attainment. This disadvantage is reflected by the fact that the earnings–school attainment line for Alabama is always below the corresponding line for New York. The lines slope upward in both Alabama and New York because additional school attainment increases earnings whether men are educated in high-spending or low-spending states.

Suppose school quality can be measured using a single, easily measured variable—say, expenditure per pupil. One hypothesis about the effect of school quality is that it lifts the logarithm of earnings by a fixed amount at every level of schooling (that is, it lifts earnings by a constant percentage amount). This hypothesis implies that the two lines in figure 1-4 should be parallel, but they should have different intercepts, say, α_1 and α_2. The greater the spending differential between two states, the larger the gap between α_1 and α_2. Another hypothesis is that because of New York's spending advantage New Yorkers receive bigger percentage increases in earnings than Alabamians as educational attainment rises. According to this hypothesis, the slope of the earnings–school attainment line should be steeper in New York than in Alabama. In their 1973 study Johnson and Stafford based their estimates on the first hypothesis; in their more recent study Card and Krueger based their estimates on the second.[41]

A third hypothesis is that *both* the slope and the intercept of the earnings–school attainment line will be affected by school quality. The third hypothesis is more general than the first or the second. In fact, it encompasses both the first two assumptions. Heckman, Layne-Farrar, and Todd estimate a model based on the third hypothesis in order to examine the validity of the first two hypotheses within a general framework in which school quality can affect earnings through a variety of channels. In addition, the authors test other special assumptions that earlier studies have relied on. For example, the relationship shown in figure 1-4 is based on the assumption that the logarithm of earnings is a strictly linear function of school attainment. This assumption ignores the

41. Card and Krueger (1992a). In their model any effect of school resources on the intercept term is completely absorbed by general state-of-birth effects. Their model does not exclude the possibility that these effects exist, but its principal goal is to accurately measure the impact of school resources on the slope of the earnings—school attainment relationship.

possibility that students enjoy sheepskin effects as a result of completing school or college. If sheepskin effects are important, workers should enjoy a larger proportional earnings gain when their school attainment rises from eleven to twelve years than when it rises from ten to eleven years. Similarly, they should enjoy a larger gain from completing the fourth year of college than from completing the third. It is straightforward to test whether this hypothesis is true by relaxing the assumption that the log earnings–school attainment relationship is strictly linear.

Heckman, Layne-Farrar, and Todd perform an exhaustive set of statistical procedures to test some of the underlying assumptions in the previous literature. They use the same data sets previously used by Card and Krueger to examine the relationship between school quality and adult earnings. They supplement these data with information from the 1970 and 1990 decennial census files, which cover the same cohorts included in earlier analyses but which also include younger cohorts which were not examined in the main Card and Krueger study.[42] In some cases they modify earlier definitions of school inputs to reflect improved methods of measuring "quality." However, they are careful to repeat their analyses using older definitions to ensure that their results are not solely due to differences in measuring school inputs.

The chapter includes many ingenious tests of the maintained assumptions in earlier studies. It also includes extensions or elaborations of previous models of the effect of school quality on adult earnings. Many of the most important findings in the chapter weaken the case for believing that school resources have a systematic or reliably determined impact on earnings.

In one respect, however, the study provides a striking confirmation of results originally obtained by Card and Krueger. Heckman, Layne-Farrar, and Todd successfully replicate the findings of the earlier study when they attempt to duplicate its assumptions and variable definitions. Card and Krueger's original findings also appear robust with respect to minor changes in procedures and in the definitions of the school input variables. When Card and Krueger's model is estimated using data from the 1970 and 1990 decennial census files, their conclusions are essentially confirmed. Heckman, Layne-Farrar, and Todd find that reductions in the

---

42. Card and Krueger (1992a) restricted their analysis to data from the 1980 census. In their study of black-white earnings gains from educational resources, Card and Krueger (1992b) also analyzed data from the 1960 and 1970 censuses.

pupil-teacher ratio and increases in term length and relative teacher salaries tend to boost adult earnings by significant and meaningful amounts. These effects are even larger in the 1990 census than in the 1980 census, which was the source of data for the original Card and Krueger study.

Though Card and Krueger's findings are confirmed when Heckman and his collaborators replicate the original Card-Krueger assumptions, they do not appear to be sustained when major assumptions in the analysis are varied. Heckman, Layne-Farrar, and Todd find that several of the assumptions commonly used to estimate the school quality–earnings relationship are rejected by the evidence. Sheepskin effects, for example, are empirically important. High school and college graduation cause large earnings gains that are missed if the analyst assumes that the relationship between the logarithm of earnings and school attainment is strictly linear. When Card and Krueger's model is reestimated after relaxing the assumption of strict linearity, the importance of school quality variables shrinks dramatically. For workers who have not completed college, school resources appear to have little or no effect on earnings. Only among college graduates do the effects of school resources appear to be important.

Card and Krueger's findings may also be sensitive to another crucial assumption. Their strategy in estimating the effect of a particular school input is to compare the earnings of men who currently live in the same state but who received their schooling in different states. This strategy is defensible if workers from a given state settle at random among the other states. A well-educated worker from Alabama can then be legitimately compared with a worker from New York who has received the identical level of schooling. On average, the difference in their earnings should be attributable to the difference in the quality of their schooling. The strategy might be less defensible if residents who settle in a given state are a highly self-selected group of workers from other states. In that case, the college graduate from Alabama and the college graduate from New York might differ in their earnings capacity, not only because the quality of their schooling differed but also because other personal differences influenced their likelihood of moving to the state where they currently reside. Heckman, Layne-Farrar, and Todd offer evidence that individuals from certain states of birth have comparative advantages in certain states of residence, which individuals exploit by migrating to the desirable states. This migration pattern undermines a key assumption used to estimate the effect of school resources on earnings. It is unclear, however, whether the effects of nonrandom migration will tend to bias Card and Krueger's estimates of resource effects by a large amount and in a particular direction.

Though the analysis undermines findings from previous aggregate studies of the effect of school resources on earnings, the authors do not regard the issue as settled. Added school resources may improve earnings in some circumstances. However, the evidence previously advanced to show that extra school resources can be beneficial is fragile. It depends on assumptions that are not always confirmed by the data. When more general statistical models are estimated, the apparent effect of added resources shrinks and becomes less significant or disappears.

Conclusion

The issues at stake in the school resource debate are important. Many policymakers and ordinary voters believe K-12 education can only be improved if there is a sizable infusion of money into the nation's schools. Others think that school financing reform is urgently needed to make educational spending more equitable across school districts, primarily by boosting expenditures in the poorest districts. These views would be easier to accept if a convincing case could be made that additional school resources are generally used to produce improved student outcomes. So far that case depends mainly on two kinds of statistical findings. In the recent past *some* infusions of extra resources have helped students in *some* schools; and additional school resources in the more distant past have been associated with significant and sizable gains in adult earnings.

The studies in this book suggest, on balance, that the case for additional school resources is far from overwhelming. Increased spending on school inputs has not been shown to be an effective way to improve student achievement in most instances where this strategy has been attempted. Individual studies show that in some cases additional school resources have been effectively used to improve student test scores, but this experience is not the dominant one in recent experience. Most studies show, however, that in the past additional school resources tended to improve the earnings capacity of students. This summary of past studies is reflected in both of the surveys included in this volume, by Card and Krueger and by Betts. However, Betts's survey and the new statistical analyses of Heckman, Layne-Farrar, and Todd suggest that this conclusion may be fragile.

Statistical evidence and recent historical experience suggest to me that school performance is unlikely to be improved solely by investing extra money in the nation's schools. Increased spending on school inputs without any change in the current arrangements for managing schools offers little promise of improving either student performance or adult earnings.

References

Aaron, Henry J. 1978. *Politics and the Professors: The Great Society in Perspective.* Brookings.

Baily, Martin Neil, Gary Burtless, and Robert E. Litan. 1993. *Growth with Equity: Economic Policymaking for the Next Century.* Brookings.

Barro, Stephen M. 1994. *Federal Policy Options for Improving the Education of Low-Income Students: Volume III, Countering Inequality in School Finance.* Santa Monica, Calif.: Rand.

Behrman, Jere R., and Nancy Birdsall. 1983. "The Quality of Schooling: Quantity Alone Is Misleading." *American Economic Review* 73 (December): 928–46.

Betts, Julian R. 1994. "Does School Quality Matter Only for Older Workers?" (mimeo) La Jolla, Calif.: University of California, San Diego, Department of Economics.

———. 1995. "Does School Quality Matter? Evidence from the National Longitudinal Survey of Youth." *Review of Economics and Statistics* 77 (May): 231–50.

Card, David, and Alan B. Krueger. 1992a. "Does School Quality Matter? Returns to Education and the Characteristics of Public Schools in the United States." *Journal of Political Economy* 100 (February): 1–40.

———. 1992b. "School Quality and Black-White Relative Earnings: A Direct Assessment," *Quarterly Journal of Economics* 107 (February): 151–200.

Childs, T. Stephen, and Charol Shakeshaft. 1986. "A Meta-Analysis of Research on the Relationship between Educational Expenditures and Student Achievement." *Journal of Education Finance* 12 (Fall): 249–63.

Chubb, John E., and Eric A. Hanushek. 1990. "Reforming Educational Reform." In *Setting National Priorities: Policy for the Nineties,* edited by Henry J. Aaron, 213–48. Brookings.

Coleman, James S., and others. 1966. *Equality of Educational Opportunity.* Government Printing Office.

Denison, Edward F. 1985. *Trends in American Economic Growth, 1929–1982.* Brookings.

Ferguson, Ronald F. 1991. "Paying for Public Education: New Evidence on How and Why Money Matters." *Harvard Journal on Legislation* 28 (Summer): 465–98.

Hanushek, Eric A. 1986. "The Economics of Schooling: Production and Efficiency in Public Schools." *Journal of Economic Literature* 24 (September): 1141–77.

———. 1989. "The Impact of Differential Expenditures on School Performance." *Educational Researcher* 18 (May): 45–51, 62.

Hanushek, Eric A., and Steven G. Rivkin. 1994. "Understanding the 20th Century Explosion in U.S. School Costs." Working Paper 388. University of Rochester: Rochester Center for Economic Research.

Hedges, Larry V., Richard D. Laine, and Rob Greenwald. 1994. "Does Money Matter? A Meta-Analysis of Studies of the Effects of Differential School Inputs on Student Outcomes." *Educational Researcher* 23 (April): 5–14.

Johnson, George E., and Frank P. Stafford. 1973. "Social Returns to Quantity and Quality of Schooling." *Journal of Human Resources* 8 (Spring): 139–55.

Koretz, Daniel M. 1986. *Trends in Educational Achievement.* Congressional Budget Office.

Morgan, James, and Ismail Sirageldin. 1968. "A Note on the Quality Dimension in Education." *Journal of Political Economy* 76 (September/October): 1069–77.

Murnane, Richard J. 1991. "Interpreting the Evidence on 'Does Money Matter?'" *Harvard Journal on Legislation* 28 (Summer): 457–64.

National Commission on Excellence in Education. 1983. *A Nation at Risk: The Imperative for Educational Reform.* Government Printing Office.

Welch, Finis. 1966. "Measurement of the Quality of Schooling," *American Economic Review* 56 (May, Papers and Proceedings, 1965): 379–92.

———. 1967. "Labor-Market Discrimination: An Interpretation of Income Differences in the Rural South." *Journal of Political Economy* 75 (June): 225–40.

———. 1973a. "Black-White Differences in Returns to Schooling." *American Economic Review* 63 (December): 893–907.

———. 1973b. "Education and Racial Discrimination." In *Discrimination in Labor Markets,* edited by Orley Ashenfelter and Albert Rees, 43–81. Princeton University Press.

Wright, John W., ed. 1994. *The Universal Almanac, 1995.* Kansas City, Mo.: Andrews and McMeel.

CHAPTER 2

School Resources and Student Performance

Eric A. Hanushek

T HE EFFECTIVENESS of school spending has been hotly debated for at
least the past quarter century. Beginning with the Coleman report,[1] evidence has accumulated to suggest that simple views of what determines
student achievement are wrong. Student achievement seems unrelated to
standard measures of the resources going into schools. Interest in this
research and the conclusions emanating from it derives from its direct
implications for policy, thus elevating the subject from an arcane research
discussion to a public debate.

The interest in schooling from a policy perspective comes from several
sources. First, schooling is perceived as an important determinant of
individual productivity and earnings. Thus it becomes an instrument for
affecting both the national economy and the distribution of individual
income and earnings. Second, while not often subjected to much analysis,
schooling is assumed to generate various externalities, ranging from its
effect on economic growth to its value for a well-functioning democracy,
thus justifying an important component of public intervention.[2] Third,
school spending is itself significant, amounting to over 4 percent of gross
domestic product and representing the largest expenditure in most state
and local budgets. Combined, these factors point to a natural policy focus
on the effectiveness of national expenditure on schools.

The policy perspective related to how school resources affect student
performance is straightforward. Can we deal with performance problems
in schools by supplying them with extra funds? Or, if uncertain about

1. Coleman and others (1966).
2. For assessments of what is known about externalities in education, see Hanushek
(1996) and Poterba (1996).

that, can we specify concrete ways of spending additional money so that we can be reasonably assured of improvements? Such questions are seldom asked about the auto industry, the computer industry, or other competitive industries. These questions arise in education because schools are typically publicly operated, because information about performance is difficult to come by and, where available, frequently hard to interpret, and because there has developed a general distrust of schools' abilities to produce sensible policies. Moreover, if schools are not performing effectively, ways of obtaining improvements are not entirely obvious. Put the other way around, confirmation that schools use resources effectively would provide considerable relief to policymakers and to the public. An easy and effective set of policy prescriptions therefore follows: decide how much to spend on schools and then turn the money over to them. Or, if schools cannot be generally counted on to spend money effectively, knowledge of the production function for schools will enable central decisionmakers to direct resources in productive ways.

The spending perspective has been central to most court cases about the financing of schools. Courts have been concerned about equity, or distributional, issues since the 1968 *Serrano* v. *Priest* decision in California. More recently, they have entered into evaluations of the total level of spending, often under the name "adequacy." It is clear why courts like the metric of spending. They can evaluate variations in spending easily, and they can develop remedies that are easily specified and easily monitored.[3] Legislatures usually have a perspective similar to that of the courts. Dealing with the distribution of funding is attractive because it permits the active design of educational policies without getting into the details of how individual districts carry out their missions.

I provide an overview of evidence on the effectiveness of resource use in schools in this chapter. My emphasis is on clarifying what can and what cannot be concluded from the data. I then link the evidence to various uses of the data.

The Aggregate Story

Consideration of schooling resources might logically begin with an overview of the history of expenditure and performance. While mainly con-

3. The history of the California court case of *Serrano* v. *Priest* and a New Jersey series of cases suggests that agreement on fiscal equity is difficult to come by and that even quantitative expenditure verdicts are difficult to implement and enforce. In both states the cases have logged more than twenty years in the courts.

Table 2-1. *Real Current Expenditure on Public Schools, Selected Years, 1890–1990*

Item	1890	1940	1950	1960	1970	1980	1990
Total current expenditure (billions of 1990 dollars)	2.09	19.65	25.79	52.47	107.1	133.5	187.4
Instructional staff expenditure (percent of total)	80.4	67.3	61.2	60.9	57.4	46.0	45.8

Source: Hanushek and Rivkin (1994).

cerned with the last quarter century, it is useful to begin with a longer perspective. Over the century 1890–1990, real expenditure per student rose at an annual rate of about 3½ percent.[4] Even though the overall growth in per student expenditure was remarkably stable over this long period, the nature of the spending increase changed over time.

Table 2-1 shows the growth in real current expenditure on public schools over the century. Over the century current expenditure increased by a factor of almost 100. Figure 2-1 shows the growth in per student real expenditure broken down into instructional staff salaries and other spending. Two things are noteworthy. First, direct expenditure on salaries for instructional staff grew steadily.[5] Second, other expenditure in schools grew even more rapidly, so that the direct spending on instructional staff fell from two-thirds of the budget in 1940 to two-fifths in 1990.

The increase in instructional staff expenditure is decomposed into more basic components in table 2-2. Specifically, growth in instructional costs is divided into three parts: that attributable to growth in the number of public school students (quantity), that attributable to increased intensity (pupil-teacher ratio and length of school year), and that attributable to input cost. During the earlier periods (1890–1940 and 1940–70) growth in the number of public school students was an important com-

4. Expenditure per pupil is deflated by the GDP deflator. Data sources and details of calculations on costs are described in Hanushek and Rivkin (1994) and put into a policy context in Hanushek and others (1994).

5. Instructional staff expenditure is wage and salary costs for instructional personnel. There are difficulties with data inconsistencies, since teacher aides were not included until 1990. Before that, in the postwar period, classroom teachers were a relatively constant proportion of all instructional personnel, with school principals making up most of the remainder. Neglecting aides has little bearing on the overall calculations. For simplicity, I frequently refer to instructional staff just as teachers since it does not materially change the interpretation. As indicated later, instructional staff expenditure does not include teacher fringe benefits, classroom materials, books, and so forth. Thus it is just one component of what would usually be labeled as total instructional costs.

Figure 2-1. *Instructional Staff and Other Current Expenditure per Student, Selected Years, 1890–1990*

1990 dollars per student

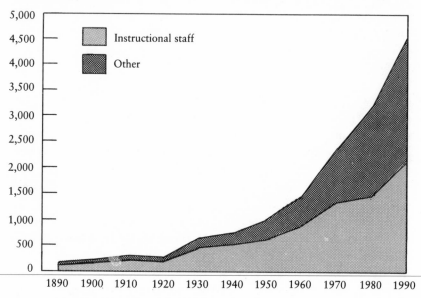

Source: National Center for Education Statistics (1995).

ponent of growth in total expenditure.[6] Over the 1970s and 1980s, however, growth in student enrollment fell, providing an offset for the significant increases that came from decreased pupil-teacher ratios and larger teacher salaries. The most important part of this table for the discussion here is that the rapid growth in spending has come from the kinds of general resource policies commonly advocated: a decrease in class size and an increase in wages to teachers.

The growth in expenditure other than that directly for instructional staff is more difficult to characterize. The decade of the 1970s was particularly important in yielding a significant, and apparently permanent, increase in the share of expenditure going to other areas. Although the data are scanty and difficult to interpret, this increase does not appear to have come from just the growth in centralized bureaucracy. A major

6. Increases in school attainment during these earlier periods would be expected to have increased per pupil costs by changing the relative weights of elementary and secondary schooling, although the magnitude of any such effects on expenditure growth is unknown. Since 1970 attainment has been constant, and there has been no change in the proportions of students at different levels.

Table 2-2. *Sources of Growth in Instructional Expenditure,*
by Period, 1890–1990

Percent

Item	1890–1940	1940–70	1970–90	1890–1990
School population[a]	34	38	−35	29
Instructional intensity[b]	23	22	85	28
Teacher cost[c]	43	40	50	43

Source: Hanushek and Rivkin (1994).
a. Combined effect of changes in the size of the school-age population, in the school enrollment rate, and in the rate of public school attendance.
b. Combined effect of changes in the pupil-teacher ratio and in the number of school days per year.
c. Effect of changes in the price of teachers.

component of the increase was "fixed charges," which include rapidly growing fringe benefits for school personnel. "Other instructional expenditure," which includes such items as aides, textbooks, and materials, also grew. A portion of the increase may also have been related to altered policies directed toward populations with various mental and physical handicaps (see the discussion of special education below). Nonetheless, the precise causes of this spending increase remain unclear; one can simply note that the rapid rise in spending other than for classroom personnel has been sizable.

Developing information about aggregate performance is more difficult. Over much of the century, school completion rates increased, but no objective information about any changes in school quality is available.[7] Since 1970 school attainment has been essentially flat, and attention has turned to student performance. The most direct information about student performance comes in the form of various test measures. The longest time series (figure 2-2) provides data on average performance on college admission tests, specifically the scholastic aptitude test (SAT). From a peak in the mid-1960s average SAT scores fell through the end of the 1970s, rose some, and then leveled off at a place lower than the peak. The fall from peak to trough was some 0.48 standard deviations for verbal and 0.28 standard deviations for mathematics.[8] Of course the

7. While it may be natural to think of an increase in school attainment as representing an increase in the output of the schools, it is more difficult to argue that this attainment resulted from the increase in spending per pupil.

8. Congressional Budget Office (1986), p. 40. Direct analysis of the effects of selective test-taking on SAT scores suggests that this factor was most important before 1971 and that changes after that were not heavily influenced by selectivity. At the same time, reliably correcting for selectivity is difficult, so the consistency with scores on other tests not subject to this effect is perhaps the strongest support for the qualitative picture from the SAT score trends.

Figure 2-2. *Scholastic Aptitude Test Scores, Total and by Race, Selected Years, 1966–93*

Average score

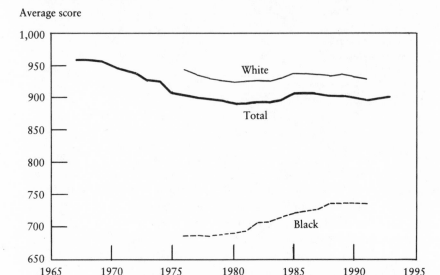

Source: National Center for Education Statistics (1995).

SAT tests are subject to well-known concerns about selectivity of the test-taking population, changes in measurement over time, and the like. Yet other tests also show declines, indicating that the qualitative test performance picture from the SAT is not a simple statistical aberration. Figures 2-3 through 2-5 show the performance of seventeen-year-olds on the National Assessment of Educational Progress (NAEP). The overwhelming picture is one of flat performance. While average math proficiency is slightly higher in 1990 than in 1970, reading proficiency is essentially unchanged, and science performance has fallen. These tests are taken by a representative sample of the school population and thus are not subject to the same criticisms as the SAT.[9] International tests give a similar picture, with the U.S. student population having low scores relative to students in a wide range of countries and failing to catch up with those students over time.[10]

9. The NAEP data do begin after the most precipitous fall in the SAT. Interestingly, from the mid-1970s through 1993 the average SAT picture looks very similar to that of the NAEP(first falling, then recovering during the 1980s—independent of any changes in participation rates for the SAT. The 1993 SAT scores almost precisely equal the 1976 scores, which are noticeably below those of the 1960s.

10. See, for example, McKnight and others (1987); Lapointe, Mead, and Phillips (1989).

Figure 2-3. *Science Achievement of Seventeen-Year-Olds by Race and Ethnicity, Selected Years, 1970–90[a]*

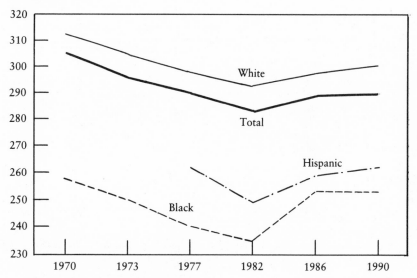

Average scale score

Source: National Center for Education Statistics (1995).
a. Scores on the National Assessment of Educational Progress.

Various explanations have been advanced to rationalize the aggregate spending and performance data. Some question whether the expenditure data are correct, in the sense that they might not represent expenditure on tested students. Specifically, during the 1970s federal legislation placed increased emphasis on providing educational services for the handicapped. These services, usually called special education, are more expensive to provide but do not go to the majority of students whose performance is assessed. Yet alternative estimates of the importance of special education do not show that these expenditures account for most of the growth in total spending or most of the decrease in pupil-teacher ratios.[11]

While some have placed great weight on recent, relatively better, U.S. performances on reading examinations, the record on both mathematics and science comparisons remains bleak.

11. Several approaches to estimating the importance of special education are found in Chaikind, Danielson, and Brauen (1993), Hanushek and Rivkin (1994), and Lankford and Wyckoff (1993). From these, an upper bound on the growth in spending over the 1980s that can be attributed to special education is around 25 percent. More recent analysis for New York State by Lankford and Wyckoff (1995), however, suggests a greater influence during the 1990s; see also Rothstein and Miles (1995).

Figure 2-4. *Reading Achievement of Seventeen-Year-Olds by Race and Ethnicity, 1971–90*[a]

Average scale score

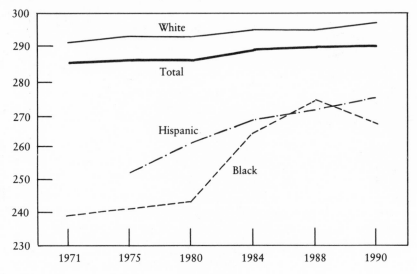

Source: National Center for Education Statistics (1995).
a. Scores on the National Assessment of Educational Progress.

An alternative explanation is that the student population has become more difficult to educate over time. To support this proposition it is common to cite increases in divorce rates, child poverty, and, sometimes, female labor force participation rates as factors presumed to affect student performance adversely. Of course these trends have been counteracted by improvements in parental education and reductions in average family size. It is difficult to say, a priori, how these factors balance out in terms of aggregate student performance, although David Grissmer and others suggest that, on net, families have actually *improved* as regards education.[12]

12. See Grissmer and others (1994). These conclusions have considerable uncertainty attached to them. They result from applying aggregate changes in family characteristics to the estimated importance of individual family factors derived from cross-sectional models of student achievement. This analysis suggests that actual student performance for the total student population and for whites is not as high as would be expected, based on family improvements. For blacks, the opposite holds. This raises the possibility that schools have been responsible for the better-than-expected gains of blacks, but the opposite for the majority of the student population. Direct analysis of the closing performance gap between blacks and whites on the NAEP nonetheless provides little support for the hypothesis that the relative gains are the result of improved school-level resources; see Cook (1995). The

Figure 2-5. *Mathematics Achievement of Seventeen-Year-Olds by Race and Ethnicity, 1973–90*[a]

Average scale score

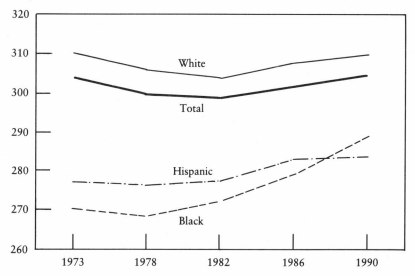

Source: National Center for Education Statistics (1995).
a. Scores on the National Assessment of Educational Progress.

The data missing are the performance of students in their subsequent careers. Has student performance with respect to labor-market productivity, home productivity, or other facets of subsequent performance been changing in a way more consistent with the use of school resources? Little aggregate information is available that permits addressing this question directly. Aggregate productivity growth certainly has not moved in line with spending, but that can be explained simply by lags in entry into the labor force.[13]

The aggregate data provide a *prima facie* case that school spending and school resources are not linked to performance. Although adjustments for changes in spending patterns or for inaccuracies of tests could modify some of the specifics, there is no way to conclude that aggregate performance has increased significantly over the past quarter-century. Indeed, some plausible evidence suggests real declines. While it is difficult

analysis in Koretz (1987) provides details of information about test score convergence by race through the mid-1980s. None of these incorporate the divergence in NAEP reading scores in the 1990s.

13. See Bishop (1989).

to provide direct aggregate labor-market analyses of the potential effect of changing school resources and quality, no simple data suggest noticeable improvements on that score. Aggregate comparisons are subject, nonetheless, to many influences.[14] This ambiguity motivates the various microeconomic studies of resources and performance.

Approaches to Analyzing the Use of School Resources

Most analyses of school resource usage follow a single basic line of attack. Measures of student performance are related to different educational inputs to ascertain whether variations in school resources are related to variations in student outcomes. Typically, some form of regression analysis is applied to data from actual school operations. The underlying studies, however, differ widely and in important ways.

The commonly accepted model of educational performance relates student performance at any time to the school and family inputs relevant to the individual student along with his or her innate abilities.[15] Current achievement results not only from current inputs but also from past inputs, so that, for example, a student's performance at the end of the sixth grade is determined not just by the sixth grade teacher but partly by previous teachers. Or, as another example, a student's performance in the labor market is affected not only by twelfth grade experiences but also those in earlier grades. As might be expected, even with agreement about the determinants of educational performance, actual application of this model varies considerably. The variation in application results most commonly from what data are available for any specific study. Moreover, specific studies often differ in several dimensions, so that attributing differences in results to particular features of the analysis or approach is often tenuous in itself.

Many ways of categorizing the underlying studies may be employed. The three dimensions that I believe are most important are measurement of student performance, faithfulness to the underlying model of inputs to the educational process, and accuracy of measurement of inputs into the process.

14. See Koretz (1987) for an assessment of some major hypotheses about the movement of aggregate test scores.
15. When measuring performance by labor-market outcomes, intervening factors such as acquisition of labor-market experience must also be considered. Discussion of such factors is ignored here.

PERFORMANCE MEASUREMENT. Most studies of school resource usage have relied on immediate output measures of schools, such as measured cognitive achievement or continuation to further schooling. The use of these measures has been justified on the grounds that they relate to important subsequent outcomes for individuals. Moreover, if that justification is plausible, their use allows direct analysis of models closely related to the conceptual model of the educational process described. Alternatively, measures based on actual career outcomes of individuals, such as earnings or employment records, can be employed. Such outcome measures correspond more directly to the ultimate benefits typically attributed to schooling. Until recently, however, such late measures of performance complicated the analytical task; concomitant measures of the educational resources of the students were unavailable directly, so that major efforts were required to assemble the relevant data. Moreover, a series of tenuous imputations was generally required.

FIDELITY TO THE UNDERLYING EDUCATIONAL PROCESS. As is commonly true with statistical approaches, the quality of the estimates of features of the educational process depends directly on how the modeling relates to the process generating the observed student performance. Although all the estimation efforts currently available are approximations to the determination of student performance, some appear better than others. Specifically, studies vary in the completeness with which they measure and estimate the effects of the inputs generally thought to be important for the educational process. Most typically, no explicit measures of innate abilities of students are available. Further, few studies have data on the history of school inputs for students. Some studies lack good measures of family backgrounds or other key nonschool inputs into education. Finally, at another level, variations in key features of the institutional and regulatory environment of schools—such as state school regulations, labor laws, funding incentives, and the like—may be unmeasured. The potential importance of such modeling limitations depends crucially on the specific analytical and modeling approach, an issue that is addressed later.

ACCURACY OF MEASUREMENT. Schools prove to be very heterogeneous. Even within the same building, the school inputs of individual students can differ dramatically, depending importantly on the actual courses being taken, the teachers of those courses, and the other students taking them. Across schools and districts, the variations are even larger.

Table 2-3. *Percentage Distribution of Estimated Effects of Key Resources on Student Performance, Based on 377 Studies*

Percent, except where indicated

Resources	Number of estimates	Statistically significant		Statistically insignificant		
		Positive	Negative	Positive	Negative	Unknown
Teacher-pupil ratio	277	15	13	27	25	20
Teacher education	171	9	5	33	27	26
Teacher experience	207	29	5	30	24	12
Teacher salary	119	20	7	25	20	28
Expenditure per pupil	163	27	7	34	19	13
Administrative inputs	75	12	5	23	28	32
Facilities	91	9	5	23	19	44

Source: Author's tabulations.

Moreover, the distribution of teachers and resources does not appear to be random. For example, the central tenet of most school-finance court cases is that resources are positively related to the economic circumstances of the student. Wealthier parents tend to ensure that more school resources are available for their children. Therefore, some care must be taken in analyses to match students with the specific resources that affect their education.

Each of these three factors enters into the existing analyses of educational performance in different ways. In the next sections I try to relate the research to these factors and their possible interpretation for policy purposes. Consistent with the thrust of this book, I give separate consideration to the direct educational production function estimation and the labor-market analyses.

Educational Production Function Estimates

I have reviewed estimates of educational production functions previously and summarize the most complete results here to facilitate discussion.[16] Table 2-3 presents the summary of estimated parameters related to school resources. This table covers published estimates through the end of

16. Past reviews are found in Hanushek (1986, 1989). These were updated through 1994 for the analysis here.

1994.[17] Each study represents a separate estimate of one of the key resource parameters on measured student performance (and more than one study typically appears in the ninety published works providing the sources of these data). The minimal requirements for acceptance are that studies must include some measures of the family background of students in addition to the common school resource factors and must include information about the statistical significance of the individual estimates.[18]

The estimates in table 2-3 summarize the effects of resources on performance that are obtained from aggregating across estimates from different school systems and different grades. No attempt has been made at this point to decide which of the published studies are better (as long as they met the minimal requirements). The first three items in the table are the most important because these inputs (teachers per pupil, teacher education, and teacher experience) together characterize variations in resources at the classroom level.[19]

The remarkable finding from combining the 377 available estimates across 90 separate published works is that neither variations in teacher-pupil ratio nor variations in teacher education are systematically related to student performance. For each input, the vast majority of parameter estimates are statistically insignificant. Of those estimates that are statistically significant, positive estimates are balanced by negative estimates. For example, of the 277 estimates of the effect of teacher-pupil ratios on student achievement, only 15 percent find statistically significant positive effects of increasing the intensity of teacher use. Fully 85 percent of available estimates give little confidence of a positive relationship between teacher-pupil ratios and student performance, while 13 percent even find statistically significant and negative effects. Only 9 percent of the estimated effects of greater teacher education give confidence of any positive effects on student performance. Teacher experience stands out in that almost 30 percent of the parameter estimates are statistically significant in the positive direction, whereas only 7 percent are statisti-

---

17. Every effort was made to locate all published articles meeting the minimal criteria about the form of the model and reporting of results described below. While the search was extensive, some studies may have been missed. Nonetheless, given that there are almost 400 estimates of resource effects, the general patterns are unlikely to be affected by a few missed estimates.

18. Thus, for example, the tabulation excludes the Coleman report because no indication of statistical significance for individual resource effects is available.

19. Teacher education and teacher experience are the most important determinants of teacher salary, and teacher-pupil ratios indicate across how many students the salaries are spread.

cally significant in the negative direction. But, again, this is far from unqualified support for the efficacy of employing more experienced teachers, since 71 percent of the estimated effects are statistically insignificant or negative.[20] Since these three inputs are combined to indicate variations in instructional expenditure per pupil, the results lead to the conclusion that no strong or systematic relationship exists between spending and student performance.[21]

Each of the inputs costs money to obtain. If each is unrelated to performance, one must draw the conclusion that significant inefficiency exists in schools. If related to performance, an additional step of analyzing the magnitude of any impact would be necessary. Because of the lack of clear relationships, this latter step has not been taken.[22]

The summary of the remaining inputs shows a similar pattern. Most estimates are statistically insignificant and are inconsistent as to sign of estimated effect. Moreover, as a general proposition, the studies under-

20. Estimates of the effects of experience are also subject to concern about direction of causality. Teachers frequently can influence their school and classroom assignment, based on their experience. This assignment option may lead more experienced teachers to select settings with students who perform better, leading to a positive relationship that is not causal.

21. The terms "strong" and "systematic"—terms used from a policy perspective—have unfortunately been confused with statistical significance by casual readers. The essence of the language here is to indicate confidence that increasing the given resource will increase student performance most of the time. The common statistical tests most often applied to the combined results of different studies relate to the null hypothesis that *all* underlying resource parameters are simultaneously zero. Evidence that resources occasionally affect student performance would lead to rejection of this null hypothesis (see Hedges, Laine, and Greenwald, 1994, and Hedges and Greenwald, this volume). Nonetheless, the evidence indicates that there is not generally likely to be any positive effect from variations in resources and that *negative effects may be as likely* as positive effects. Thus statistical significance against the overly strong null hypothesis of absolutely no relationship in common combined significance tests is a totally inappropriate criterion from a policy perspective.

22. Hedges, Laine, and Greenwald (1994, p.11) do attempt to ascertain the magnitude of performance gains suggested by studies of expenditure per student. They provide the quite incredible estimate that a 10 percent increase in school expenditure would lead to a 0.7 standard deviation increase in student performance. To put this estimate in perspective, real expenditure per student between 1966 and 1980 rose by 73 percent, while the average verbal SAT score declined by almost 0.5 standard deviations instead of increasing by the 5 standard deviations predicted. Through 1993, SAT scores had recovered somewhat, but spending continued its upward movement. The NAEP scores, as described, remained essentially flat during a period when per student spending roughly doubled. As noted, Grissmer and others (1994) suggest that, if anything, family backgrounds have improved overall, so that cannot explain the mismatch of actual data and predicted results from Hedges, Laine, and Greenwald. The most plausible interpretation of these highly erroneous predictions is that the underlying estimates are biased toward showing excessive effects of spending; see especially Hanushek, Rivkin, and Taylor (forthcoming).

lying these latter estimates are poorer. Measures of expenditure per pupil, of salaries, of administrative inputs, and of facilities are typically available only at the aggregate district level or, at best, at the aggregate school level (an issue I return to shortly).

Two points are relevant for interpreting these results. First, the results come from the operations of currently existing schools. They do not say that school resources *could not* be effective in raising student achievement; they say only that there is little reason to expect improved achievement from added resources in schools as currently organized and run. Organized in a different way—particularly with different incentives—added resources could lead to higher achievement by students. Alternative organizational approaches aimed precisely at altering this existing situation are described elsewhere.[23]

Second, the results do not say that school resources *never* have an impact. They say only that there is no reason to expect that added resources will have any consistent effect across typical schools currently being operated. Some studies find positive and statistically significant effects, which means that some systems may employ these resources effectively. Indeed, while having some problems with the mechanics of the analysis by Larry Hedges, Richard Laine, and Rob Greenwald, I have no disagreement with the conclusion they draw from reanalyzing these studies; namely, that one can be confident that some schools do employ resources effectively (that is, get positive results from added resources).[24] For example, 15 percent of the estimated effects of teacher-pupil ratios are positive and statistically significant, or more than the 5 percent expected by chance if no effective use were ever made of more teachers. This conclusion is neither new nor inconsistent with prior interpretations of the data, although independent confirmation of this result is useful.

Knowing that resources could and sometimes do affect student performance is not, however, helpful from a policy perspective. The existing research does not indicate under which circumstances resources are likely to be used effectively. It just indicates, by implication, that the existing

23. See Hanushek and others (1994).

24. Hedges, Laine, and Greenwald (1994) and Hedges and Greenwald (this volume). As described in Hanushek (1994), two issues are central to the interpretation of their results. Most important, they address the question whether resource differences ever matter in determining performance—a question that has little relevance to any policy discussions about education. Second, although the use of formal statistical tests is appealing, the methodology they choose is inappropriate for the data, requiring them to manipulate the data in ways that clearly bias the results of their tests toward the conclusion they are seeking.

proclivities of school decisionmakers do little to ensure effective use of resources. Returning, for example, to teacher-pupil ratios, 85 percent of the estimates give little reason to expect gains from employing teachers more intensively, and a number almost equal to the significantly positive parameter estimates even give strong reasons to worry about perverse effects.

The evidence in table 2-3 mixes many different kinds and qualities of studies. The original intent of the summary was to incorporate all the available evidence so as to avoid any possible distortion from the selection of studies. Specifically, the idea was to look at all evidence, no matter how weak, that could be marshaled to support the notion that increased resources systematically improve student performance. But the studies vary considerably in terms of the potential problems described previously. Two problems stand out. First, the studies differ in how comprehensively the inputs are measured. The general absence of historical data and of data on innate abilities of individuals is especially important. Also, a number of studies do not measure the relevant inputs for students accurately. For example, the average experience of the teachers in a large comprehensive high school may have little to do with the teachers any specific student has in the classroom, which leads to many measurement errors. Or, as another example, the percentage of students receiving a free or reduced-price lunch is an inaccurate measure of family background. Second, in the United States, states are the primary locus of policy development, and they create distinctly different environments for schools. For example, each state operates a different funding formula for local districts, resulting in varying incentives to localities and widely different funding levels within and across states. States also use very different regulations for teacher certification, for required curriculum in the schools, for graduation requirements, and the like. They have varying starting ages and mandatory attendance laws. These factors, almost never measured in studies of student performance, are also likely to be correlated with resources and other important schooling inputs.

To compensate for these data problems, a subset of studies has concentrated on value-added models of individual student performance in which the relevant teacher and classroom inputs are explicitly measured (along with detailed family backgrounds). These models consider gains in performance over limited time periods, conditional on earlier achievement and family factors. Such studies provide more reliable information about the effects of resources. Additionally, since studies within an individual state face the same policy environment, they will not run the

Table 2-4. *Summary of the Estimated Relationship between Student Performance and Various Components of School Expenditure, Based on Thirty-Nine Value-Added Studies of Individual Student Performance within Individual States*

| Input | Number of studies | Statistically significant | | Statistically insignificant | | |
		Positive	Negative	Positive	Negative	Unknown
Teacher-pupil ratio	23	1	3	7	9	3
Teacher education	33	0	3	11	9	10
Teacher experience	36	14	1	8	6	7

Source: Author's tabulations.

risk of biases from lack of measurement of relevant state policy. Table 2-4 summarizes the results of the thirty-nine studies that use these value-added models of individual schooling situations found within a single state.[25] It is clear from the table that neither the teacher-pupil ratio nor teacher education are important policy instruments; neither gives reason to expect improved student performance from increased resource use. Teacher experience again looks more important, but even so, thirty-five of the fifty-five estimates are statistically insignificant.[26] Thus, when attention is restricted to the higher-quality studies, the conclusions are unchanged. There is no consistent relationship between the key resources to schools and student performance.

These findings do not indicate, however, that differences in schools and teachers are unimportant. They consider only measured differences. Several analyses have concentrated on the overall differences among teachers regardless of the ability to measure the components of these differences.[27] These analyses, using a general covariance structure, find huge differences among teachers. For example, in my 1992 study I find that in a single academic year a good teacher can develop student performance a full grade level above the performance of students with a poor teacher. Good teachers certainly exist; it is just that good teachers are not different from bad in terms of class sizes, salaries, education, and

---

25. Aggregate inputs such as expenditure per pupil are generally unavailable for these analyses because these measures do not reflect resource variations for individual classrooms. A larger number of studies look at aggregate school performance in a value-added format, but these frequently do not involve the same students and are excluded from this analysis.

26. Clearly, though, a formal test of combined significance would reject the hypothesis that *all* experience parameters in the underlying systems are simultaneously zero.

27. See Hanushek (1971, 1992); Murnane (1975); Armor and others (1976); Murnane and Phillips (1981).

the like. The policy dilemma, discussed below, is that there is no reliable way to identify more or less effective teachers.

The key interpretative question remaining in the production function analyses is the measurement of student performance. Virtually all the production function studies included in the previous review employ measures of performance that are available at or soon after the student's schooling experience. This approach, which has obvious advantages, relies on the appropriateness of a two-stage analysis. In the first stage, characteristics of schools (and families) are related to measures of student performance obtained during or close in time to the schooling experience. In the second stage, these early student performance measures are related to outcomes later in life. But potential disadvantages come from the possibility that these early measures are not good measures of long-term performance.

The actual performance measures used in the studies encompass many kinds of standardized test scores and other measures of student performance. Of the 377 studies, 282, or 75 percent, use test measures of performance; the others include dropout behavior, school continuation, college performance, attitudes, and early career earnings. What is the overall tie of the more proximate measures of school performance and long run outcomes?

Over an extended time, studies of the labor market have been concerned about how individual differences in cognitive ability affect earnings (and modify the estimated returns to quantity). The early work was subsumed under the general topic of "ability bias" in the returns to schooling. The simple question was whether the tendency of more able individuals to continue in schooling led to an upward bias in the estimated returns to school (because of a straightforward omitted variables problem).[28] The correction most commonly used was to include a cognitive-ability measure in the earnings function estimates. Most of the early work concentrated on how the estimated returns to schooling were altered by including cognitive ability. The estimated direct effects of cognitive achievement on earnings, however, usually indicated modest effects of variations in cognitive ability after holding constant years of schooling.[29] In this work, there was no real discussion of what led to any

28. See, for example, Griliches (1974).
29. An exception to the generally modest relationship of cognitive performance and income is found in the work of Young and Jamison (1974). Using a national sample of data on reading competence, they find a strong influence of test scores on income for whites

observed differences in cognitive ability, although much of the work implicitly treated it as innate and not much related to variations in schooling.[30] Further, all this work relied on nonrepresentative samples of the population.

More recent direct investigations of cognitive achievement, however, have suggested generally larger labor market returns to individual differences. For example, a study by John Bishop, June O'Neill, Ronald Ferguson, Jeffrey Grogger, and Eric Eide and another by Richard Murnane, John Willett, and Frank Levy find that the earnings advantages to higher achievement on standardized tests are substantial.[31] Their results are derived from different approaches. On the one hand, Bishop, in his 1989 article, worries about the measurement errors that are inherent in most testing situations and demonstrates that careful treatment of that problem has a dramatic effect on the estimated importance of test differences. O'Neill, Ferguson, Grogger and Eide, and Bishop in his 1991 essay, on the other hand, simply rely on labor-market data for more recent periods, along with more representative sampling, and suggest that the earnings advantage to measured skill differences is larger than that found in earlier time periods and in earlier studies (even without correcting for test reliability). Murnane, Willett, and Levy, considering a comparison over time, demonstrate that the results of increased returns to measured skills hold regardless of the methodology (that is, whether simple analysis or error-corrected estimation). The National Academy of Sciences study on employment tests also supports the view of a significant relationship between tests and employment outcomes, although the strength of the relationship appears somewhat less strong than that in the direct earnings investigations.[32]

(but not blacks). This held in both recursive and simultaneous equations models of the joint determination of achievement and income.

30. Manski (1993) represents more recent work with this same general thrust. He recasts the issue as a selection problem and considers how ability or quality interacts with earnings expectations to determine continuation in schooling. Currently, however, no empirical work along these lines identifies the quantitative importance of selection or the interaction of school quality and earnings in such models.

31. Bishop (1989, 1991); O'Neill (1990); Ferguson (1993); Grogger and Eide (1995); Murnane, Willett, and Levy (1995).

32. Hartigan and Wigdor (1989). The study considers the relation between the General Aptitude Test Battery (GATB), the standard employment test of the Department of Labor, and job performance. The authors' synthesis of a wide number of studies suggests a systematic but somewhat modest relationship, with correlations to performance on the order of 0.2 to 0.4. The analysis also finds that the validity of these tests in predicting performance has gone down over time. These results, being somewhat at odds with recent studies, may

An additional part of the return to school quality comes through continuation in school. There is substantial evidence that students who do better in school, either through grades or scores on standardized achievement tests, tend to go farther in school.[33] Steven Rivkin finds that variations in test scores capture a considerable proportion of the systematic variation in high school completion and in college continuation.[34] Indeed, he finds that test score differences fully explain black-white differences in schooling. Bishop and Hanushek, Rivkin, and Lori Taylor find that individual achievement scores are highly correlated with school attainment.[35] Jere Behrman and others find strong achievement effects on both continuation into college and quality of college; moreover, the effects are larger when proper account is taken of the endogeneity of achievement.[36] Hanushek and Pace, using the High School and Beyond data, find college completion is significantly related to higher test scores at the end of high school.[37] At the same time school resources, as opposed to student achievement, are much less connected to school continuation.[38]

I conclude from these diverse studies that variations in cognitive ability, as measured by standardized tests, are important in career success. Although variation in measured cognitive ability is far from being everything that is important, it is significant statistically and quantitatively. Therefore, it seems that the two-stage analysis found in the existing educational production function estimates is appropriate and useful.

Wage Determination Models with School Resources

Work involving estimates of earnings models that include measures of school resources has been conducted for a long time, but it has received

simply reflect the specialized nature of the GATB. The GATB is a very old test that may not reflect changes in the economy. It also suffers from some psychometric problems. The central purpose of the study was to assess the Department of Labor's practice of providing test information normed to racial groups.

33. See, for example, Dugan (1976); Manski and Wise (1983).
34. Rivkin (1991).
35. Bishop (1991); Hanushek, Rivkin, and Taylor (forthcoming).
36. Behrman and others (1994).
37. Hanushek and Pace (1995).
38. Of the available production function studies, only 33 of the 377 (9 percent) consider school attainment directly; that is, look at high school dropout rates or at college continuation. While the small numbers make generalizations difficult, the pattern of estimated resource effects looks qualitatively similar to the overall results presented previously. In contrast, virtually all examinations of the relationship with achievement tests show significant positive effects, in part because colleges select on the basis of achievement.

much more attention with the publication of David Card and Alan Krueger's study.[39] The usual approach in this line of research has been to begin with a general database, such as that from the census, and to fill in information about the schooling experiences of the individuals from some other source. Until recently, few data sets have been available that simultaneously contain detailed individual information about schooling experiences and later labor market success, the exception being the National Longitudinal Survey of the High School Class of 1972 (NLS-72) sample. Now the High School and Beyond data set and the National Longitudinal Survey of Youth (NLS-Y) data set contain such information, but the workers are relatively early in their careers.

The labor-market studies are, in most ways, superior in their measurement of student outcomes or achievement to the educational production function approaches. The direct observation of career accomplishment is clearly better than the measure of immediate proxies. But this advantage comes at a cost.

First, the precise schooling experiences of the individual are virtually never known from the retrospective addition of schooling information. Instead, it is necessary to go to broad aggregate data, say, state-level observations. Aggregate data for states do not accurately portray the resources available to any student, since, by most conventional measures, within-state variations in resources are considerably larger than between-state variations. This makes extraction of any systematic effects difficult.

Second, such an approach, while possibly dealing with random measurement errors, has the potential for exacerbating any specification errors. Even if data on individual classrooms or students contained significant measurement error, aggregation would not necessarily help unless the model was well specified. The interaction of aggregation with model specification is considered below.

Third, the measurement error that exists is not random. Resources applied to schools vary in some systematic ways. That fact is the heart of all the school-finance court cases. Better-off parents are more likely to provide better resources for schools. Such a pattern is far from perfect, and in fact varies considerably across states. Nevertheless, there is no

39. For examples of earlier studies, see Welch (1966); Johnson and Stafford (1973); Wachtel (1976). Card and Krueger (1992) provided the most extensive estimates of resource effects until the analysis of data from the 1970, 1980, and 1990 censuses by Heckman, Layne-Farrar, and Todd (this volume). Betts (this volume) provides a complete listing of such studies along with an evaluation of the overall results.

presumption that resources are randomly distributed within (or across) states.

Fourth, most of the earnings-resources studies neglect any influences of families on student achievement. Certainly families are important to education, and one would expect this component to show up in skills that are valued in the labor market. If families are important in education, and if family circumstances also tend to dictate the level of school resources in the local district, estimation of models based just on school resources are subject to standard misspecification problems. In the simplest case, one would expect the impact of school resources to be overestimated when family circumstances are neglected. This expectation, which comes directly from a simple model that assumes that only families and schools effect outcomes, is complicated in the more realistic, multivariate circumstances discussed here. It is also complicated by being overlaid with the aggregation issues discussed previously. Nevertheless, one would normally expect an upward bias from neglecting family influences on child outcomes.

Fifth, earnings analyses generally draw data from individuals who attended schools across the United States. As such, they combine schooling governed by distinct state policies, but they never include direct measures of such state differences. To the extent that state regulatory and policy regimes affect student performance—a widely held belief—and to the extent that they are correlated with resource usage in the state's schools, the estimated effects of school resources on subsequent performance will be biased. While there is no theoretical reason to expect that these omitted state factors bias the estimated resource effects upward, the evidence presented below suggests that they have just this impact.

An easy demonstration of these issues comes from work that Rivkin, Taylor, and I have done.[40] We have been investigating what influences student achievement and school continuation. In doing so, we have confirmed the significance of variations in individual achievement for attainment. But a second focus has been whether there are significant variations across schools in educational continuation and, if these exist, whether variations in resources promote more schooling (over and above individual family and achievement differences). Our approach has been to estimate individual school attainment models (using the High School and Beyond data from the 1980s). In addition to descriptions of family income and education levels, race, and sex, these models include either a

---

40. Hanushek, Rivkin, and Taylor (forthcoming).

Table 2-5. *Generalized Least Squares Estimates of School-Specific Educational Attainment*[a]

Factor	(1)	(2)	(3)	(4)	(5)	(6)
Local community						
College completion rate	...	2.31	...	2.29	...	2.46
		(3.34)		(3.24)		(3.45)
Unemployment rate	...	4.22	...	4.25	...	4.18
		(2.54)		(2.59)		(2.51)
Wage	...	−.0008	...	−.0016	...	−.0009
		(−.38)		(−.84)		(−.42)
State community						
College completion rate	...	−1.50	...	−1.68	...	−1.50
		(−1.17)		(−1.33)		(−1.17)
Unemployment rate	...	−1.83	...	−1.75	...	−2.17
		(−.71)		(−.68)		(−.84)
Wage	...	−.0019	...	−.0012	...	−.0019
		(−.82)		(−.52)		(−.80)
In-state tuition	...	−.0001	...	−.0001	...	−.0001
		(−.88)		(−1.06)		(−.91)
School						
Teacher-pupil ratio	2.86	2.39	3.01	2.55	...	...
	(1.50)	(1.26)	(1.59)	(1.35)		
Teacher salary	0.47	0.45	...	...	0.51	0.51
	(1.24)	(1.03)			(1.34)	(1.16)

Source: Hanushek, Rivkin, and Taylor (forthcoming).
a. Based on 307 observations. Numbers in parentheses are *t* statistics.

school-specific or a state-specific fixed effect. These school- and state-specific effects are subsequently regressed (with generalized least squares) on a set of school resources and community factors, an approach that mimics the two-step procedures of Card and Krueger. The first-stage estimation shows clearly that there are significant differences among schools in expected educational attainment. Table 2-5 shows the results from the second-stage models for school-specific factors. The conclusion from this table is that school resources (teacher-pupil ratio and teacher salaries) have small and statistically insignificant effects on educational attainment. Significantly, omitting all the community factors does make the teacher-pupil ratio look stronger and closer to being statistically significant. The real story lies in the comparison with table 2-6, which presents the models for state-specific differences in educational attainment. Here teacher-pupil ratios and teacher salaries, when aggregated to the state level, seem to have important influences on educational attainment. The estimated parameters for the effects of both teacher-pupil ratio and teacher salary are four to five times as large as in the school-level

Table 2-6. *Generalized Least Squares Estimates of State-Specific Educational Attainment*[a]

Factor	(1)	(2)	(3)	(4)	(5)	(6)
State community						
College completion rate	...	4.89	...	4.89	...	5.54
		(2.64)		(2.65)		(2.91)
Unemployment rate	...	8.51	...	9.40	...	7.72
		(2.95)		(3.50)		(2.51)
Wage	...	−.0041	...	−.0049	...	−.0063
		(−1.71)		(−2.29)		(−2.36)
In-state public tuition	...	−.0001	...	−.0000	...	−.0000
		(0.47)		(0.25)		(0.24)
School						
Teacher-pupil ratio	11.63	11.66	12.33	11.94	...	...
	(2.50)	(2.53)	(2.59)	(2.61)		
Teacher salary	1.91	0.94	...	...	2.21	1.21
	(1.91)	(0.88)			(2.03)	(1.04)

Source: Hanushek, Rivkin, and Taylor (forthcoming).
a. Based on thirty-eight observations. Numbers in parentheses are *t* statistics.

analysis shown in the previous table, and the teacher-pupil ratio here is consistently statistically significant across the various specifications. How could it be that the pupil-teacher ratio is unimportant at the individual school level but important in the aggregate? Our explanation is simple: model misspecification and measurement errors are amplified by aggregation to the state level, so that severely biased parameter estimates occur. This result appears to be similar to Julian Betts's findings for the effects of disaggregated and aggregated resources on earnings differences.[41]

The generality of these findings can also be seen from previous production function studies. Table 2-7 divides the studies of the effects of teacher-pupil ratios and of expenditure per student into different classes depending on whether or not the data are drawn from samples crossing state boundaries and are aggregated to the state level (that is, lacking within-state variation). Since the state policy and regulatory environment is the same for all schools within a given state, analyses of performance for students schooled entirely within a state will not be biased by a lack of measures of state policies. Analyses across states will, however, be biased by such an omission. This division of the estimates demonstrates the pattern of bias dramatically. Cross-state studies omitting measures of state policies are much more likely to find that resources affect student outcomes, and this tendency is greatly increased when school data are aggregated to the state level.

41. Betts (1995).

Table 2-7. *Distribution of Estimated Effect of Teacher-Pupil Ratio and Expenditure per Pupil, by State Sampling Scheme and Aggregation*[a]

Percent, except where indicated

State sampling scheme and aggregation of resource measures	Number of estimates	Statistically significant		Statistically insignificant		
		Positive	Negative	Positive	Negative	Unknown
Teacher-pupil ratio						
Total	277	15	13	27	25	20
Single state[b]	157	12	18	31	31	8
Multiple state[c]	120	18	8	21	18	35
Within-state variation[d]	109	14	8	20	19	39
No within-state variation[e]	11	64	0	27	9	0
Expenditure per pupil						
Total	163	27	7	34	19	13
Single state[b]	89	20	11	30	26	12
Multiple state[c]	74	35	1	39	11	14
Within-state variation[d]	46	17	0	43	18	22
No within-state variation[e]	28	64	4	32	0	0

Source: Hanushek, Rivkin, and Taylor (forthcoming).
a. Rows may not add to 100 because of rounding.
b. Estimates from samples drawn within single states.
c. Estimates from samples drawn across more than one state.
d. Resource measures at level of classroom, school, district, or county allowing for variation within each state.
e. Resource measures aggregated to state level with no variation within each state.

Consider the effects of teacher-pupil ratios. The combined results reported previously indicate that 15 percent of the studies find positive and statistically significant effects, while 13 percent find negative and statistically significant effects. Studies within individual states (which necessarily do not aggregate school resource data to the state level), however, find that statistically significant results are split 12 percent to 18 percent (positive to negative). Statistically insignificant studies are evenly split. Studies drawing data from across states, on the other hand, show disproportionately positive and significant effects, with almost two-thirds of the studies that use aggregated state-level data finding statistically significant positive effects. The findings for estimated effects of expenditure per pupil follow the same pattern. Support for the notion that there is a positive relationship comes disproportionately from studies using cross-state samples and even more so from studies using aggregated expenditure data. Thus the difference in findings between the production function literature and the wage determination literature is quite consistent with the varying analytical approaches underlying them, as opposed to just the measurement of performance or the range of resource data commonly available.

Finally, such an analytical approach employing later outcomes, typi-fied by the wage determination models, is not generally helpful from a policy point of view. For evaluating current programs or resource usage, it is impractical to wait thirty years to obtain information about subse-quent labor market success or failure. Alternatively, even if one were to presume that today's schools are like those of the 1920s, save perhaps for teacher-pupil ratio and teacher salaries, what would be the recom-mended policy? Would it be to reduce average pupil-teacher ratio by some fixed amount (past the significant reductions already incurred)? Does it matter how this is done across districts, across students, or across grades? Since reducing class sizes and increasing salaries are just the policies that have been pursued throughout the century (see table 2-2), but more strongly in recent decades, shouldn't we now be in a position of not worrying about schooling? Clearly, we are not in such a position.

Conclusions

The discussion whether school resources are systematically related to school quality and to student achievement has tended toward a battle of slogans: "Money matters" or "Money doesn't matter." Early in this century Alfred Marshall noted that all short sentences in economics are wrong.[42] With an appropriate definition, either slogan can be correct. Neither, however, is useful from a policy perspective. Questions about the effectiveness of resources have been widely embraced by many people who just want to limit or reduce public expenditure. The suggestion that differences in resources are unrelated to student performance, on the other hand, defies common sense, conventional wisdom, the hopes of parents and policymakers, and the apparent self-interest of many partic-ipants in the schooling system. Given this background, it is not surprising that any evidence that appears to suggest that "resources count" gets unduly wide circulation.

---

42. In private correspondence, Marshall (1925, p. 484) stated: "My favourite *dictum* is: Every statement in regard to economic affairs which is short is a misleading fragment, a fallacy or a truism. I think this dictum of mine is an exception to the general rule: but I am not bold enough to say that it *certainly* is."

The policy question remains, nonetheless: what is the best way to improve schools? Few people who have thought about school policies would recommend just dumping extra resources into existing schools. America has in fact followed that program for several decades, with no sign that student performance has improved. Unless one weights it in specific and peculiar ways, the evidence from the combined studies of resource usage provides the answer for the aggregate data: any evidence of effective resource usage is balanced by evidence of other, naturally occurring, situations in which resources are squandered. Moreover, nobody has produced a guide to situations that yield effective as opposed to ineffective resource usage.

The central issue in all policy discussions is usually not whether to spend more or less on school resources but how to get the most out of marginal expenditures. Nobody would advocate zero spending on schooling, as nobody would argue for infinite spending on schooling. The issue is getting productive uses from current and added spending. The existing evidence simply indicates that the typical school system today does not use resources well (at least if promoting student achievement is their purpose). It is tautological to say that we will get good performance if we spend the money wisely. Today the existing knowledge base does not ensure that any added funds will, on average, be spent wisely. That is true even if some schools may spend their funds wisely.

The reason why this situation could persist seems to lie in the lack of incentives to improve student performance.[43] School personnel— teachers, principals, superintendents, librarians, and other staff—have little at stake in student outcomes. Whether students do particularly well or particularly poorly, the career progression and rewards of virtually all school personnel remains unaffected. Given this situation, it is not particularly surprising that resources are at best weakly linked to student performance. The most promising alternative policy to make current and additional resources more productive reverses this feature by emphasizing performance incentives. In essence U.S. schools are unlikely to improve in terms of either student outcomes or costs unless much stronger incentives for improved student performance are instituted. This policy focus is fraught with uncertainties, because very little is known about how best

---

43. Hanushek and others (1994) examine this point and evaluate the most frequently discussed options for introducing performance incentives.

to structure the various incentives. But improved performance incentives are central to school reform designed to improve student outcomes.

References

Armor, David, and others. 1976. *Analysis of the School Preferred Reading Program in Selected Los Angeles Minority Schools.* Santa Monica, Calif: Rand.

Behrman, Jere R., and others. 1994. "How Family Background Sequentially Affects College Educational Investments: High School Achievement, College Enrollment, and College Quality Choices."

Betts, Julian R. 1995. "Does School Quality Matter? Evidence from the National Longitudinal Survey of Youth." *Review of Economics and Statistics* 77 (May): 231–50.

Bishop, John H. 1989. "Is the Test Score Decline Responsible for the Productivity Growth Decline?" *American Economic Review* 79 (March): 178–97.

———. 1991. "Achievement, Test Scores, and Relative Wages." In *Workers and Their Wages*, edited by Marvin H. Kosters, 146–86. American Enterprise Institute.

Card, David, and Alan B. Krueger. 1992. "Does School Quality Matter? Returns to Education and the Characteristics of Public Schools in the United States." *Journal of Political Economy* 100 (February): 1–40.

Chaikind, Stephen, Louis C. Danielson, and Marsha L. Brauen. 1993. "What Do We Know about the Costs of Special Education? A Selected Review." *Journal of Special Education* 26 (Winter): 344–70.

Coleman, James S., and others. 1966. *Equality of Educational Opportunity.* GPO.

Congressional Budget Office. 1986. *Trends in Educational Achievement.*

Cook, Mike. 1995. "Families or Schools? Accounting for the Convergence in White and Black Test Scores since 1970." Paper prepared for the annual meeting of the Association for Public Policy Analysis and Management, Washington, D.C., November.

Dugan, Dennis J. 1976. "Scholastic Achievement: Its Determinants and Effects in the Education Industry." In *Education as an Industry*, edited by Joseph T. Froomkin, Dean T. Jamison, and Roy Radner, 53–83. Cambridge, Mass.: Ballinger.

Ferguson, Ronald F. 1993. "New Evidence on the Growing Value of Skill and Consequences for Racial Disparity and Returns to Schooling." H-93-10. Malcolm Wiener Center for Social Policy. Harvard University.

Griliches, Zvi. 1974. "Errors in Variables and Other Unobservables." *Econometrica* 42 (November): 971–98.

Grissmer, David W., and others. 1994. *Student Achievement and the Changing American Family.* Santa Monica, Calif.: Rand.

Grogger, Jeffrey T., and Eric Eide. 1995. "Changes in College Skills and the Rise in the College Wage Premium." *Journal of Human Resources* 30 (Spring): 280–310.

Hanushek, Eric A. 1971. "Teacher Characteristics and Gains in Student Achievement: Estimation Using Micro Data." *American Economic Review* 61 (May): 280–88.

———. 1986. "The Economics of Schooling: Production and Efficiency in Public Schools." *Journal of Economic Literature* 24 (September): 1141–77.

———. 1989. "The Impact of Differential Expenditures on School Performance." *Educational Researcher* 18 (May): 45–51, 62.

———. 1992. "The Trade-Off between Child Quantity and Quality." *Journal of Political Economy* 100 (February): 84–117.

———. 1994. "Money Might Matter Somewhere: A Response to Hedges, Laine, and Greenwald." *Educational Researcher* 23 (May): 5–8.

———. 1996. "Rationalizing School Spending: Efficiency, Externalities, and Equity, and Their Connnection to Rising Costs." In *Individual and Social Responsibility: Child Care, Education, Medical Care, And Long-Term Care in America*, edited by Victor R. Fuchs, 59–91. Chicago: University of Chicago Press.

Hanushek, Eric A., and Richard R. Pace. 1995. "Who Chooses to Teach (and Why)?" *Economics of Education Review* 14: 107–17.

Hanushek, Eric A., and Steven G. Rivkin. 1994. "Understanding the 20th Century Explosion in U.S. School Costs." Rochester Center for Economic Research, Working Paper 388.

Hanushek, Eric A., Steven G. Rivkin, and Lori L. Taylor. Forthcoming. "Aggregation and the Estimated Effects of School Resources." *Review of Economics and Statistics*.

Hanushek, Eric A., and others. 1994. *Making Schools Work: Improving Performance and Controlling Costs*. Brookings.

Hartigan, John A., and Alexandra K. Wigdor, eds. 1989. *Fairness in Employment Testing: Validity Generalization, Minority Issues, and the General Aptitude Test Battery*. Washington: National Academy Press.

Hedges, Larry V., Richard D. Laine, and Rob Greenwald. 1994. "Does Money Matter? A Meta-Analysis of Studies of the Effects of Differential School Inputs on Student Outcomes." *Educational Researcher* 23 (April): 5–14.

Johnson, George E., and Frank P. Stafford. 1973. "Social Returns to Quantity and Quality of Schooling." *Journal of Human Resources* 8 (Spring): 139–55.

Koretz, Daniel. 1987. *Educational Achievement: Explanations and Implications of Recent Trends*. Congressional Budget Office.

Lankford, Hamilton, and James Wyckoff. 1993. "Where Has the Money Gone? An Analysis of School District Spending in New York, 1979–80 to 1991–92." In *Putting Children First*. vol. 2: *Reports Prepared for the New York State Special Commission on Educational Structure, Policies and Prac-*

tices. Albany: New York State Commission on Educational Structure, Policies and Practices.

———. 1995. "The Allocation of Resources to Special Education, Administration and Regular Instruction." Paper prepared for a conference on Performance-Based Approaches to School Reform. Brookings Institution, Washington, D.C., April 6–7.

Lapointe, Archie, Nancy A. Mead, and Gary W. Phillips. 1989. *A World of Differences: An International Assessment of Mathematics and Science*. Princeton, N.J.: Educational Testing Service.

Manski, Charles F. 1993. "Adolescent Econometricians: How Do Youth Infer the Returns to Schooling?" In *Studies in Supply and Demand in Higher Education*, edited by Charles T. Clotfelter and Michael Rothschild, 43–57. Chicago: University of Chicago Press.

Manski, Charles F., and David A. Wise. 1983. *College Choice in America*. Harvard University Press.

Marshall, Alfred. 1925. "Letter to the Right Hon. Louis Fry." In *Memorials of Alfred Marshall*, edited by A. C. Pigou, 484–87. London: Macmillan.

McKnight, Curtis C., and others. 1987. *The Underachieving Curriculum: Assessing U.S. School Mathematics from an International Perspective*. Champaign, Ill.: Stipes.

Murnane, Richard J. 1975. *The Impact of School Resources on the Learning of Inner City Children*. Cambridge, Mass.: Ballinger.

Murnane, Richard J., and Barbara R. Phillips. 1981. "What Do Effective Teachers of Inner-City Children Have in Common?" *Social Science Research* 10 (March): 83–100.

Murnane, Richard J., John B. Willet, and Frank Levy. 1995. "The Growing Importance of Cognitive Skills in Wage Determination." *Review of Economics and Statistics* 77 (May): 251–66.

National Center for Education Statistics. 1995. *Digest of Education Statistics 1995*. Washington.

O'Neill, June. 1990. "The Role of Human Capital in Earnings Differences between Black and White Men." *Journal of Economic Perspectives* 4 (Fall): 25–46.

Poterba, James M. 1996. "Government Intervention in the Markets for Education and Health Care: How and Why?" In *Individual and Social Responsibility: Child Care, Education, Medical Care, and Long-Term Care in America*, edited by Victor R. Fuchs, 277–304. University of Chicago.

Rivkin, Steven G. 1991. "Schooling and Employment in the 1980s: Who Succeeds?" Ph.D. dissertation. University of California, Los Angeles.

Rothstein, Richard, and Karen Hawley Miles. 1995. *Where's The Money Gone? Changes in the Level and Composition of Education Spending*. Washington: Economic Policy Institute.

Wachtel, Paul. 1976. "The Effect on Earnings of School and College Investment Expenditures." *Review of Economics and Statistics* 58 (August): 326–31.

Welch, Finis. 1966. "Measurement of the Quality of Schooling." *American Economic Review* 56 (May, *Papers and Proceedings, 1965*): 379–92.

Young, K. H., and Dean T. Jamison. 1974. "The Economic Benefits of Schooling and Compensatory Education." Paper prepared for meetings of the Econometric Society, December.

CHAPTER 3

Have Times Changed?
The Relation between School Resources and Student Performance

Larry V. Hedges and Rob Greenwald

Ｉ N THE PREVIOUS chapter Eric Hanushek surveys the relation between school resources and achievement using two sources of evidence. The first is aggregate data about resources and achievement. The second is the body of production function studies that explicitly model the relation between measures of resources and achievement, controlling for student background variables. In this chapter we analyze Hanushek's evidence and arguments.

Aggregate Data

Hanushek presents aggregate data on school resource use and student achievement to develop an argument that resources are unrelated to educational outcomes. He provides data on the level of resource inputs to schools for the period 1890 to 1990. After examining these data on total expenditures for elementary and secondary education and the percentage of those expenditures allocated to instructional staff, enrollments, and teacher costs, Hanushek concludes that aggregate expenditures per student have increased over the century under consideration. He then presents data on student achievement based on Scholastic Aptitude Test (SAT) scores and National Assessment of Educational Progress (NAEP) information, and argues that achievement has declined in the last twenty to twenty-five years.

Hanushek argues that since resources are up and achievement is down, the two variables cannot be positively related. This argument necessarily assumes that everything else relevant to the cost of education and the

74

production of student achievement has remained constant. This assumption is incorrect; there have been important changes over the period, including a dramatic expansion in the *level and comprehensiveness* of education and a decline in the *social capital* available in families, which substitute for school resources. Both these changes confound any simple relation between gross spending and gross achievement.

Social Capital

Considerable research in psychology and education supports the hypothesis that home environment has strong effects on student achievement, stronger in fact than social class effects.[1] The most important home environment variables involve a parent (or parents) expending time participating in or facilitating activities with children that enhance learning (reading with a child, playing games with educational content, helping with homework, and so on). These home environment variables have been characterized as social capital,[2] since they reflect a consistent allocation of parental time and expertise to the child for the purpose of fostering greater achievement (investment of time on the part of parents to produce a return). While few national data exist on the most important home environment or social capital variables, there are some indicators that are likely to be correlated with them. These indicators have shown marked declines in the past quarter-century.

Data Availability

Although gross expenditure data for the last century are available, data on school outcomes were more difficult to obtain until the advent of the NAEP in the early 1970s.

THE PERIOD 1890–1970. Hanushek acknowledges that it is difficult to obtain aggregate information about performance, particularly educational achievement, over the past century. There is, however, some suggestive evidence about the period 1890–1970. This period is associated with the expansion of secondary education in the United States. The rate of enrollment in secondary schools went from about 6–7 percent in 1890 to approximately 92 percent in 1970, increasing steadily throughout the

1. See, for example, Kellaghan and others (1993).
2. Coleman (1987, 1988).

period, except for minor deviations apparently caused by World War II and the Korean War.[3] The rate of secondary school graduation grew from approximately 5 percent in 1890 to about 78 percent in 1970, increasing steadily throughout the period.[4] Thus while expenditures were increasing throughout this period, they were used to educate larger numbers and different types of students. This fact demonstrates the difficulty in making aggregate comparisons across such large time spans.

It seems misleading to compare aggregate cost data in 1900, when only a small fraction of the population (mostly in cities and towns) attended secondary school, to cost data in 1970, when secondary schooling was nearly universally available, even in the most distant rural areas. It is surely more expensive to attain universal geographic coverage for students at all ability levels and physical limitations (the contemporary setting) than to provide schools for a more or less elite urban segment of the population (the reality in 1900).

It is also misleading to compare aggregate educational achievement of the national population across such large time periods. One suspects that the proportion of seventeen-year-olds who could solve simple algebra or high school science problems was many times greater in 1970 than in 1900, when few people were in secondary school (few learn the symbolic representations of algebra or science if they have not been taught them in school). The effect size is probably many standard deviations, but it would surely be misleading to conclude that education in 1970 was therefore much more effective than in 1900.

It is clear from Hanushek's data that the nation has progressively spent more money on education and that a larger fraction of the nation has attended schools of different types over that period. Aggregate comparisons of achievement over that period are therefore difficult to interpret.

THE PERIOD 1970–92. In contrast to the earlier period, the period 1970–92 had relatively stable enrollment patterns. Thus aggregate comparisons across this period are not as problematic. Hanushek presents two specific kinds of data on achievement trends during this time: SAT scores and NAEP data.

SAT scores. Although the SAT score decline in the 1960s and early 1970s has been widely discussed, the SAT is a flawed social indicator. It is flawed because the population that takes the SAT in any given year is

---

3. For percent in 1890, see Kleibard (1995, pp. 7–8); for 1970, see Goldin (1994).
4. Goldin (1994).

a matter of self-selection. Changes over time in the composition of the tested population are now generally believed to have accounted for much, if not most, of the declines.[5] Indeed, the second part of the study cited by Hanushek for the data on the SAT concludes that selection and composition factors "exaggerated the drop in scores on the SAT-Verbal by about 75 percent and the decline in the reading comprehension scores of students taking the SAT by about 125 percent."[6] These estimates of selection effects suggest that the adjusted total decline in the SAT verbal score is closer to 0.25 standard deviations than the 0.48 standard deviations (the unadjusted decline) cited by Hanushek. Using the same rule of thumb, the adjusted total decline in SAT math score would be closer to 0.12 standard deviations than the 0.24 standard deviations cited by Hanushek.

There has been much discussion among statisticians, psychometricians, and even a few economists about whether methods available to correct for selection effects could render the SAT a meaningful social indicator. The consensus among statisticians seems to be that the difficulties posed by selection are too great to overcome in SAT scores.[7] If SAT scores *even after adjustment for selection* are too problematic to be useful for policy inferences, then we believe the *unadjusted* scores are even more misleading.

NAEP scores. The NAEP trend data are collected from nationally representative samples using the same design and measurement instruments during each wave of data collection. We agree with Hanushek that the NAEP provides the best available data on the academic achievement of seventeen-year-olds in the United States and changes in achievement over time. But we do not agree that the NAEP data fail to show a pattern of increases over the last two decades. Table 3-1 shows the means and standard deviations of NAEP trend scores in reading, mathematics, and science from 1970 to 1992. The effect size is the change in mean from the earliest trend assessment to the last (in 1992), expressed in standard deviation units. These are the same data that Hanushek presents graphically in his chapter, except that the 1992 data have been added for completeness.

The overall average achievement scores in reading and mathematics

---

5. See Beaton, Hilton, and Schrader (1977); Advisory Panel on the Scholastic Aptitude Test Score Decline (1977).

6. Koretz (1987, p. 103).

7. Wainer (1986).

Table 3-1. *Trends in National Assessment of Educational Progress Achievement Scores, Selected Years, 1970–92*

	SCIENCE					
	1970	1977		1992		
Group	Mean	Mean	Standard deviation	Mean	Standard deviation	Effective size[a]
All	305.0	289.5	45.0	294.1	44.7	−0.24
Whites	312.0	297.7	40.5	304.2	40.6	−0.19
Blacks	258.0	240.2	41.6	256.2	39.4	−0.05
Hispanics	n.a.	262.3	41.8	270.2	41.6	0.19[b]

	READING					
	1971		1975		1992	
Group	Mean	Standard deviation	Mean	Standard deviation	Mean	Standard deviation	Effective size[a]
All	285.2	45.8	n.a.	n.a.	289.7	43.0	0.10
Whites	291.4	42.5	n.a.	n.a.	297.4	39.8	0.15
Blacks	238.7	43.5	n.a.	n.a.	260.6	42.2	0.52
Hispanics	n.a.	n.a.	252.4	42.0	271.3	43.7	0.43[c]

	MATHEMATICS					
	1973	1978		1992		
Group	Mean	Mean	Standard deviation	Mean	Standard deviation	Effective size[a]
All	304.0	300.4	34.9	306.7	30.1	0.09
Whites	310.0	305.9	32.3	311.9	28.4	0.07
Blacks	270.0	268.4	31.8	285.8	27.5	0.58
Hispanics	277.0	276.3	32.9	292.2	26.9	0.60

Source: Mullis and others (1994).
n.a. Not available.
a. The change in mean from the earliest trend assessment to the last (1992), expressed in standard deviation units.
b. Computed for the change between 1977 and 1992.
c. Computed for the change between 1975 and 1992.

have increased slightly since 1971 and 1973, respectively, when the NAEP trend data collection began. However, the overall means obscure important changes in scores. Although the achievement of white students has remained fairly stable, the reading and math achievements of blacks and Hispanics have increased by about one-half a standard deviation. These are substantial increases.

Overall achievement in science has declined somewhat since 1970, when the NAEP trend data collection began. Achievement for whites is down a bit less than the total average, and the achievement of blacks in science is essentially unchanged. But achievement of Hispanics in science has increased.

Table 3-2. *Indicators of Social Capital, Selected Years, 1940–70*

Percent

Item	1940	1950	1960	1970	1980	1990
Children with mothers in the work force	10	16	26	36	49	59
Children living with mother only	6.7	6.4	7.7	11.8	16.2	20.0
Births to unmarried women	n.a.	n.a.	5.3	10.7	18.4	n.a.

Sources: For data on children and mothers, Hernandez (1994); for data on births, Hobbs and Lippman (1990, table 30, p. 49).
n.a. Not available.

Thus overall achievement in the core academic subjects of reading and mathematics has increased in the last two decades, and the achievement of blacks and Hispanics in these subjects has risen substantially. Achievement in science, which constitutes a much smaller part of the elementary and secondary school curriculum, has decreased overall, but even in science Hispanics have shown increases.

In sum, it would appear that schools *have* produced modest increases in achievement for all students in the core academic areas of mathematics and reading, and produced rather substantial increases in the achievement of blacks and Hispanics.

Social capital. Measurement of social capital has not received great attention until fairly recently. Several indicators suggest, however, that the social capital available to American school children has decreased remarkably since 1960 (table 3-2).

One aspect of social capital is the amount of time mothers have to devote to their children, presumably some of which is given over to informal educative activities. Maternal employment competes for time with the educative aspects of child rearing; consequently social capital is diminished when mothers work. As the table shows, the percentage of children with mothers in the work force has increased steadily over the last few decades, from 16 percent in 1950 to 26 percent in 1960 and 59 percent in 1990.[8]

Presumably, the presence of a father in the home increases the total amount of adult time that could be deployed for all family activities, including educative activities in the home. Thus social capital would be smaller when no father is present. The proportion of children living with their mothers only has more than tripled since 1950, increasing from 6.4 percent in 1950 to 20.0 percent in 1990.[9] Finally, it might be expected that children born to unwed mothers would normally have fewer adult

8. Hernandez (1994).
9. Hernandez (1994).

resources in the home and hence less social capital than children born to married couples. The proportion of births to unmarried women has more than tripled since 1960, increasing from about 5 percent to about 22 percent in 1986.[10]

Each of these indicators provides evidence of a substantial decline in social capital in the last few decades. The declines are at least as pronounced for disadvantaged groups such as blacks and Hispanics as for the population as a whole, making the increases in achievement of the latter groups even more impressive.

Implication. We argue that achievement would be expected to decline over the 1970–92 period because of the decline in favorable home environment or social capital. The fact that achievement has not declined substantially (and has increased substantially for some subgroups) is evidence *for*, not against, the positive effects of increasing school expenditures. We argue that, as family structures have changed and social capital has eroded, increases in school expenditures have substituted for the informal educational resources we characterize as social capital investments.[11]

Educational Production Function Estimates

The second source of evidence that Hanushek considers is the body of studies that attempt to determine the relation between resources and achievement while explicitly controlling for characteristics of students, studies that estimate education production functions.

The cumulative nature of education presents a problem for education production function modeling, especially given the current high mobility of students in urban school systems. Cross-sectional studies usually attempt to control for background characteristics by including a measure of the socioeconomic status (SES) of the family. Though sometimes elaborate constructions, most often these indexes are devised using parental income or parental education, or both. These controls are not designed to directly measure the educational background of students but are relied on because of their historic relation to student achievement.

10. Hobbs and Lippman (1990).
11. We are not alone in drawing this conclusion; Flyer and Rosen (1994) have made precisely this point.

Critique of Hanushek's Findings

Longitudinal studies provide better control for student background effects. In such studies, a pre-test and a post-test are employed to measure student progress over a prescribed period (usually one academic year). Most equations also use an SES control. Over a period of ten years, Hanushek assembled and analyzed a universe of studies on the effects of school resources.[12] His analysis led him to question whether there was a relation between school inputs and student outcomes. The data presented in his chapter in this book are an analysis of the studies in his universe that were longitudinal.

We (with Richard D. Laine) have assembled a new universe of studies in which one-third of the studies are longitudinal. Our meta-analysis of studies of the full data set and the longitudinal subset of the new universe have similar results. In both cases the findings suggest strong and substantially positive relations between educational resource inputs and academic achievement. Global resource variables such as per pupil expenditure (PPE) show strong and consistent relations with achievement. School size and teacher-pupil ratio are negatively related to student achievement (these results reflect greater achievement in *smaller* schools and *smaller* classes, respectively). Teacher background characteristics, including verbal ability, education, and experience are all positively related to student achievement.

In his chapter Hanushek focuses on the resource input variables, teacher-pupil ratio, teacher education, and teacher experience, arguing that they "together characterize variations in resources at the classroom level." We feel that differences in the effects of the global resource variable (PPE) will also result in resource differences in classrooms. We would argue that the differences in PPE between a high-spending suburban district and a moderate-spending urban district (even within the same geographic area, such differences in PPE are often on the order of a factor of 2) are more important than the variation in teacher experience, which may be comparable on a districtwide basis. Thus while arguing that most of the studies do not track resources down to the classroom level, Hanushek appears to have arbitrarily selected three of the input measures (of the seven, including PPE, he assesses in earlier work). Although Hanushek is incorrect in maintaining that no longitudinal study uses the variable PPE (see his footnote 16), the number of studies, and thus our

12. Hanushek (1989).

Table 3-3. *Summary of the Production-Function Coefficients Used in the Combined Significance Analyses of Longitudinal Studies*[a]

	Significant		Nonsignificant			
Input variable	Positive	Negative	Positive	Negative	Unknown	Total
Teacher-pupil ratio[b]						
Hanushek-incl NS?[c]	2 (11)	3 (16)	7 (37)	7 (37)	27	46
Hanushek	2 (11)	1 (6)	8 (44)	7 (39)	...	18
New universe of studies	4 (15)	3 (12)	12 (46)	7 (27)	...	26
Teacher education						
Hanushek-incl NS?[c]	0 (0)	4 (19)	9 (43)	8 (38)	10	31
Hanushek	2 (11)	3 (16)	7 (37)	7 (37)	...	19
New universe of studies	1 (5)	5 (26)	7 (37)	6 (32)	...	19
New universe (dichotomous)[d]	1 (8)	1 (8)	7 (54)	4 (31)	...	13
Teacher experience						
Hanushek-incl. NS?[c]	19 (40)	1 (2)	17 (35)	11 (24)	7	55
Hanushek	20 (37)	1 (2)	21 (39)	12 (22)	...	54
New universe of studies	8 (27)	1 (3)	13 (43)	8 (27)	...	30

Source: Author's calculations.

a. The numbers in parentheses are percents. The percentages exclude the category nonsignificant unknown sign.

b. The signs have been reversed in those studies that use the variable pupil-teacher ratio or class size, to be consistent with teacher-pupil ratio, so that $b > 0$ means that smaller classes have greater outcomes.

c. NS? refers to coefficients that the primary research study reported as insignificant without indicating the magnitude of sign.

d. A "dichotomous" subsample was created, which used only those equations that indicated the possession of a master's degree. Those equations with continuous variables (such as B.A. to Ph.D.) were excluded from this subsample.

confidence in making policy recommendations based on the available evidence from longitudinal data, are limited.[13]

Hanushek appears to be arguing that all longitudinal studies eliminate the level of aggregation problem, but that is simply not true. Even in longitudinal studies, resource inputs and student outcomes are often measured at different levels. For example, Richard Murnane and Barbara Phillips do not match teacher-level data to students, and Rebecca Maynard and David Crawford measure inputs at the school level.[14] It should be noted that some studies exemplify the type of data tracking we hope all future research will follow. Charles Link and Edward Ratledge track to the classroom level, and Hanushek in an earlier work and Anita Summers and Barbara Wolfe use both inputs and outcomes at the student level.[15]

Table 3-3 presents a summary of the direction and the statistical sig-

13. Two studies in Hanushek's universe: Bieker and Anschel (1973) and Maynard and Crawford (1976); three studies in our new universe: Bieker and Anschel (1973); Maynard and Crawford (1976); and Ehrenberg and Brewer (1994).

14. Murnane and Phillips (1981); Maynard and Crawford (1976).

15. Link and Ratledge (1979); Hanushek (1971); Summers and Wolfe (1977).

nificance of the production function coefficients for the three resource variables discussed in Hanushek's chapter. The distribution of data used in the combined significance analyses is presented in this way to demonstrate that the universe of coefficients in Hanushek's universe, our reanalysis, and the new universe we have assembled are similar with respect to vote-count distribution.

The large number of coefficients with nonsignificant results but unknown direction is puzzling. We believe that perhaps the analyses were not reported in detail because they were conducted as part of specification searches in which many models with potentially overlapping variables were estimated. That these results were not taken seriously by the researchers as definitive model estimates is reflected by the fact that they did not bother to report coefficient estimates (and in some cases the details of the model specification).

We have discussed elsewhere the weaknesses of counting the number of significant p-values to summarize the *estimates* from a collection of studies.[16] Briefly, because individual studies may have low statistical power, the proportion of significant p-values may not be very large, even when small-to-moderate effects are present in every study. Indeed, our summary of the collection of studies that Hanushek has reviewed showed much more evidence of positive effects.

To overcome some of these weaknesses, we summarized the longitudinal studies that Hanushek had assessed by counting the number of significant p-values. We also summarized the longitudinal portion of our new universe of production function studies.

Combined Significance Tests

Our meta-analysis uses combined significance testing. Combined significance tests provide a way to combine statistical significance values (p-values) from studies that test the same conceptual hypothesis but that may differ in the details of their designs or measurement methods.[17] The inverse chi-square (Fisher) method was used to determine if the data are consistent with one or both of the null hypotheses in every study, or if there are effects in a specified direction in at least some of the studies. Two directional hypotheses were tested for each of the resource input variables:

16. Hedges, Laine, and Greenwald (1994).
17. Hedges and Olkin (1985).

(a) the positive case, where the null hypothesis states that no positive relation exists between the resource input and student outcome, and

(b) the negative case, where the null hypothesis states that no negative relation exists between the resource input and student outcome.

It is possible to reject the null hypothesis in both the positive and negative cases, which would mean that there is evidence of both some positive and some negative relations. But to reach the conclusion that there was no systematic relationship between educational resource inputs and student outcomes, the data would have to be consistent with the null hypothesis in both the positive and the negative cases.

The results of the combined significance tests are reported in tables 3-4 and 3-5. Table 3-4 provides the data, including degrees of freedom and chi-square critical values. We examined the data in the combined significance tests in two ways. In the full analysis we analyzed all independent *p*-values or effect magnitudes. To assess the robustness of the results, we analyzed the central 90 percent of values to determine the impact of outlier values.

Table 3-5 provides a summary of the results presented in table 3-4, listing whether there was evidence of a positive or negative effect in each of the variable categories.

Examining the results in table 3-5 of the combined significance tests in the positive direction (left rows) shows that the null hypothesis for the positive test (that no positive relation exists between resource inputs and student achievement) is rejected for the full sample in Hanushek's universe for the variable teacher-pupil ratio. Thus there is evidence that at least some of the coefficients associated with this input variable in the combined significance analyses are positive. However, this result is not robust, for it does not hold for the trimmed subsample. Examining the results of the combined significance tests for the teacher-pupil ratio in the negative direction (right rows) shows that the null hypothesis for the negative test (that no negative relation exists between resource inputs and student achievement) is rejected for the full sample. Thus there is evidence of coefficients associated with this input variable in the combined significance analyses that are negative. As in the positive case, this finding is not robust, for it does not hold for the trimmed subsample. It is difficult to draw conclusions about the relation between the teacher-pupil ratio and student achievement from a reanalysis of the longitudinal studies in Hanushek's universe. In contrast, conclusions may be drawn from the evidence provided by the data presented in the universe of studies we examined. In the new universe the trimmed subsamples pro-

Table 3-4. Results of Combined Significance Tests of Longitudinal Studies[a]

Input variable (outcomes)	Equations (studies)	Sample					
		Positive case (H₀: β ≤ 0)		Full analysis (df, X²)[c]	Robustness[b] (df, X²)[c]	Negative case (H₀: β ≥ 0)	
		Full analysis	Robustness[b]			Full analysis	Robustness[b]
Teacher-pupil ratio[d]							
Hanushek	18 (6)	57.95	**39.45**	(36, 51.00)	(32, 46.19)	**53.54**	**35.36**
New universe of studies	26 (10)	90.81	**73.70**	(52, 69.83)	(48, 65.17)	**73.19**	**47.92**
Teacher education							
Hanushek	19 (6)	59.26	**44.73**	(38, 53.38)	(34, 48.60)	**89.33**	**56.87**
New universe	19 (2)	**44.06**	**34.92**	(38, 53.38)	(34, 48.60)	**111.40**	**82.59**
New universe (dichotomous)[e]	13 (7)	43.43	**34.30**	(26, 38.89)	(22, 33.92)	**27.63**	**13.34**
Teacher experience							
Hanushek	54 (9)	356.93	**283.37**	(108,133.26)	(96,119.70)	**76.72**	**54.73**
New universe	30 (14)	177.50	**128.26**	(60,79.08)	(52, 69.83)	**55.27**	**37.78**

Source: Author's original research.

a. **Bold** indicates failure to reject the null hypothesis in the (+) case, and rejection of the null hypothesis in the (−) case.

b. The robustness samples are the middle 90 percent with 5 percent trimmed from each side of the distribution.

c. df = degrees of freedom. The chi-square values provided are at the α = 0.05 level. The degrees of freedom and chi-square values are identical for the positive and negative cases.

d. The signs have been reversed in those studies that use the variable pupil-teacher ratio or class size, to be consistent with the teacher-pupil ratio, so that $b > 0$ means that smaller classes have greater outcomes.

e. A "dichotomous" subsample was created, which used only those equations that indicated the possession of a master's degree. Those equations with continuous variables (for example, B.A. to Ph.D.) were excluded from this subsample.

Table 3-5. *Summary of Results of Combined Significance Tests of Longitudinal Studies*[a]

Input variable (outcomes)	Evidence of positive effects?		Evidence of negative effects?	
	Full analysis sample	Robustness[b] sample	Full analysis sample	Robustness[b] sample
Teacher-pupil ratio[c]				
Hanushek	Yes	No	Yes	No
New universe of studies	Yes	Yes	Yes	No
Teacher education				
Hanushek	Yes	No	Yes	Yes
New universe of studies	No	No	Yes	Yes
New universe (dichotomous)[d]	Yes	Yes	No	No
Teacher experience				
Hanushek	Yes	Yes	No	No
New universe of studies	Yes	Yes	No	No

Source: Author's original research.

a. Evidence of positive effects indicates that the null hypothesis was rejected at $\alpha = 0.05$ level; evidence of negative effects indicates that the null hypothesis was rejected at $\alpha = 0.05$ level.

b. The robustness samples are the middle ninety percent, with 5 percent trimmed from each side of the distribution.

c. The signs have been reversed in those studies that use the variable pupil-teacher ratio or class size, to be consistent with the teacher-pupil ratio, so that $\beta > 0$ means that smaller classes have greater outcomes.

d. A "dichotomous" subsample was created, which used only those equations that indicated the possession of a master's degree. Those equations with continuous variables (for example, B.A. to Ph.D.) were excluded from this subsample.

vide evidence that at least some of the coefficients associated with the teacher-pupil ratio in the combined significance analyses are positive but no evidence that any coefficients associated with this input variable in the combined significance analyses are negative. These results lead us to conclude that smaller classes are associated with higher achievement.

We regard the results on the class size effect found in the new universe as sensible, particularly in light of the extensive experimental literature on class size suggesting that smaller class sizes are associated with higher achievement. A number of leading studies report data in a form that could not be used in the analyses we conducted.[18] And indeed Hanushek, in table 2-5 of his chapter, presents school-level data on the teacher-pupil ratio indicating that smaller classes are associated with greater educational attainment.

The results of the combined significance tests for the variable teacher education in both Hanushek's universe and the new universe appear to be difficult to interpret. The trimmed subsamples in each of these data

18. Finn and Achilles (1990); Glass and Smith (1979); Hedges and Stock (1983); McGiverin, Gilman, and Tillitski (1989).

sets provide no evidence of positive coefficients and some evidence of negative coefficients. This result would suggest that less-educated teachers are associated with higher student achievement. We have reason to believe, however, that this finding is due to a problem in variable characterization. To investigate this hypothesis, we separated the studies analyzed according to the way in which teacher education was measured. While some studies used continuous scales (for example, from B.A. to Ph.D.), we felt the most efficient measure of teacher education was whether a person possessed a master's degree. When we analyzed only those studies that measured teacher education in this dichotomous manner, the results provided evidence of positive relations and no evidence of negative relations. These findings were robust, holding for both the full analysis and the trimmed subsample. We conclude that the instruction by teachers possessing a master's degree is associated with higher student achievement.

The results for the variable teacher experience were unambiguous. For both Hanushek's universe and the new universe, there was evidence that at least some of the coefficients associated with this teacher experience in the combined significance analyses are positive and no evidence that any coefficients associated with this variable are negative. This finding was robust, holding for both the full sample and the trimmed subsample in each case. This result suggests that more-experienced teachers are associated with higher student achievement. The conclusions we draw from the variable teacher experience are congruent to those we reached in our reanalysis of Hanushek and the new universe (in which seven variables, including PPE, teacher verbal ability, and school size were analyzed).[19] In both the reanalysis and the new analysis, the relations between inputs and outcomes are consistently positive and large enough to be educationally important.

It would be desirable to have some information about the magnitudes of the relations between resources variables and achievement. Although we summarized the standardized regression coefficients in our earlier work and in our new universe, very few longitudinal studies in either universe reported the information necessary to compute the magnitude of the individual effects. Consequently, we feel that the quantity of information, while suggesting positive effects, was insufficient to create meaningful summaries.

19. Hedges, Laine, and Greenwald (1994).

Improving Research on Resource Utilization

As Hanushek notes in his chapter, to evaluate properly the effects of resources on student outcomes, it is important to match students with the resources they actually use in their education. Unfortunately the data available to address questions about resource allocation at or within the school site are limited. Few school districts have developed financial data collection and reporting systems that track resources to the classroom, the level of greatest interest in understanding student learning. Bruce Cooper has tested a model in which data gathering originates at the school and classroom level and differentiates between allocations at the central office and those at the school site.[20] Robert Berne and Leanna Stiefel caution that the variability in data quality is likely to increase as the measurements move closer to the students.[21] Their apprehension is not meant as a barrier to change, merely a warning about the need to carefully scrutinize data until the quality of collection techniques is ensured.

Classroom-level data are essential to accurately address the question of how educational inputs matter. One example is the importance of matching the educational experiences of teachers with the performance of their students. David Monk uses longitudinal data to determine the effects of specific background characteristics of teachers (major field of study and extent of course work in the areas of life science, physical science, and mathematics at both the undergraduate and graduate level) on their NAEP achievement tests.[22] Rather than use broad categories such as the acquisition of a master's degree to represent teacher education, detailed analyses of specific aspects of a teacher's educational background are more likely to accurately explain the relation between teacher education and student outcomes.

Owing to the complexity in modeling the educational experience, researchers frequently seem to use a "kitchen sink" approach. This method includes employing a multitude of overlapping variables in the initial regression, then limiting future equations to those variables with significant coefficients. This practice explains the large number of coefficients with nonsignificant results but unknown direction in Hanushek's data. A better approach is to develop a conceptual paradigm of what is im-

20. Cooper and associates (1994).
21. Berne and Stiefel (1994).
22. Monk (1994).

portant in the classrooms and corridors of a school and design a model that reflects it. Inherent in such a process is understanding the difficulty of quantifying certain aspects of school experience. It may not be feasible to collect certain types of data on a large scale. However, it may be practical to determine the interactions between certain variables in small-scale intensive studies and use the relations identified to better understand the larger data set.

Hanushek questions the estimates of the magnitude of the effects of PPE on student achievement that we obtained from the collection of studies that he assembled. Note that these are not estimates we produced from our own modeling exercise, but a summary of the estimates of others. We agree that the median effect in his collection of studies is probably too large to be credible (the median effect in our new universe of studies is much smaller and seems more plausible); however, half of the estimates were even larger than the median we reported.

Hanushek also expresses general concern about the methods we used, without being specific. They are not particularly obscure; we simply took the median of the standardized regression coefficients reported in the studies Hanushek had assembled. It is unfortunate that more studies did not explicitly report the values of coefficients in models that they estimated, but we do not think it inappropriate to summarize the values that were reported. If the aim is to determine the magnitude of an effect, we believe that most members in the statistical community will find a summary of estimates more informative than a count of the number of significant p-values.

Hanushek himself has estimated rather large differences between the effects of individual teachers; "the estimated difference in annual achievement growth between having a good [teacher] and having a bad teacher can be more than one grade-level equivalent in test performance."[23] We wish to note this effect may also be extrapolated to absurd lengths. It says that parents who pick "good" teachers for their children every year should expect them to gain half a standard deviation (which is about equal to a grade equivalent in many achievement tests) more each year than students who have only average teachers. In ten years of schooling, such students would be predicted to be five standard deviations ahead of the students who had only average teachers and ten standard deviations ahead of those who had consistently bad teachers.

The general conclusion of the meta-analyses we have conducted, in-

---

23. Hanushek (1992, p. 107).

cluding the results presented in this chapter, is that school resources are systematically related to student achievement and that these relations are large enough to be educationally important. Although the findings of our research should provide a clear direction for policymakers, the results do not provide detailed information on the most educationally or economically efficient means to allocate existing and new dollars. We hope that the emphasis will shift from the question of "does money matter?" to the issue of how resources matter in specific circumstances. Hanushek appears to agree with this sentiment, stating in the conclusion of his chapter that "the policy question remains . . . what is the best way to improve schools?" Yet he goes on to state that dollars wisely spent are canceled by dollars wasted. This statement is not what our data, or his for that matter, suggest. We believe that discussions of school reform should not proceed under a mandate of flat resources but should instead incorporate an assessment of the current relation between inputs and outcomes and determine how to best allocate resources in specific contexts.

References

Advisory Panel on the Scholastic Aptitude Test Score Decline. 1977. *On Further Examination.* New York: College Entrance Examination Board.

Beaton, Albert E., Thomas L. Hilton, and William B. Schrader. 1977. *Changes in the Verbal Abilities of High School Seniors, College Entrants, and SAT Candidates between 1960 and 1972.* New York: College Board and Educational Testing Service (Princeton, N.J.).

Bieker, Richard F., and Kurt R. Anschel. 1973. "Estimating Educational Production Functions for Rural High Schools: Some Findings." *American Journal of Agricultural Economics* 55 (August): 515–19.

Berne, Robert, and Leanna Stiefel. 1994. "Measuring Equity at the School Level: The Finance Perspective." *Educational Evaluation and Policy Analysis* 16 (Winter): 405–21.

Coleman, James S. 1987. "Families and Schools." *Educational Researcher* 16 (August/September): 32–38.

———. 1988. "Social Capital in the Creation of Human Capital." *American Journal of Sociology* 94 (supplement): 95–120.

Cooper, Bruce S., and associates. 1994. "Making Money Matter in Education: A Micro-Financial Model for Determining School-Level Allocations, Efficiency, and Productivity." *Journal of Education Finance* 20 (Summer): 66–87.

Ehrenberg, Ronald G., and Dominic J. Brewer. 1994. "Do School and Teacher

Characteristics Matter? Evidence from High School and Beyond." *Economics of Education Review* 13 (March): 1–17.

Finn, Jeremy D., and Charles M. Achilles. 1990. "Answers and Questions about Class Size: A Statewide Experiment." *American Educational Research Journal* 27 (Fall): 557–77.

Flyer, Frederick, and Sherwin Rosen. 1994. "The New Economics of Teachers and Education." Working Paper 4828. Cambridge, Mass.: National Bureau of Economic Research.

Glass, Gene V., and Mary Lee Smith. 1979. "Meta-Analysis of Research on Class Size and Achievement." *Educational Evaluation and Policy Analysis* 1 (January–February): 2–16.

Goldin, Claudia Dale. 1994. "How America Graduated from High School: 1910 to 1960." Working Paper 4762. Cambridge, Mass.: National Bureau of Economic Research.

Hanushek, Eric A. 1971. "Teacher Characteristics and Gains in Student Achievement: Estimation Using Micro-Data." *American Economic Review* 61 (May): 280–88.

———. 1989. "The Impact of Differential Expenditures on School Performance." *Educational Researcher* 18 (May): 45–51, 62.

———. 1992. "The Trade-Off between Child Quantity and Quality." *Journal of Political Economy* 100 (February): 84–117.

Hedges, Larry V., and Ingram Olkin. 1985. *Statistical Methods for Meta-Analysis.* Orlando: Academic Press.

Hedges, Larry V., and William Stock. 1983. "The Effects of Class Size: An Examination of Rival Hypotheses." *American Educational Research Journal* 20 (Spring): 63–85.

Hedges, Larry V., Richard D. Laine, and Rob Greenwald. 1994. "Does Money Matter? A Meta-Analysis of Studies of the Effects of Differential School Inputs on Student Outcomes." *Educational Researcher* 23 (April): 5–14.

Hernandez, Donald J. 1994. "Children's Changing Access to Resources: A Historical Perspective." *Social Policy Report* 8 (Spring): 1–23.

Hobbs, F., and L. Lippman. 1990. "Children's Well-Being: An International Comparison." *International Population Reports*, series P-95, no. 80. Bureau of the Census.

Kellaghan, Thomas, and others. 1993. *The Home Environment and School Learning: Promoting Parental Involvement in the Education of Children.* San Francisco: Jossey-Bass.

Kliebard, Herbert M. 1995. *The Struggle for the American Curriculum 1893–1958.* Routledge.

Koretz, Daniel. 1987. *Educational Achievement: Explanations and Implications of Recent Trends.* Congressional Budget Office.

Link, Charles R., and Edward C. Ratledge. 1979. "Student Perceptions, IQ, and Achievement." *Journal of Human Resources* 14 (Winter): 98–111.

Maynard, Rebecca, and David L. Crawford. 1976. *Rural Income Maintenance Experiment: Summary Report.* University of Wisconsin, Institute for Research on Poverty.

McGiverin, Jennifer, David Gilman, and Chris Tillitski. 1989. "A Meta-Analysis of the Relation between Class Size and Achievement." *The Elementary School Journal* 90 (September): 47–56.

Monk, David H. 1994. "Subject Area Preparation of Secondary Mathematics and Science Teachers and Student Achievement." *Economics of Education Review* 13 (June): 125–45.

Mullis, Ina V.S., and others. 1994. *NAEP 1992 Trends in Academic Progress.* Washington, D.C.: National Center for Education Statistics.

Murnane, Richard J., and Barbara R. Phillips. 1981. "What Do Effective Teachers of Inner-City Children Have in Common?" *Social Science Research* 10 (March): 83–100.

Summers, Anita A., and Barbara L. Wolfe. 1977. "Do Schools Make a Difference?" *American Economic Review* 67 (September): 639–52.

Wainer, H., ed. 1986. *Drawing Inferences from Self-Selected Samples.* New York: Springer-Verlag.

CHAPTER 4

Evidence from Fifteen Schools in Austin, Texas

Richard J. Murnane and Frank Levy

T HE QUESTION here is whether existing empirical work and summaries of this empirical work suggest different realities about the relation between educational spending levels and outcomes for students. We would like to explain our view by describing fifteen elementary schools serving low-income, minority-group children in Austin, Texas. In 1989 student achievement in these schools was extremely low, as measured on state-mandated achievement tests, relative both to other schools in Austin and to the state average. As part of the resolution to a desegregation court case, these fifteen schools were designated priority schools and were given $300,000 each, above normal school spending in Austin, each year for five years. So the experience of these fifteen schools is something of a natural experiment.

Four years later, at the end of the 1993 school year, student achievement and student attendance remained extremely low in thirteen of the fifteen schools. In those schools there was no discernible evidence of improved outcomes despite the extra money.

In two of the schools, the Zavala Elementary School and the Ortega Elementary School, the situation was different. By the end of 1993 student attendance at the two schools was among the highest in the city, and test scores had risen to the city's average, even though median family income for the families with children in those schools remained about $12,000. In other words, the accomplishments of these two schools were extraordinary.

On the basis of the evidence from these fifteen schools, what would

These comments are based on the forthcoming book by Richard J. Murnane and Frank Levy, *Teaching the New Basic Skills* (Free Press, 1996).

an analysis of the question *does money matter?* show? From the vote-counting perspective that Eric Hanushek favors, the conclusion would be negative. In thirteen out of fifteen cases, extra money did not result in higher achievement.

A meta-analysis of the evidence, conducted along the lines Larry Hedges advocates, would come to a different conclusion. The correlation between changes in spending and changes in student achievement at Zavala and Ortega is sufficiently high, even when combined with thirteen cases of a zero correlation, for the null hypothesis of no effect to be rejected at conventional levels of statistical significance.

Who would be right? Hanushek would emphasize the lack of a consistent relation between spending and achievement. Hedges would point out that the evidence simply does not support a conclusion that money does not matter, on average. Both are right. Both of their summaries fit the facts for the fifteen schools.

Of course, both the vote-counting and the meta-analysis techniques are designed to summarize disparate evidence rather than to highlight the sources of the differences. A compelling question is, why did achievement rise so dramatically over four years at Zavala and Ortega, while extra money seemed to make no difference in the other thirteen schools? To answer that, we need to look at what the schools did with the money.

At the thirteen schools that experienced no achievement gains, the money was spent primarily on reducing class size by hiring extra teachers. Little was done to change what happened in the classes. In the words of Austin's superintendent, Terry Bishop:

> They didn't change the way they were doing things. . . . All they did was take that support, lower pupil-teacher ratios, still use the same curriculum, still use the same instructional methods. You'd go over there and they'd actually have . . . ten students in a class, but guess what they would be doing? You'd have two rows of five students, and the teacher would still be sitting up there in the front of the room, and still using ditto sheets like they were before. You can do that with thirty students as easy as you can ten. Politically I think they were afraid to use the money in any other way.[1]

Zavala and Ortega also used much of the extra money to lower class size. But that was not all they did. The principals actively confronted the

---

1. Interview with Terry Bishop, April 7, 1994.

problem of low achievement and worked with teachers and parents to change it. One thing they did was to put all children with special needs into regular classes, something that freed up a considerable amount of money, and that was possible with small classes but not with large. Adopting the reading and math curriculum that was provided only to gifted and talented children in the rest of the district, the principals used it as a lever to change instructional methods. They had to get a waiver from the School Board to do so. They also brought health services to their schools. That turned out to be important in raising attendance with school populations in which 40 percent of the children come to school without state-mandated immunizations and for which the alternative to school-based health services is waiting all day in the emergency room at the nearest hospital. These two schools also invested heavily in getting parents involved in their children's schooling, including having parents participate in the governance structure of the schools, right down to sitting on hiring and budget committees.

What would multiple regressions of relationships between school resources and student achievement based on these fifteen schools have shown?

—First, if estimated with 1990 data, they would have shown nothing, because it took even Zavala and Ortega several years to implement a new plan.

—Second, if estimated with 1993 data, they would have shown that class size had a modest negative relationship to achievement as a main effect. This modest impact is an average of large effects in two schools and no effects in thirteen schools.

—Third, if a model was estimated that included interactions between class size, instructional techniques, and investments in raising student attendance and increasing parental involvement, the results would show that the package of changes had enormous effects. In contrast, lowering class size and not changing anything else, especially not changing instructional techniques, had no effect on achievement.

But are there any data sets that would have permitted investigation of the consequences at Zavala and Ortega of lowering class size, changing curriculum and instructional techniques, and involving parents? Even if the data were available, would such complicated interaction effects ever be explored?

These questions of timing, data, and modeling strategy are just a few of the issues that must be dealt with to correctly specify relationships between resources and the outcomes of schooling. Our guess is that very few if any of the studies that Hanushek and Hedges summarized are specified correctly. Consequently, we cannot get too excited by attempts to summarize the conclusions of these studies, either by the vote-counting method or by meta-analysis.

We conclude with a summary by Alejandro Melton, the principal of Zavala: "I think money is a good thing. Money is the answer to the problems in education, with the caveat that it's spent and invested wisely."[2]

We do not believe either Hanushek or Hedges would disagree with this statement. Both would probably agree that some schools use money wisely and others do not. This conclusion is consistent with both their statistical summaries; it is also consistent with the theme of the Card-Krueger work.

The policy question emanating from the research we have discussed is whether a large enough percentage of schools use resources wisely to make providing more funds a good social investment. This is an issue about which economists can legitimately disagree. Many state legislatures have gone beyond this question, however. They are tying state school aid to reform measures aimed at increasing the efficiency with which school resources are used. The wisdom of the many different reform strategies would be a subject for another interesting study.

2. Interview with Alejandro Melton, April 8, 1994.

CHAPTER 5

Labor Market Effects of School Quality: Theory and Evidence

David Card and Alan B. Krueger

T HE EFFECTIVENESS of school spending is a critical issue for public policy. Education is the single largest component of government spending in the United States, accounting for 14 percent of combined federal, state, and local government expenditures.[1] In addition, the private sector makes a major financial contribution to education through private schooling and through the opportunity cost of students' time in school. Any improvement in the effectiveness of schools could have vital implications for the nation's 48 million school children, or generate huge savings for taxpayers, or both. In the past two decades the issue of school quality has taken on even greater significance as the labor market rewards to skill have risen and U.S. schools have come under renewed criticism for failing to meet international standards.

This paper presents an overview and evaluation of the literature on the impact of school quality on students' subsequent labor market success. School quality is measured by the level of resources available in the school, district, or state where the student grew up, such as expenditures per student or the pupil-teacher ratio. Achievement is measured by students' subsequent earnings in the labor market and by their educational attainment. This approach contrasts with much of the research on school quality conducted by psychologists, sociologists, and political scientists,

We are grateful to Aaron Saiger for data assistance. Helpful comments were provided by Julian Betts, Gary Burtless, James Heckman, Larry Katz, and Cecilia Rouse. This research was supported in part by a grant from the National Institute of Child Health and Development.

1. See *Statistical Abstract of the United States: 1994*, 114th ed., Bureau of the Census, table 464.

who tend to measure student achievement by standardized test scores.[2] To economists, however, the labor market is a natural yardstick for measuring the effectiveness of schools. Schools that increase the earnings of their students meet an objective "market test." In the standard economic model of schooling education is treated as an investment: current resources are spent while the student is in school in anticipation of higher income later in life.[3] This framework lends itself naturally to a consideration of the costs and benefits of expenditures on school resources. A reduction in the pupil-teacher ratio, for example, has immediate and readily measured costs. Monetary benefits, if any, are only realized over students' lifetimes as they use their improved knowledge to gain employment and achieve higher pay.

We hasten to add, however, that raising students' earnings is not the only measure of the effectiveness of schools, nor the only purpose of schooling. Schools may have other economic or noneconomic effects that are just as important.[4] For example, Milton Friedman argues for compulsory schooling and government-subsidized education because of the presumed positive externalities of an educated electorate.[5] Nevertheless, this chapter focuses narrowly on the monetary benefits of education.

Section one presents a simple theoretical model of school quality, educational attainment, and earnings that provides a unifying framework for analyzing many of the issues that arise in the literature. An important intuition arises from this model: higher school quality is expected to increase the payoff to each additional year of schooling, and to lead some students to acquire more schooling. The extra schooling creates a potential selection problem, in that the characteristics of students with a given level of schooling will change with a rise in school quality. Our theoretical model suggests that it is important to examine the impact of school

---

2. If standardized test scores were highly correlated with economic success, the distinction between test scores and earnings would be less important. But many studies find only a weak link between standardized tests and earnings. For example, the addition of test score information to the earnings equations estimated by Griliches and Mason (1972, table 3) improves the R-squared of their models by less than one-half of a percentage point. Using more recent data, Murnane, Willet, and Levy (1995, tables 3 and 4) find that the addition of a math test score raises the R-squared by 1.7 percentage points for men and 4.0 percentage points for women. Furthermore, recent research on the GED test indicates that simply passing the test has no significant effect on labor market outcomes (Cameron and Heckman, 1993). These findings underscore the importance of examining labor market outcomes directly.

3. See, for example, Becker (1967).

4. See Haveman and Wolfe (1984).

5. Friedman (1962).

quality on both the payoff to additional years of schooling *and* students' eventual educational attainment.

The second section of the chapter summarizes previous studies of the connection between school resources and students' earnings and educational attainment. A variety of evidence suggests that students who are educated in schools or areas with more resources tend to earn more once they enter the labor market, holding other factors constant. Moreover, the earnings premium associated with higher quality schooling appears to be greatest for those who have spent the most time in school, which is consistent with the view that the earnings differences are a result of school quality, rather than some omitted characteristic of students.

Other evidence based on a finer level of analysis of the variation in school spending also suggests that higher-quality schooling is associated with significantly higher earnings. For example, in a series of studies of army veterans, Paul Wachtel finds a statistically significant relationship between district-level expenditures and students' subsequent earnings.[6] A notable exception to this conclusion is a set of recent studies that focus on the earnings of relatively young workers from microeconomic data sets, including the National Longitudinal Survey of Youth (NLS-Y). These studies generally find statistically insignificant effects of school resources on earnings. On this basis, some analysts have concluded that school resources do not matter.[7] We reconsider the evidence from these studies and reach a somewhat different conclusion. In particular, we argue that specific aspects of these data sets, including the young age of the individuals and the relatively small number of observations, make it very difficult to obtain precise estimates of any school quality effects. Most importantly, when comparable specifications are estimated with the NLS-Y and census data, the estimated effects of school quality typically are not statistically different.

Most of the studies surveyed in the second section of this chapter also suggest that greater school resources are positively associated with students' educational attainment. For example, this conclusion emerges in studies that examine the effect of high-school resources on student graduation rates, as well as in those that relate years of educational attainment to the average quality of education in a state or school district. As suggested by our theoretical model, higher school quality seems to lead to higher earnings by increasing the payoff per year of schooling, and by

6. Wachtel (1975, 1976).
7. See, for example, chapter 6.

encouraging students to stay in school longer. Reduced form models, which relate earnings directly to school quality, typically show that a 10 percent increase in educational expenditures per student is associated with a 1 to 2 percent increase in the students' eventual annual earnings.

The third section of the chapter reviews the evidence on the effects of school quality for African Americans who were educated in the segregated school systems of the South. The quality of schooling available to black children in different states and across different cohorts varied widely—mainly for political and historical reasons. Thus some of the concerns that arise in interpreting the correlation between school quality and the subsequent earnings for white children, such as the role of family background or unmeasured ability factors, are reduced. The available evidence suggests that the effects of school quality are very similar for black workers and for white workers, providing support for a causal interpretation of the link between school resources and student outcomes.

The conclusion offers some suggestions for additional research that might shed further light on the effects of school resources on labor market outcomes, and that might help to reconcile the apparent conflict between studies that relate school quality to earnings and those that focus on test scores.

A Theoretical Model of School Quality, Education, and Earnings

As a starting point for discussing the labor market effects of school quality it is useful to outline a simple theoretical model of individual earnings and schooling determination. Let y_{is} represent the earnings of individual i who attended school system s. We defer discussion of the level of aggregation represented by s: in principle, s refers to the specific set of schools potentially attended by i. Let E_{is} represent the level of education of individual i. Assume that the logarithm of earnings is determined by a simple linear equation:

$$(5\text{-}1) \qquad \log y_{is} = a_i + b_s E_{is} + u_{is} ,$$

where a_i represents a person-specific intercept (person i's "ability"), b_s represents the marginal productivity of schooling acquired from system s, and u_{is} represents a random term.[8] It is natural to assume that higher

8. We abstract from differences in the structure of earnings across labor markets, such as higher or lower levels of earnings for all workers, or differences in the return to education.

quality leads to a higher marginal return to each additional year of schooling, that is, $b_s = b(Q_s)$, where Q_s is a quality index and $b'(Q) \gtrsim 0$. In a simple static model, equation 5-1 represents the budget constraint facing individual i before the choice of a specific level of education.

To close the model, assume that individual preferences are represented by a utility function of the form

(5-2) $$U(y_{is}, E_{is}) = \log y_{is} - f(E_{is}),$$

where f is a quadratic function with a person-specific slope

$$f(E_{is}) = c_i E_{is} + k/2 \cdot E_{is}^2.$$

Variation in c_i captures differences across people in the "cost" of schooling, associated with differences in access to funds, differences in tastes or family background, or differences in aptitude for schooling.[9]

Maximization of (5-2) subject to the constraint (5-1) gives rise to the optimal schooling choice,

(5-3) $$E_{is} = (b_s - c_i)/k.$$

In this very simple framework, *all* of the variation of schooling outcomes within a particular school system is attributable to differences in the cost of schooling. A more general model would allow for idiosyncratic differences in the return to schooling, possibly in combination with decreasing returns to schooling, as in the work of Gary Becker. As discussed by David Card, however, most of the literature on earnings and schooling can be reconciled within the simplified framework of equations 5-1 and 5-2, ignoring person-specific components in the return to education.[10]

Equations 5-1 and 5-3 form a simple model of schooling and earnings with several important implications for analyzing the effect of school quality. Observe that the conventional ordinary least squares (OLS) estimate of the return to schooling for individuals educated in system s has the probability limit

(5-4) $$\rho_s = b_s - k \cdot r_{ac},$$

where r_{ac} represents the (theoretical) regression coefficient of a_i on c_i. The OLS estimate of the return to schooling for people who attended school

---

9. See Becker (1967) on access to funds and Spence (1973) on aptitude.
10. Becker (1967); Card (1995).

system s differs from the true productivity effect b_s by an "ability bias" component: if a_i and c_i are negatively correlated (so that people with lower costs of schooling tend to have higher levels of earnings, regardless of their schooling choice), then ρ_s will be upward-biased as an estimate of b_s. Nevertheless, if the joint distribution of a_i and c_i is the same across school systems, then the ability bias component is constant, and estimates of the relationship between b_s and Q_s can be obtained by studying the relationship between ρ_s and Q_s across school systems.

Higher school quality, in this model, increases the slope of the observed relationship between log earnings and schooling. If schooling and ability are positively correlated, however, then higher quality also *lowers* the intercept of this relationship.[11] The reason for this is that an increase in b_s leads all individuals to increase their schooling. For example, consider people who would acquire only the minimum level of schooling when faced with a given level of school quality (that is, a given b_s). With higher school quality, some individuals in this group with the lowest costs of schooling will acquire an additional year of schooling. If costs and ability are negatively correlated, this shift will lower the average ability of those who remain at the minimum level of schooling, causing the intercept of the earnings-schooling relationship to fall.

Formally, the conditional expectation of individual ability given observed schooling and b_s is

$$E(a_i|E_{is}, b_s) = \text{constant} + r_{ac}(b_s - k \cdot E_{is}),$$

which is a decreasing function of b_s if $r_{ac} < 0$. Thus the theoretical regression function that relates log earnings to schooling (conditional on b_s) is

$$E(\log y_{is}|E_{is}, b_s) = E(a_i|E_{is}, b_s) + b_s E_{is},$$
$$= \text{constant} + r_{ac}b_s + (b_s - k \cdot r_{ac})E_{is}.$$

A rise in Q_s lowers the intercept and raises the slope of this function, as illustrated in figure 5-1. The crossover point occurs at the level of education such that $E = -r_{ac}$.[12] For example, if we assume that a_i and c_i are normally distributed, and calibrate the model so that the standard deviation of education is 3.3, the standard deviation of log earn-

11. This point was raised by Lang (1993) in the context of a more complex model of schooling.
12. If $r_{ac} = 0$, schooling and ability are uncorrelated, then an increase in Q_s rotates the earnings-schooling relationship at the origin.

Figure 5-1. *Earnings-Schooling Relationship in High- and Low-Quality Schools*

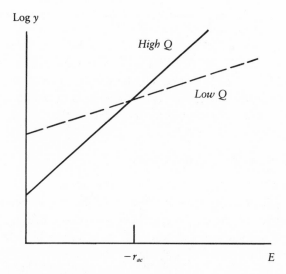

Source: Authors' model as described in text.

ings is 0.50, the average level of education is 12, and ability bias leads to a 20 percent upward bias in the OLS estimate of the return to schooling, then the cross-over occurs between nine and ten years of education.

Examination of figure 5-1 leads to three observations regarding the measurement of the earnings gains associated with higher school quality. First, higher school quality does not necessarily lead to higher average earnings conditional on education. If schooling and ability are positively correlated, an increase in school quality may be associated with lower average earnings at low levels of education and little or no effect on average earnings at intermediate levels of schooling. A second, related, observation is that evaluations of school quality based on samples that exclude highly educated workers may substantially understate the true effects of higher quality. Third, measures of the effect of school quality on the slope of the earnings-schooling relationship may capture only some of the benefits of higher quality. If schooling is endogenously determined, a full assessment of the effect of school quality should compare the unconditional distributions of earnings associated with high- and low-quality school systems.

Summary of the Literature

The empirical economics literature has focused on two main questions concerning education and earnings. The first, and most widely studied, concerns the interpretation of the correlation between education and earnings. The second, less widely studied question, is how factors like school spending affect the relationship between schooling and earnings. Although the focus of this paper is on the second question, it is helpful to begin with a brief overview of the literature on the first.

The Return to Years of Education

The finding that average earnings are higher for individuals with more schooling is one of the most strongly established facts in social science. Figure 5-2 illustrates the relationship between weekly earnings and years of schooling, using data on the (adjusted) mean log weekly wage of three birth cohorts of white men from the 1980 census.[13] The figures show that earnings rise almost linearly with years of education beyond a minimal threshold (corresponding roughly to the second percentile of the education distribution). There are dips at eleven and fifteen years of schooling, and a jump at the sixteenth year, suggesting the presence of "sheepskin" effects. Thus, a linear model of log earnings and education provides a reasonable description of the data, although formal goodness-of-fit tests will reject linearity with large enough samples.[14] Because of its relatively good fit and its close connection to simple theoretical models, such as those presented by Jacob Mincer and Robert Willis, the log-linear functional form has dominated the empirical literature.[15] Most estimates indicate that the marginal return per year of schooling is in the range of 6 to 10 percent, with a trend toward higher returns during the 1980s.[16]

A vast literature has investigated the relationship between earnings and years of schooling with the aim of understanding the forces behind their positive association. The first studies tried explicitly to control for

---

13. These figures are from Card and Krueger (1992a). The log earnings have been adjusted for marital status, experience, state of residence, and residence in a standard metropolitan statistical area (SMSA).

14. Using a Box-Cox procedure, Heckman and Polachek (1974) find that earnings and schooling have an approximately log-linear relationship. See Hungerford and Solon (1987) and Park (1994) for further evidence on sheepskin effects.

15. Mincer (1974); Willis (1986)

16. See, for example, Levy and Murnane (1992).

Figure 5-2. *Return to Single Years of Education, White Males, Nationwide*

Earnings differential[a]

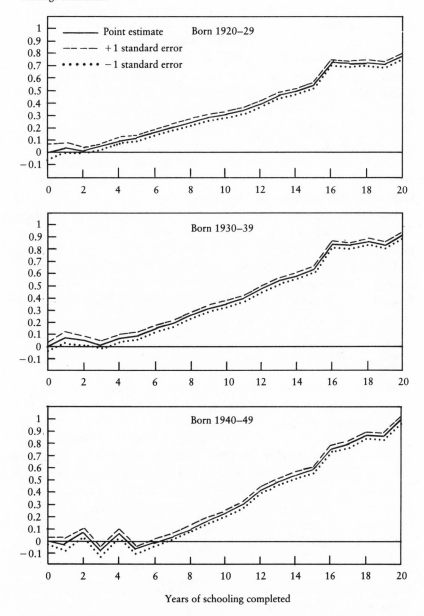

Years of schooling completed

Source: Card and Krueger (1992a), using data from the 1980 census.

a. Mean log weekly earnings are adjusted for marital status, experience, state of residence, and residence in an SMSA.

individuals' characteristics, such as IQ and parental education. A second set of studies has compared identical twins with different levels of education, to control for family background and genetic characteristics. Yet another strand of this literature has tried to estimate the monetary payoff to schooling by comparing workers who obtained different levels of education for reasons having little to do with innate abilities or background characteristics, such as being compelled to stay in school for a longer period because of compulsory schooling laws.[17] In a fourth approach, estimates of the return to schooling and schooling choices are derived from structural econometric models.[18]

Our interpretation of this literature is that additional years of schooling tend to lead to higher earnings, and that this relationship results primarily from the extra schooling itself, rather than extraneous factors. Omitted factors, such as imperfectly measured ability, may bias the OLS estimate of the return to education upward, but our reading of the evidence is that the bias is on the order of just 10 to 20 percent. Moreover, measurement error in reported education appears to bias the OLS estimate down by roughly the same magnitude. Thus these two potential sources of bias appear to us to approximately cancel out.[19] Zvi Griliches reached essentially the same conclusion in his presidential address to the Econometric Society nearly two decades ago.[20]

School Quality and Earnings

The literature on school quality and earnings is much less voluminous than the literature on years of education and earnings. This is partly due to data limitations. Studies of school quality must combine data on the quality of schools that workers attended, or could have attended, with data on their labor market outcomes. In the literature, school quality is typically measured by expenditures per pupil, or by school resources such as the pupil-teacher ratio and teacher pay. In reviewing the literature, we focus on expenditures per pupil as an index of school quality when this measure is available. We also summarize the evidence on the effect of the pupil-teacher ratio, because this is the policy variable typically of interest

17. See Grilliches (1977) for the first approach; Behrman and others (1980), Ashenfelter and Krueger (1994) and Miller, Mulvey, and Martin (1995) for the second; and Angrist and Krueger (1991) for the third.
18. See, for example, Willis and Rosen (1979).
19. This evidence is reviewed in Card (1995).
20. Grilliches (1977).

to decisionmakers, and because variation in the ratio accounts for close to one-half of the variability in total expenditures per student.[21] We suspect that many of the conclusions would hold for some other measures of school resources, such as average teacher pay, but we do not extensively review the evidence here.

The research on earnings and school quality can be divided into four general classes of studies, based on the statistical model used to link school quality to earnings.[22] "Class I" models simply add one or more school quality variables to the right-hand side of a conventional wage equation that also controls for education, experience, and other worker characteristics. The typical model estimated in such class I studies is

$$(5\text{-}5) \qquad Y_{is} = \beta X_{is} + \rho E_{is} + \theta Q_s + \epsilon_{is},$$

where Y_{is} represents the logarithm of earnings of worker i who was educated in school system s; X_{is} is a set of covariates such as experience, region of residence dummies, and marital status; E_{is} represents years of education, Q_s is a measure of the quality of schooling (for example, expenditures per student) in school system s, measured at the state, school district, or school level; and ϵ_{is} is a random error term. The parameter θ measures the effect of a unit change of school quality on log earnings. Notice that this specification implies that school quality has the same impact on expected earnings, regardless of an individual's education level.

"Class II" models recognize that school quality may influence the slope as well as the intercept of the earnings function. These specifications are more consistent with the theoretical model in the previous section, in that school quality has a potentially larger effect on individuals' earnings if they stay in school longer. A typical statistical model in such class II studies is

$$(5\text{-}6) \qquad Y_{is} = \beta X_{is} + \rho E_{is} + \theta Q_s + \varphi E_{is} Q_s + \epsilon_{is},$$

where all variables are defined as above. In this model, the parameter θ

21. For example, in 1990 the Nevada legislature passed a law lowering the pupil-teacher ratio in the first three years of primary education for all schools in the state. Furthermore, in New Jersey, while differences in the pupil-teacher ratio account for 43 percent of the variation in total expenditures per student across school districts, differences in average teacher salary account for only about 8 percent. We thank Cecilia Rouse for providing these calculations.

22. For a less technical presentation of this material, see Card and Krueger (1995).

measures the impact of school quality on the intercept of the earnings function, while the parameter φ measures the impact of school quality on the slope of the earnings-education relationship. If school quality has no effect on educational attainment, the effect of a unit change in school quality on the log wage of individuals with E years of schooling is θ + φE. If school quality affects educational attainment, the total effect of school quality is θ + φE + (ρ + φQ)· $\partial E/\partial Q$, where the third term reflects the marginal effect of a change in school quality on educational attainment ($\partial E/\partial Q$).

"Class III" studies focus on estimating the impact of school quality on the slope of the return to education (the parameter φ), having absorbed any level effect of school quality (θQ_s) by including unrestricted dummies for the area in which individuals went to school. This approach enables researchers to control for differences across labor markets in the average level of earnings (through market-specific intercepts for the place of work), as well as for differences in the rate of return to education across local labor markets (through market-specific interactions with education). In these models the school quality effect, φ, is identified by comparing earnings of individuals who were educated in one locale and observed working in another. We implement a two-step variant of such a model in another study.[23] In the first step, we estimate the return to education for individuals from each state of birth and cohort with the following model:

$$(5\text{-}7) \quad Y_{ijbc} = \delta_{bc} + \mu_{jc} + \beta X_{ijbc} + (\gamma_{bc} + \rho_{rc})\cdot E_{ijbc} + \epsilon_{ijbc},$$

where i indexes individuals, j represents the state where the individual currently lives and works, b represents the state where the individual was born (and by assumption, was educated), and c represents a birth cohort. This model includes unrestricted state-of-birth intercepts for each cohort (δ_{bc}) as well as unrestricted state-of-residence intercepts for each cohort (μ_{jc}). The model also allows the rate of return to education to differ across regions of residence (r) by cohort (the ρ_{rc} interactions). The key parameters are the state-of-birth-specific rates of return to education, estimated separately for each cohort (γ_{bc}).

In the second step, we relate the returns to education for each state of birth and cohort to state-level school quality measures and other variables using generalized least squares (GLS):

23. Card and Krueger (1992a).

(5-8) $$\gamma_{bc} = \alpha_b + \alpha_c + \varphi Q_{bc} + \Omega W_{bc},$$

where α_b represents an unrestricted state-of-birth effect in the return to education, α_c represents an unrestricted cohort effect, Q_{bc} represents average school quality at the time cohort c attended school in state b, and W_{bc} is a vector of state-of-birth-by-cohort-level variables, such as the average education of parents. As in equation 5-6, the parameter φ measures the effect of school quality on the slope of the earnings-education gradient. Unlike equation (6), this model absorbs the effect of school quality on the intercepts via the unrestricted state-of-birth effects in the first-step model. Notice that this model could also be estimated in one step by substituting equation 5-8 into equation 5-7. The two-step estimator, however, is asymptotically unbiased and efficient if proper GLS weights are used in the second step.[24] Moreover, the two-step approach is computationally attractive, and allows researchers to investigate easily the robustness of any relation between school quality and the return to education.

Finally, "class IV" models are reduced form relationships between earnings and school quality, without conditioning on educational attainment, and are of the form

(5-9) $$Y_{is} = \beta X_{is} + \pi Q_s + \epsilon_{is}.$$

Because this model excludes educational attainment, the parameter π reflects both the direct effect of school quality on earnings and any indirect effect of school quality on earnings via its effect on educational attainment. One limitation of such models (compared with class III models) is that they do not control for cohort-specific unobserved factors associated with the area in which an individual was educated: unrestricted place-of-birth effects would absorb the school quality variables.

Table 5-1 summarizes twenty-four estimates of the effect of school spending on earnings from eleven different studies. The estimates are derived from eight independent data sets and sixteen mutually exclusive samples. We selected the set of studies by searching the *Journal of Economic Literature* index and by examining citations in known papers and past issues of selected education journals. We included only those studies that report information on their coefficients and standard errors in order

---

24. See Hanushek (1974).

Table 5-1. *Summary of Studies that Estimate the Effect of Expenditures per Student on Earnings*

Study	Sample	Methodology and comments		Estimated elasticity of earnings with respect to dollars per pupil[a]
1. Morgan and Sirageldin	1965 Survey Research Center. Family heads, not self-employed. N = 1,438	Class I. State expenditures (average of 1930, 1940, 1950) matched to individuals by state where they grew up. Dependent variable: log hourly wage in 1964. Stepwise regression. First step: remove years of education, age, sex, race, grew up on farm.		0.29 (0.05)
2. Johnson and Stafford	1965 Survey Research Center. White male nonfarm heads. N = 1,039	Class I. State* decade average expenditures matched to individuals by age and state where they grew up. Dependent variable: log hourly wage in 1964. Other controls: years of education, experience, urban residence or birthplace, father's education.		0.20 (0.05)
3. Morgenstern	1968 Urban Problems. Survey conducted by Institute for Survey Research. Heads of households; black households oversampled. N = 1,624	Class I. State expenditures matched to individuals by state where grew up. Dependent variable: average hourly wage previous year. Other controls: gender, age, place of birth, experience, parents' education.	Blacks Whites	0.12 (0.04) 0.13 (0.07)
4. Jud and Walker	1970 NLS. Males ages 18–28. N = 1,215	Class I. District-level expenditures matched to high schools. Dependent variable: annual earnings in 1970 in levels. Controls: experience, education, race, SMSA, married, South, health, IQ, work hours.		0.07 (0.07)
5. Ribich and Murphy	1959 Project Talent. 9th grade men, reinterviewed in 1968; blacks and Southerners under-represented. N = 8,466	Class I. Expenditures per pupil collected from school survey. Dependent variable: estimated lifetime earnings, imputed from 1967 earnings (if employed) and education data. Other controls: years of education, Armed Forces Qualifying Test, parental and school-average socioeconomic status.		0.01 (0.02)
6. Link and Ratledge	1968 NLS. Young men ages 16–26, out of school ≥ 1 year. N = 1,157	Class I. School-district expenditures for 1968 matched by school district of school attended. Dependent variable: 1968 log annual earnings. Other controls: years of education, experience (quadratic), urban residence, IQ, hours worked.	Whites Blacks	0.15 (0.05) 0.55 (0.17)
7. Wachtel	Thorndike-Hagen. Men ages 18–26 in 1943 (army veterans). N = 1,633	Class I. School-district expenditures matched to individuals by name or location of high school (1936–38 Biennial Survey of Education data). Dependent variable: 1955/1969 earnings.	1969 1955	0.20 (0.04) 0.09

Study	Data	Comments	Group	Estimate (SE)
		Other controls: years of education, experience, hours worked, test score, college quality, father's education.		(0.03)
8. Rizzuto and Wachtel	1960, 1970 censuses. White and black men ages 14–65, not self-employed. $N=26,204$ (1960), $N=27,729$ (1970)	Class I. State expenditure data matched to individuals by state of birth and age interval. Dependent variable: 1959/1969 log earnings. Other controls: years of education, experience, urban residence.	1959 Whites	0.12 (0.01)
			1959 Blacks	0.09 (0.03)
			1969 Whites	0.08 (0.01)
			1969 Blacks	0.11 (0.04)
9. Akin and Garfinkel[b]	Panel Survey on Income Dynamics (PSID). Male heads ages 30–55 during 1968–72. $N=1,049$	Class II. State* decade average expenditures matched to individuals by state of residence at age 12. Dependent variable: log average wage 1968–72. Expenditures interacted with years of education. Other controls: IQ, father's income, indicators for family income.	Whites	0.30
			Blacks	0.14
10. Link, Ratledge, and Lewis[c]	1969 NLS. Young men ages 19–29. $N=2,127$ PSID male heads as in study 9.	Class II. See comments for studies 6 and 9. Dependent variable for NLS is log average wage in 1971, for PSID is log average wage 1968–72. Expenditures interacted with years of education. Other controls: in NLS, IQ, father's education; in PSID, as in study 9.	NLS Whites	0.13–0.17
			NLS Blacks	0.15–0.23
			PSID Whites	0.24–0.32
			PSID Blacks	0.13–0.15
11. Tremblay	1976 NLS. Young men, ages 24–34. $N=247$ Southern, 496 non-Southern	Class II. See comments for study 6. Expenditures interacted with education. Dependent variable: log monthly income. Other controls: occupation and industry dummies, IQ, race, age, seniority, SMSA, marital status, occupational training dummy, and union status.	High school	
			South	0.12
			Non-South	0.04
			College	
			South	0.05
			Non-South	0.03

Source: Morgan and Sirageldin (1968); Johnson and Stafford (1973); Morgenstern (1973); Jud and Walker (1977); Ribich and Murphy (1975); Link and Ratledge (1975); Wachtel (1976); Rizzuto and Wachtel (1980); Akin and Garfinkel (1980); Link, Ratledge, and Lewis (1980); and Tremblay (1986).
a. A positive coefficient means that higher earnings are associated with higher spending per student. Elasticities are with respect to a percentage change in spending per student. Estimated standard errors are shown in parentheses.
b. Elasticities are calculated at 12 years of education for whites, and at 10.5 years for blacks.
c. Elasticities are calculated at mean number of years of education for each group.

to evaluate the power of the estimates.[25] The table summarizes the estimated elasticities of earnings with respect to spending per student. For example, if a study regresses log earnings on log expenditures per student, we simply report the estimated expenditure coefficient. For studies that estimate log-linear models, we convert the coefficient estimate to an elasticity using mean spending per student.[26] The table also describes the data and model that each study uses and designates the class of model according to the discussion above. Inevitably there is some arbitrariness in the construction of our summary tables, but we have tried to include the estimates that were highlighted by the authors, or that correspond to the reduced form model.

All twenty-four of the estimates in table 5-1 show a positive effect of additional school spending on subsequent earnings. The odds of this happening purely by chance are less than 1 in 16 million. It is possible that many of the studies find a positive effect of school quality for spurious reasons (for example, omitted variables), but one can clearly rule out chance as an explanation for the consistent finding that more resources are associated with higher earnings. Most of the studies that report sufficient data to calculate a *t* ratio for the estimate have statistically significant coefficients. Julian Betts similarly finds that sixteen of twenty-one estimates have statistically significant effects of expenditures per pupil at the 10 percent level.[27]

The mean of the estimates in table 5-1 is 0.152, and the median is 0.125; the interquartile range is 0.085 to 0.195.[28] The consistency across studies is impressive in view of the fact that many use different data sets, estimate varying specifications, and include different sets of control variables.

All of the estimates represented in table 5-1 control for education and

25. Furthermore, if an author published more that one article using the same data set to estimate a similar empirical specification, we only report results from one of the articles in Table 1, usually the most recent one. If a study did not report its coefficient or standard error, we do not consider it in this table because it is not possible to evaluate the power of the study. The table also is limited to studies of U.S. data. See Behrman and Birdsall (1983) for an excellent article on the effect of school quality on students' subsequent income in Brazil.

26. Jud and Walker (1977) regress the level of earnings on the level of expenditures per student. The elasticity for this study was calculated at the mean earnings in the sample, and at the mean expenditure per enrolled student for 1969–70, as reported in the *Digest of Education Statistics*, U.S. Department of Education, 1994.

27. See chapter 6, table 6-2.

28. These figures are calculated taking the midrange for Link, Ratledge, and Lewis (1980). The unweighted mean elasticity in table 6-2 is 0.121.

are either class I or class II models. Many of the studies also control for differences in family background, by including father's education, family income, IQ, or the Armed Forces Qualifying Test (AFQT) score. Questions could be raised about many of the specifications used in the literature. For example, it does not seem appropriate to include occupation dummies as explanatory variables, as Carol Tremblay has done, because more and higher quality education may enable people to obtain jobs in better paying occupations.[29] More generally, the functional forms used in some of the studies are open to question.

Despite the varying sets of control variables and specifications used in the literature, it is possible that the estimated school quality coefficients reflect the influence of omitted factors, rather than the true effect of school resources. In our view, the most important omitted variables are likely to be measures of family background and characteristics of the areas in which individuals attended school. An important motivation for the class II and class III models is that many of these omitted variables are absorbed by state-of-birth effects (or by the "main" effect in the class II models), while still identifying the effect of school quality on the rate of return to education.

Estimates of the elasticity of students' earnings with respect to the pupil-teacher ratio (or teacher-pupil ratio) are summarized in table 5-2.[30] The models underlying these estimates are either class IV reduced form models that exclude education or class I models that condition on educational attainment.[31] For comparability across studies, log-linear coefficient estimates were converted to elasticities by assuming 17.9 students per class (or 1/17.9 for the teacher-pupil ratio).[32] Specifically, if π is the coefficient on the pupil-teacher ratio in a log wage regression, a point elasticity η was calculated as $\eta = \pi (17.9)$. Notice that a log-linear specification implies a larger proportionate effect of the pupil-teacher ratio for larger class sizes. Thus, as average class sizes have shrunk in recent decades, these models would imply a lower elasticity of earnings with respect to changes in the pupil-teacher ratio.

All the studies except Grogger's find that a lower pupil-teacher ratio is associated with higher earnings, although only two are statistically

---

29. Tremblay (1986).
30. As in table 5-1, we summarize only those studies that report both a coefficient estimate and standard error (or t statistic) for the pupil-teacher variable.
31. The reduced-form estimate from Betts (1995) is from his table A-4.
32. A pupil-teacher ratio of 17.9 was selected for comparability to the NLS-Y.

Table 5-2. *Summary of Studies that Estimate the Effect of Pupil-Teacher Ratio on Earnings*

Study	Sample	Methodology and comments	Estimated elasticity of earnings with respect to pupil-teacher ratio[a]
1. Wachtel	1943 Thorndike-Hagen. Men ages 18–26 (army veterans). $N=1,812$	Class I. School district teacher-pupil ratio matched to individuals by name or location of high school. (1936–38 Biennial Survey of Education data). Dependent variable: 1969 earnings. Other controls: years of education, experience, hours worked, test score, parents' education, college quality.	−0.044 $(t < 2)$
2. Card and Krueger (a)	1980 census. White men ages 31–60, not self-employed. $N=1,018,477$	Class IV. State average school data for 1926–66 matched to individuals by state of birth and years of school attendance. Dependent variable: log weekly wage in 1979. Other controls: state of birth, state of residence, experience (quadratic), marital status, urban residence.	−0.074 (0.012)
3. Card and Krueger (b)	1960–80 censuses. Black and white men born in South, 1910–49. $N=728,284$	Class IV. State average school data for 1916–66 matched to race*state-of-birth*10-year cohort. Dependent variable: state*cohort*census black-white log weekly wage gap. Other controls: cohort dummies, year dummies.	−0.050 (0.018)
4. Grogger	NLS-72: high school class of 1972; $N=4,685$. HSB: high school class of 1979; $N=2,396$	Class I. Pupil-teacher ratio for high school provided by school survey. Other controls: educational attainment dummies, experience, region, family income, achievement test scores, high school grades.	NLS-72 0.052 (0.027) HSB 0.056 (0.034)
5. Betts	1979–89 NLS-Y. White men ages 17–31. $N=11,314$ worker/year observations	Class IV. School data from survey of latest high school attended in 1979. Other controls: teacher salary, teacher education, region of residence, age. Uses teacher-pupil ratio.	−0.043 (0.025)

Source: Wachtel (1975), Card and Krueger (1992a, 1992b), Grogger (1994); Betts (1995).
a. The sign is changed for studies that use the teacher-pupil ratio. A negative coefficient means that higher earnings are associated with a lower pupil-teacher ratio. Elasticities are calculated assuming a pupil-teacher ratio of 17.9. Estimated standard errors are shown in parentheses.

significant. The four negative estimates have an average elasticity of −0.053, and are all fairly close. A notable pattern that emerges from table 5-2 is that the two recent studies, by Betts and Grogger, find statistically insignificant effects.[33] These studies have two features in common: they analyze relatively small microeconomic data sets of young workers, and they use quality data from the worker's high school. Although Betts has argued that the weaker school quality effects in these two studies arise from the use of school-level quality data, we suspect that the insignificant findings are mainly a result of the age ranges and sample sizes of the data sets.[34]

In the NLS-Y sample used by Betts, the average age of workers is twenty-three; the average age in Grogger's sample from the High School and Beyond survey (HSB) is similar. The youthfulness of the sample in studies of school quality is a potential problem for at least two reasons. First, many determinants of labor market performance are only revealed with experience. For example, it is widely acknowledged that the return to the *quantity* of schooling is understated among very young workers.[35] One might expect a similar understatement of the effect of school *quality* in the first few years of the work career. This assumption holds in Paul Wachtel's comparison of returns to school quantity and school quality for the Thorndike-Hagen sample of veterans in 1955 and 1969.[36] Between 1955 and 1969, as the average age of the sample rose from 32 to 46, the rate of return to education rose from 0.030 to 0.079 (an increase of 163 percent), while the return to school quality (measured as the coefficient of school expenditures per pupil in a class I regression model) rose from 0.291 to 0.684 (135 percent). Second, samples of young workers tend to underrepresent individuals of a given age with higher education. If higher school quality leads individuals to acquire more education, such samples will contain too few earnings observations for individuals from higher-quality schools, leading to an understatement of any school quality effects.

The small sample sizes of the NLS-Y and HSB data sets make it

33. Betts (1995); Grogger (1994).
34. See chapter 6.
35. Mincer (1974). Using the NLS-Y sample from Saiger and Irwin (1994) and a cumulative experience measure similar to the one used by Betts (1995), the rate of return to schooling in the NLS-Y data set is 4.5 percent—far below generally accepted estimates of the return to schooling in the 1980s. Similarly, Murnane, Willet, and Levy (1995) report a 4.4 percent estimate of the return to a year of schooling for men in the 1986 High School and Beyond survey.
36. Wachtel (1976).

potentially difficult to detect small but economically significant effects of school quality. Moreover, the set of models that can be estimated in the NLS-Y is fairly limited. For example, James Heckman, Anne Layne-Farrar, and Petra Todd estimate earnings models that include about four hundred parameters, capturing differences across states and cohorts in the level of earnings and the return to schooling. Models of this complexity cannot be precisely estimated with samples of only one or two thousand individuals.[37]

In light of these features, it is interesting to compare the estimated school quality effects from the microeconomic-level data sets to the estimates in the other literature. The reduced form models in Betts's and our earlier studies are the most comparable sets of estimates in the two studies.[38] Using the NLS-Y data, Betts estimates a reduced form model that excludes education and its interactions, and controls for age, marital status, and region of residence. As shown in table 5-2, this model yields an earnings elasticity of 0.043 (t = 1.70) at the mean teacher-pupil ratio. The 95 percent confidence interval for this estimate runs from −0.01 to 0.09. The comparable elasticity evaluated at the same mean classroom size in a similar reduced form model from our study is 0.074.[39] Thus, for comparable specifications, the NLS-Y data yield results that are *not* statistically distinguishable from estimates derived from census data using state-level school quality data, although the confidence interval based on the NLS-Y is relatively large.[40]

---

37. Heckman, Layne-Farrar, and Todd (1995). A third aspect of the NLS-Y and HSB data sets is the range of variation in measured school quality. The variance of measured quality across schools in both data sets is relatively wide—comparable to the historical variability of quality measures across states. For example, the variance in the pupil-teacher ratio for white men in the NLS-Y is 16.6, compared with a variance of 17.5 across states and cohorts in Card and Krueger (1992a). However, the observed variances of school quality in the HSB and NLS-Y may overstate the true variability of school quality across individuals since the quality measures pertain to just a single year of high school and may also contain measurement errors that average out at the state level.

38. Betts (1995, table A-4); Card and Krueger (1992a, table 6).

39. The reduced form equations in Card and Krueger (1992a) include essentially the same covariates. The reason for conditioning on age, rather than experience, is that experience is a function of educational attainment; workers with less education have more opportunity to gain work experience. Because the reduced form equations are intended to capture all direct and indirect effects of school quality (including educational attainment), we believe it is appropriate to condition only on age. When Betts (1995) controls for experience (measured by cumulative weeks of work) instead of age, the reduced form coefficient is less than half as large and is statistically different from ours.

40. Betts (1995) argues that estimates from the NLS-Y reject comparable estimates of the effect of the teacher-pupil ratio on earnings from the earlier literature. However, he

In a replication study, Aaron Saiger and Timothy Irwin also estimate a reduced form model with the NLS-Y data, using the pupil-teacher ratio rather than the teacher-pupil ratio.[41] Their point estimate of the elasticity of earnings with respect to the pupil-teacher ratio evaluated at the mean is 0.05 ($t = 0.52$): the associated 95 percent confidence interval is huge, ranging from -0.14 to 0.24. Moreover, adjusting their standard errors for the fact that the NLS-Y sample includes repeated earnings observations for the same individuals increases the width of the confidence interval.

Betts argues that the reduced form models just discussed provide an "overly optimistic" view of school quality effects. In table 6-3 of this volume, he reports an elasticity of 0.014 with a standard error of 0.025 to summarize the effect of the teacher-pupil ratio in his earlier study of NLS-Y data. This estimate, which we interpret as his preferred specification, is based on a class I model that includes the levels of school quality variables, but not their interactions. Betts notes that this estimate is significantly different from those in our earlier studies. However, he fails to adjust his estimated standard error for the fact that there are as many as ten wage observations per individual in the NLS-Y sample. Since wages for the same individual are highly correlated over time, it is inappropriate to treat the repeated observations for each individual as independent. Betts kindly provided his data to us, and we have used his sample to calculate appropriate standard errors for this specification. The standard error for the pupil-teacher coefficient is almost twice as large as the one he reports (0.049), indicating a substantial degree of dependence between the wage observations for the same person in different years. With this appropriate standard error, Betts's preferred estimate of the effect of the teacher-pupil ratio based on the NLS-Y data is *not* significantly different from earlier estimates.

Although we believe that the differences between the estimated school quality effects in the earlier literature and those derived by Betts and Grogger are mainly due to differences in specification and to the age and sample size limitations of the NLS-Y and HSB data sets, a number of

---

reaches this conclusion by comparing class III estimates from Card and Krueger (1992a) to estimates of a restricted class II model in the NLS-Y data that excludes the teacher-pupil main effect. The state-of-birth effects in our model (and in that of Heckman, Layne-Farrar, and Todd, 1995) absorb any direct effect of Q. The standard error of φ is more than six times greater in Betts's model that includes the main effect for the teacher-pupil ratio than in the restricted model.

41. Saiger and Irwin (1995).

authors, including Betts and Hanushek, Rivkin, and Taylor, have argued that the use of aggregated school quality measures in the earlier literature led to a systematic overstatement of school quality effects.[42] In a longer version of this chapter, we lay out the econometric issues involved in comparing the estimated effects of school quality using school-level (or district-level) data as opposed to state-level data.[43] This analysis leads to three main conclusions. First, the use of aggregated school quality information does not automatically lead to biased estimates. Indeed, if the unobserved components of student earnings are uncorrelated with school quality, then specifications using school-level and aggregated data are both unbiased. On the other hand, if the unobserved components of earnings are correlated with school quality, then the use of aggregated school quality data may either reduce or magnify the biases that arise using school-level data. Second, if school quality information is measured with error, or if the quality data at a point in time (for example, the data for the school attended at age seventeen) are an imperfect measure of the quality of schools attended over a student's career, then the estimated effect of school quality with school-level data will be attenuated, and the use of aggregated quality data can help to reduce this attenuation bias. Finally, in more complex models of school quality, such as the class III models described above, any bias that arises from the use of aggregated data is determined by a correlation between unobserved earnings components and the interaction between years of schooling and school quality, conditional on educational attainment. It is unclear in what direction, if any, such omitted effects might bias the implied effects of school quality.

School Quality and the Return to Education

Focusing on the impact of school quality on the *slope* of the earnings-education relationship may reduce the bias attributable to omitted variables, since these factors will primarily affect the estimate of the main effect of school quality on the *level* of earnings, or be absorbed by unrestricted state-of-birth effects. Table 5-3 summarizes the available estimates of the effect of school quality on the slope of the log earnings-education relationship. The table reports the change in the percentage return to a year of education for a proportionate change in the pupil-

---

42. Chapter 6; Hanushek, Rivkin, and Taylor (1995).
43. Card and Krueger (1996).

Table 5-3. *Effect of Pupil-Teacher Ratio on Return to One Year of Schooling*

Study	Model	Without state effects	With state effects
		Estimate[a]	
Card and Krueger (a)	2 percent threshold for education GLS	−0.40 (0.28)	−1.59 (0.54)
	Linear education GLS	−0.20 (0.27)	−1.37 (0.52)
Card and Krueger (b)	Linear education GLS	−1.44 (0.39)	−1.25 (0.54)
Heckman, Layne-Farrar, and Todd	Linear education OLS (White standard errors)		
	1970	−0.36 (0.12)	−1.51 (0.26)
	1980	0.23 (0.09)	−1.07 (0.25)
	1990	0.26 (0.13)	−1.81 (0.25)
Betts[b]	OLS (White standard errors)	0.50 (1.24)	...
	School random effects	−4.06 (1.56)	...
	State average quality	5.30 (6.79)	...

Source: Card and Krueger (1992a, 1992b), Heckman, Layne-Farrar, and Todd (1995); Betts (1995).
a. Estimates are the change in the percentage return to one year of education for a 1 percent change in the pupil-teacher ratio. The state effects (α_b) are in the return to education, as described in text. A negative estimate indicates that reducing the pupil-teacher ratio increases the slope of the earnings-education function. Calculations assume seventeen students per class. Estimated standard errors are shown in parentheses.
b. Because Betts uses the teacher-pupil ratio as his explanatory variable, the negative sign is taken.

teacher ratio. The studies by Heckman, Layne-Farrar, and Todd and our two studies implement a class III two-step estimation procedure with state-level data; Betts uses a one-step class II model with high-school level quality data.[44]

44. See chapter 7; Heckman, Layne-Farrar, and Todd (1995); Card and Krueger (1992a, 1992b); Betts (1995). Our estimates for Betts are taken from his table 1, column 1 (for the OLS estimate), and from his appendix table A-3, column 1, for the GLS estimate. Betts uses the teacher-pupil ratio, rather than the pupil-teacher ratio. Thus we first convert his estimate of the effect of the teacher-pupil ratio on the return to education into an elasticity (by multiplying by 0.059 = 1/17), and then multiply by −100 to obtain the elasticity of the percentage return to education with respect to the pupil-teacher ratio.

When state-of-birth effects are omitted from the models estimated by us and by Heckman, Layne-Farrar, and Todd (column one), the pupil-teacher ratio tends to have a statistically insignificant effect on the return to education, but when state effects are added (column two) the effect is statistically significant. In other words, the census samples *only* show a systematic effect of the pupil-teacher ratio on the return to education when permanent differences in the rate of return to schooling across states are taken into account (through the α_b's in equation 5-8). It is interesting to note that Betts's GLS estimate from the NLS-Y shows a relatively strong effect of the pupil-teacher ratio on the return to education, even though his model does not control for permanent state effects. Indeed, his GLS estimate of φ, based on school-level quality data, is larger than the estimates based on census earnings data with state-level quality measures, although his OLS estimate for the same model has the opposite sign.[45]

The estimates in table 5-3 pertain only to the *slope* of the education-earnings relationship. Corresponding estimates of the effect of the pupil-teacher ratio on the *intercepts* are often positive, suggesting that varying class sizes are associated with a rotation of the relationship, as predicted by our theoretical model. Estimates from census data in one of our studies and in those by Heckman, Layne-Farrar, and Todd suggest that the crossover point of this rotation is about twelve years of education.[46] The GLS estimates of the intercept effects reported by Betts imply a higher point of rotation (14.2 years), while his OLS estimates imply a rotation in the opposite direction (although the coefficients in the OLS model are insignificant).[47] We discuss the interpretation of this rotation effect in more detail below.

Although not included in table 5-3, Kevin Lang uses the NLS-Y data set to estimate the effect of school quality on the slope of the education-earnings relationship.[48] His estimates, derived from a nonlinear set of equations with cross-equation restrictions, indicate that a reduction of the pupil-teacher ratio increases the education slope and lowers the intercept of the earnings function. Both of these effects are statistically significant at the 0.05 level. However, the reduction of the intercept

45. We are not certain why the GLS estimate is so different from the OLS estimate. In principle, both estimates have the same probability limit.
46. Card and Krueger (1992a); chapter 7; Heckman, Layne-Farrar, and Todd (1995).
47. Betts (1995).
48. Lang (1993).

dominates the steeper slope at all reasonable levels of education, suggesting that school quality has a negative effect on earnings conditional on any level of education.

As we noted earlier, some authors have argued that the use of aggregated quality data overstates school quality effects.[49] In this regard, the estimates reported by Betts using school-level and state-level quality measures are informative. The OLS estimate of the elasticity of the education slope with respect to the state-average pupil-teacher ratio is 5.30, compared with 0.50 using the school-level pupil-teacher ratio.[50] Both of these estimates are "wrong-signed" for the hypothesis that higher school quality raises the return to schooling. If anything, however, the estimate based on aggregate data understates rather than overstates the effect of class size on the education slope, relative to the estimate based on school-level data.

Lastly, another interesting study that is not included in table 5-3 is that by Bernt Brattsberg and Dek Terrell. This study uses 1980 census data to estimate fifty-eight separate returns to education for immigrants living in the United States, based on their country of origin.[51] It then relates these estimated returns to characteristics of the home countries, including the pupil-teacher ratio, an index of teacher pay, educational attainment, GNP per capita, income inequality, distance from the United States, region dummies, and political variables. The authors find a statistically significant relationship between the pupil-teacher ratio and the return to education and between the teacher wage and the return to education, both with the expected signs. For example, the elasticity for the pupil-teacher is −0.80 (standard error = 0.17). Although it is unclear whether this estimate should be compared with those in columns one or two of table 5-3, Brattsberg and Terrell's study provides suggestive evidence that immigrants from countries with higher quality schools have higher returns to education in the U.S. labor market. A potential limitation of this study is that differential selection biases may lead to systematic differences that are not attributable to school quality in the returns to education for immigrants from different countries.

49. See, for example, Hanushek, Rivkin, and Taylor (1995).
50. Betts (1995).
51. Brattsberg and Terrell (1995). To increase the likelihood that the immigrants were educated abroad, the sample is restricted to those who were at least twenty-five years old when they emigrated to the United States.

School Quality and Educational Attainment

The evidence in the preceding subsection supports the notion that improved school quality is associated with a steeper slope for the return to education function. As discussed in the first section, an increase in the payoff to a year of education would also be expected to induce students to stay in school longer and increase their educational attainment. We do not attempt an exhaustive survey of the empirical literature on this prediction, but it does appear that the evidence is consistent with this hypothesis. For example, over half of the studies on educational attainment in Betts's table 6-10 find a statistically significant relationship between the pupil-teacher ratio and educational attainment.[52]

Nevertheless, Betts questions the conclusion that school resources affect educational attainment. Like Eric Hanushek, Steven Rivkin, and Lori Taylor, Betts argues that studies of the link between school resources and schooling outcomes that use aggregated quality measures are biased toward finding a positive quality effect. This argument runs counter to William Sander's findings.[53] Sander relates high school graduation rates to the pupil-teacher ratio across 154 Illinois school districts. In eighty-six of the districts there is only one high school, so estimates for this subsample are equivalent to school-level estimates. If the level of aggregation matters, then one would expect a weaker relationship in the subsample of single-school districts. Sander reports that the estimates are quite similar in single-school districts and in the full sample: a 10 percent decrease in the pupil-teacher ratio is associated with a 1.5 percentage point increase in the graduation rate in the single-school subsample, and a 1.4 percentage point increase in the full sample.

Two other recent studies are also inconsistent with the conclusion that the level of aggregation of the school quality variable is critical. First, in the framework of a highly restrictive structural model, Lang finds a statistically significant relationship between educational attainment and high school quality with the 1988 wave of the NLS-Y.[54] Second, Michael Boozer finds generally positive effects of smaller class size on the dropout

52. See table 6-10. Additionally, Ribar (1993) finds a positive association between state-level expenditures per student and high school graduation rates for women in the NLS-Y, and Murray, Evans, and Schwab (1995) find a significant relationship with district-level data for 15 states using census data.
53. See chapter 6; Hanushek, Rivkin, and Taylor (1995); Sander (1993).
54. Lang (1993).

rate for whites and blacks in the National Educational Longitudinal Survey and in the High School and Beyond data sets. In three of the four subsamples that he examines, a lower pupil-teacher ratio is significantly associated with a lower dropout rate.[55]

Wachtel's study, one of the older ones to find an insignificant effect of the pupil-teacher ratio on educational attainment using disaggregated quality data, deserves further comment. Individuals in this data set, the Thorndike-Hagen data, were selected, in part, on the basis of their education. The sample has an extremely high level of average education for this cohort of men, averaging more than fifteen years. Thus it may not be too surprising that this sample shows an insignificant effect.[56]

In interpreting the relationship between educational attainment and resources per student, it is important to recognize that the observed correlation between these variables may give a downward-biased estimate of the true effect of per capita spending on educational attainment. To see this point, consider an increase in enrollment in a particular district or state induced by a change in family background or tastes for education. The rise in enrollment will tend to raise the pupil-teacher ratio and depress spending per student, unless school taxes and the number of teachers are increased in proportion to the new enrollment. Thus unobserved taste factors or family income changes that lead to variation in enrollment rates across districts or states could spuriously induce a negative correlation between educational attainment and per student expenditures. This conclusion may be reversed, of course, if a rise in interest in education leads to a rise in enrollment and a greater than proportional increase in taxation and spending.

In summary, our reading of the literature is that it provides evidence that school quality is related to educational attainment, although it is unclear whether this relationship results because students respond to the economic incentives created by a rise in the return to schooling, or because they find it more enjoyable to attend schools with smaller classes or better-paid teachers.

55. Boozer (1993). One subsample shows a significant effect with the opposite sign. Also, the use of sample weights that adjust for nonrandom attrition has an important effect in the HSB data set.

56. Wachtel (1975). We thank Paul Wachtel for bringing this to our attention.

Heckman, Layne-Farrar, and Todd

In a recent series of papers, Heckman, Layne-Farrar, and Todd extend the third class of models described above in many important directions.[57] Table 5-4 summarizes the main features of their analysis and their principal findings. First, they estimate a variant of our earlier two-step model using data from the 1970, 1980, and 1990 censuses.[58] Their model allows the return-to-education-by-state-of-birth coefficients in equation 5-7 to also vary by region of residence, as follows:

$$(5\text{-}7') \qquad Y_{ijbc} = \delta_{bc} + \mu_{jc} + \beta X_{ijbc} + \gamma_{rbc} \cdot E_{ijbc} + \epsilon_{ijbc}.$$

In the first step of their analysis they estimate some 1,323 (= 49 states of birth × 9 regions of residence × 3 cohorts) slope coefficients, denoted γ_{rbc}.[59] In the second step, they relate these coefficients to cohort effects, state-of-birth effects, and measures of state-average school quality for the particular cohort and state of birth. Rather than include unrestricted region of residence effects in the second-stage model, they adjust the quality measures for individuals from cohort c and state of birth b who live in region r by subtracting the average quality measure for all groups in the region. They report that deviating the quality measures from regional means leads to a slight increase in the estimated quality effects. Indeed, their estimated effects are slightly larger than our original results for the 1980 census. Their estimate of the effect of school quality on the return to education is especially large in 1990, a year in which the payoff to skills is considered to be at a very high level.

Heckman, Layne-Farrar, and Todd next relate the state-of-birth intercepts to the level of quality in the state. Their results suggest that higher school quality is associated with a lower intercept, as in the theoretical model depicted in figure 5-1. Our earlier study found a similar result, although the analysis was somewhat complicated by the 2 percent threshold that we assumed in the education variable.[60]

The next extension is to include aggregate region-of-residence variables in the second-stage model, to capture aggregate supply and demand effects on the regional return to education. Since their quality variables

57. See chapter 7; Heckman, Layne-Farrar, and Todd (1995).
58. Card and Krueger (1992a).
59. It is impressive to note that these estimates are obtained from a model that also includes many other covariates.
60. See Card and Krueger (1992a, figure 5).

Table 5-4. Summary of Heckman, Layne-Farrar, and Todd's Study of Effect of School Quality on Return to Education

Analysis	Findings
1. Replicate Card and Krueger study in 1970, 1980, and 1990 censuses, using region-of-residence × region-of-birth interactions with linear education in first-step model.[a]	School quality effects on the return to education in 1970 and 1990 are stronger than Card and Krueger's findings in 1980 census.
2. Relate state of birth intercepts to school quality variables.	Higher school quality tends to reduce the intercept; similar to Card and Krueger's result.
3. Include region-of-residence effects and aggregate region-of-residence variables in second-step estimator.	School quality continues to have a beneficial and sizable effect on the rate of return to education.
4. Free up linearity assumption by allowing jumps in the return to education.	School quality has a weak and inconsistent relationship with the return to education around grade 12, but a significant relationship for postcollege years. Similar to Card and Krueger's results for grade 12 in 1980 census.
5. Include quadratic in distance between region of birth and region of residence and free up effect of school quality by region of residence in second-step equation.	Effects of quality are positive in most regions, and often large. Can reject that the effect of the pupil-teacher ratio is constant in all regions, but average across regions is about the same as in the unrestricted model.
6. Calculate Kendall coefficients of concordance between ranks of average wages across regions of residence and regions of birth, by cohort in 1980.	Weak positive correlations. Also, weak correlations between ranks of school quality and ranks of earnings.
7. Relate fractions of state population with college degree, with high school degree only, and high school dropouts to school quality, by cohort.	Higher quality is strongly related to greater proportion of college graduates, weakly related to proportion of high school graduates, and strongly related to reduction in dropouts.

Source: Heckman, Layne-Farrar, and Todd (1995).
a. With reference to Card and Krueger (1992a).

Table 5-5. *Effect of Pupil-Teacher Ratio on Return to Education, Based on Heckman, Layne-Farrar, and Todd*

Year	Restricted[a]	Average across nine census regions[b]
1970	−8.10	−7.23
1980	−5.66	−4.65
1990	−9.22	−26.62

Source: Restricted data are from Heckman, Layne-Farrar, and Todd (1995, tables 8a, b, c, column 1); average regional data are from Heckman, Layne-Farrar, and Todd (1995, tables 17a, b, c, column 1).
a. Restrictive model excludes the distance variables and imposes constant quality effects across regions.
b. Unweighted average represents the return to education for someone with an equal probability of moving to each region.

are deviated from regional means in their initial specification, however, the regional-level variables are orthogonal to the quality measures by construction, and the inclusion of these variables does not affect the estimated quality coefficients.

A fourth issue that Heckman, Layne-Farrar, and Todd raise is nonrandom migration. If interstate mobility induces a correlation between the state-of-birth-specific return to education and the quality of education, then the second-step estimates may be biased. In their specification, biases associated with interregional mobility are eliminated through the inclusion of features of the region of origin and region of residence in the second-step equation. In particular, they include a quadratic in the distance between the region of birth and the region of residence. They simultaneously free up the effect of school quality across regions by interacting the school quality variables with a set of nine region-of-residence dummies. Although they reject the hypothesis that the pupil-teacher ratio has the same effect on the return to education in different regions, this hypothesis cannot be rejected for teacher salary.[61] Furthermore, in almost all regions better school resources are associated with a higher return to education. To summarize these estimates, table 5-5 reports the unweighted averages of the pupil-teacher coefficients for the nine census regions.[62] The average pupil-teacher coefficients are similar to the coefficients from more restrictive models that exclude the distance variables and impose constant quality effects across regions. The only exception is 1990, when the average unrestricted coefficient is three times larger than the restricted one. This pattern suggests that the assumptions

61. Indeed, the F-tests for the teacher salary restrictions are far in the left tail of the distribution with values of p around 0.99.
62. The unweighted average represents the return for someone with an equal probability of moving to each region. Of course, one could use different weights.

of similar returns to school quality across regions and random migration may lead to downward biases in the estimated effect of school quality.

Their fifth contribution is to relax the linear education specification in the first-step equation by allowing for a piece-wise linear earnings-education function with discrete jumps at twelve and sixteen years of education. Each jump introduces an additional 76 to 120 parameters to be estimated in the first-step equation. They then relate the returns to education at grades 12 and 16 from these less-restrictive models to the school quality variables. These results show a weak and inconsistent pattern of the school quality variables at grade twelve, but stronger results at grade sixteen.[63] Taken together, eleven of the eighteen coefficients (two grade levels × three census years × three quality variables) have the right sign for the hypothesis that higher school quality raises the return to education. The results from the nonlinear specifications are probably the weakest set of findings in their study of school quality effects. In our earlier paper we similarly found that school quality had small and inconsistent effects on earnings for those with exactly twelve years of schooling.

A critical issue in the interpretation of these results is the selectivity of schooling. Although it may seem intuitively appealing that higher-quality public schooling has the greatest impact on students who go no further than high school, this intuition misses the fact that students with better elementary and secondary education may be more likely to enter college.[64] The results discussed in the previous subsection and the findings of Heckman, Layne-Farrar, and Todd suggest that higher school quality is associated with greater educational attainment.[65] If the average ability of individuals at each level of education falls as school quality rises, small, or even zero, effects of school quality on earnings would be expected for those with intermediate levels of education, consistent with the nonlinear specifications reported by Heckman, Layne-Farrar, and Todd. In our view, then, the question of how to interpret the effect of school quality on the level of earnings, conditional on education, remains open.

A sixth contribution of Heckman, Layne-Farrar, and Todd is to provide a nonparametric test of the hypothesis that average wages of workers educated in different regions have the same rank order across regional

63. See chapter 7, table 7-14.
64. An analogy may be helpful. It is arguable that advanced-level undergraduate courses yield the greatest benefit for students who go on to graduate school. In an evaluation of an undergraduate program these benefits would be missed if students who continued their training were excluded from the analysis.
65. See the last entry in table 5-4, p. 125.

labor markets. The tests are carried out by cohort, conditional on various levels of education. Taken as a whole, the evidence in support of this hypothesis is weak. They also correlate regional average quality measures with the mean wages of individuals who were educated in different regions and observed working in a given region (by education level and cohort). Again the correlations are weak. However, it is not clear that these tests have much power because school quality effects tend to be relatively small compared with the background noise in earnings and because the effects of school quality, conditional on education, may be relatively weak at the middle levels of education.

As a final comment, we note that simple reduced form models of the effect of school quality (that is, class IV models) may be quite useful in understanding the overall effects of school quality. Inferences about school quality effects from reduced form models do not depend on the functional form of the earnings-education relationship, they do not depend on particular assumptions about mobility, and they fully incorporate any effect of school quality on education attainment. It is also possible to estimate reduced form models for different quartiles of the earnings distribution, revealing potential differences in the effect of school quality for individuals in the lower or upper tails of the distribution. One limitation of reduced form models is the presence of unobserved state-of-birth effects (or unobserved differences across school districts) that may lead to biases in the correlation between school quality and earnings. However, we believe that estimates from reduced form models are an important part of the collage of evidence linking school quality and earnings.

Lessons from the Experiences of Southern-Born Blacks

A final aspect of the link between school quality and earnings that is worth considering in more detail is the unique experience of African American children who were schooled in the segregated school systems of the South. Racially segregated schooling led to profound differences in the school resources available to black and white children and among black children educated in different states. In 1915, for example, the eighteen jurisdictions with legally segregated schools had an average pupil-teacher ratio of sixty-one in black schools and thirty-eight in white schools. By the 1953–54 school year, on the eve of the *Brown* v. *Board of Education* decision, the average pupil-teacher ratio had fallen to thirty-

Figure 5-3. *Pupil-Teacher Ratios by Race, North Carolina and South Carolina*

Ratio

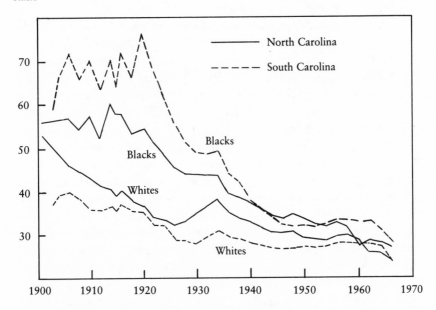

Source: Card and Krueger (1992b).

two in black schools and twenty-eight in white schools. The differences in school quality were also enormous across states. For example, in 1953–54 the average pupil-teacher ratio in black schools was thirty-nine in Mississippi and twenty-seven in Kentucky.

A particularly revealing comparison is provided by two neighboring states: North Carolina and South Carolina. Figure 5-3 shows the pupil-teacher ratio for black and white schools in North Carolina and South Carolina annually for most of the century. Although these two states are similar in many respects, they differed dramatically in the resources they provided for schooling, especially for black children. Whereas North Carolina was among the most progressive of the nonborder Southern states vis-à-vis black schooling, South Carolina was among the least progressive.[66] By contrast, schools for whites were actually better funded in South Carolina than in North Carolina throughout the first half of the century. In both states the pupil-teacher ratios in black and white schools had roughly converged by the late 1960s.

66. See, for example, Harlan (1958).

Horace Mann Bond and others have observed that in areas where blacks were more numerous, a greater share of school resources was diverted from black schools to white schools.[67] An exclusionary political system enabled this discrimination to persist until the 1960s.[68] North Carolina and South Carolina are consistent with this pattern, as the population of South Carolina included a much higher proportion of blacks than that of North Carolina.[69] Compared with white families, black families could exercise much less discretion over the level of school resources in segregated states. To the extent that the endogenous determination of school resources (that is, a correlation between school resources and omitted variables) is a problem for studies based on samples of white workers, it is much less of a problem for estimates based on black workers who were educated during the era of segregation.

In an earlier study, we draw on the large interstate differences in the pupil-teacher ratio and other resources in black and white schools in the first half of the century, as well as changes in resources across cohorts, to estimate the effect of school quality on earnings.[70] To control for differential labor market effects, much of our analysis focuses on workers who attended school in the South but later were observed working in a common set of Northern labor markets. This technique has the advantage of controlling for labor market differences that may be correlated with school quality differences. For example, states that discriminate in the allocation of school resources may be more likely to allow discrimination in labor market conditions. We relate the payoff to a year of schooling, by racial group, for individuals who were educated in different states to the quality of the educational resources available to students of that racial group at the time when they attended school (that is, class III models). The results indicate that the payoff to education was greater for individuals (of either racial group) who were from states that devoted more resources to education.

Figure 5-4 displays the cross-state relationship between the difference in returns to education between blacks and whites and the difference in the pupil-teacher ratio for black and white men born between 1910 and 1939. The downward-sloping relationship signifies that the differential payoff to a year of education was greatest for those from states where

67. See, for example, Bond (1934).
68. See Boozer, Krueger, and Wolkon (1992).
69. This difference reflected, in part, the history of different cropping patterns in the two states (see Fogel and Engerman, 1974).
70. Card and Krueger (1992b).

Figure 5-4. *Difference in Returns to Schooling versus Difference in Pupil-Teacher Ratios for Blacks and Whites, by State*[a]

Difference in returns[a]

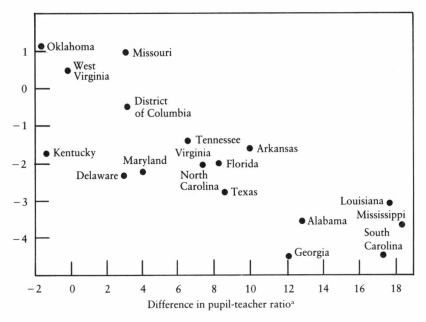

Source: Card and Krueger (1992b).
a. Black minus white.

black schools lagged furthest behind white schools in class size. Similar results are found when the focus is only on black workers, rather than on the difference between blacks and whites. Moreover, when we estimate separate models for blacks and whites from the segregated states, we are not able to reject the hypothesis that the effect of school quality on the return to education is the same for both racial groups.

The comparison between North Carolina and South Carolina provides additional evidence that the returns to education reflected the differences in quality. As noted, the quality of black schools was higher in North Carolina than in South Carolina, while the reverse was true for white schools throughout most of the century (see figure 5-3). For blacks, the estimated payoff to a year of education in 1980 was 2.1 percent for those born in South Carolina and 4.0 percent for those born in North Carolina; while for whites the order was reversed: 6.6 percent for South Carolina and 6.0 percent for North Carolina. Thus the differences in the payoff to education accord fairly well with the differences in the resources devoted to education in these two states.[71]

Because the analysis described so far is based on individuals who were educated (or, actually, born) in the South and then observed working elsewhere, the validity of our inferences depends on the migration decisions of the workers. To the extent that these decisions are correlated with the payoff to education (conditioning on the labor market where the individuals work) and the quality of individuals' schooling, the estimated effects of school quality may be biased. We suspect that a consideration of the nature of black mobility from the South would lead to the conclusion that patterns of earnings and school quality among migrants tend to underestimate any school quality effects estimated with state-level data. Most research suggests that Southern out-migrants were better educated than nonmigrants.[72] More generally, people with higher overall productivity (including both the level and quality of education, as well as other unobserved components of productivity) may have been more likely to leave the South. Thus, low-educated blacks who migrated from states with low average school quality (for example, Mississippi) are likely to have had higher levels of unobserved ability and to have attended schools with above average school quality within the state. In this scenario, the unobserved components of ability and school quality for individuals in our sample will be negatively correlated with measured school quality, biasing downward any measured effect of school quality.

More direct evidence that selective migration is not driving our findings is provided by reduced form estimates (class IV models). These estimates are based on all workers from a particular state, both those who moved out of state and those who did not. Specifically, we relate the gap in average weekly earnings between blacks and whites from each state to the gap in average school quality between blacks and whites that existed in the state during the years in which the workers would have attended school. The results were consistent with our findings based on differences in the returns to education: earnings are higher for groups from states with higher quality schooling. According to the reduced form

71. A similar comparison is possible between white and black students born in Virginia and West Virginia. In the early part of this century white schools had lower pupil-teacher ratios in Virginia than in West Virginia, while the reverse was true for black schools. Consistent with the school quality hypothesis, the estimated returns to schooling are higher for whites born in Virginia than West Virginia, while the returns are higher for blacks born in West Virginia than Virginia.

72. See, for example, Margo (1990).

estimates, a reduction of the pupil-teacher ratio by ten students was associated with nearly 3 percent higher weekly earnings during each year of an individual's working life. Notice, also, that this approach reflects any effects of school quality on the level of education, on the payoff to a year of education, and on the intercept.

In summary, evidence based on patterns of school quality and earnings for Southern-born black workers provides further confirmation of a link between school resources and labor market success. Because of the wide variation in school quality available to black children in different states and at different times, and because of the arguably exogenous—and certainly different—nature of the resource decisions that affected black students, this evidence is especially valuable. The estimated effects of school quality on the earnings of Southern-born blacks educated before the mid-1960s are consistent with the estimates obtained in the rest of the literature.

Conclusions

Our review of the literature reveals a high degree of consistency across studies regarding the effect of school quality on students' subsequent earnings. The literature suggests that a 10 percent increase in school spending is associated with a 1 to 2 percent increase in annual earnings for students later in their lives. The studies estimate a wide range of specifications and hold constant a number of different variables, including IQ, parental income, and parental education. Nonetheless, it is possible that school quality is only spuriously correlated with earnings as a result of unobserved background factors that affect school resources and student outcomes. Class III studies, which identify the effect of education on the slope of the earnings-education relationship, are less susceptible to such biases because the inclusion of unrestricted state effects eliminates the influence of omitted state-level characteristics. Most studies that estimate class III models tend to find a positive effect of school quality on the payoff to a year of education, once fixed state effects are removed.

Another finding is that educational attainment is positively related to school quality. This holds in several data sets, including those that measure quality at the state, district, and school levels. It is also consistent with a simple model that predicts that students will invest in more years of education if they perceive that higher quality schooling increases the payoff to each additional year of education.

Some authors have argued that the estimated positive effects of school quality on earnings and educational attainment are a spurious result of using aggregated school quality data. To support this argument, they point to studies using school-level quality data, such as the NLS-Y, that often (although not always) find a statistically insignificant relationship between school quality and earnings. Our review casts doubt on this conclusion. The small number of data sets that have information on workers' earnings and the quality of the specific schools they attended have three features in common that limit their usefulness: they include only young workers (often in their early twenties); they have school quality for just one year (typically a year during high school); and they have relatively small samples. Wachtel finds that the return to school quality increases as workers gain experience, and similar results have been found for the return to years of education.[73] School quality in a given year is an imprecise measure of the student's history of school quality, leading to potential attenuation biases. Perhaps most important, the small sample sizes of these data sets lead to imprecise estimates that cannot distinguish between small but economically important differences in school quality effects that are estimated with comparable specifications using more aggregative quality data in larger data sets. For example, our reanalysis shows that estimates based on the NLS-Y do not reject estimates of comparable specifications in the previous literature when appropriate standard errors are calculated. Furthermore, when state-level average quality is used in place of school-level data in these studies, the estimates are even less precise and often have the wrong sign, suggesting that the use of aggregated quality measures does not automatically lead to upward-biased quality effects.

Our reading of the literature leads us to suggest several important directions for future research to help resolve some of the remaining puzzles in the literature on school quality and earnings. First, as suggested by Wachtel, we hypothesize that the labor market returns to school quality tend to be lower for younger workers and to rise with experience.[74] This can be tested by examining young cohorts of workers (for example, ages seventeen to thirty-one) in census data, or by following cohorts in the NLS-Y, HSB, and similar data sets as they age.

73. Wachtel (1975).
74. Wachtel (1975).

Second, as Heckman, Layne-Farrar, and Todd and our earlier study find, the precise form of the earnings-school quality relationship exerts an important influence on the estimated effects of school quality.[75] For example, these studies conclude that school quality has a weak and inconsistent effect on the earnings of those with exactly twelve years of schooling. Conditioning on education is inappropriate, however, if educational attainment is affected by school quality and if the people with higher education would tend to earn more even without more schooling. Our theoretical model suggests that such unobserved ability biases will lead the observed earnings-schooling relationship to *rotate* as school quality increases—a prediction that is consistent with findings in these studies.

Third, reduced form models incorporate the effects of school quality on both educational attainment and the shape of the earnings-schooling relationship. For this reason, we recommend that researchers report such models and compare the reduced form estimates with their other specifications. Nevertheless, reduced form models are particularly susceptible to omitted variable biases. Perhaps the only way to fully overcome the problems of inferring the net effects of school quality is through randomized experiments. In the meantime, natural experiments that generate large and more-or-less exogenous shifts in school resources, such as the system of segregated schooling in the South, may provide the strongest evidence on school quality and labor market outcomes.

Our conclusion that most studies of labor market outcomes show a positive effect of school quality is in apparent conflict with the widely held view that school resources have little or no impact on students' test scores.[76] We do not think this conflict is resolved by concluding that the relationship between school quality and earnings is spurious. Instead, we believe that the following observations are relevant:

First, test scores are not strong predictors of students' success in the labor market, so the finding that school resources have a low association with test scores does not imply that school resources have a low association with earnings.[77] Test scores may be a poor indicator of what is

75. See chapter 7; Card and Krueger (1992a).
76. See, for example, Hanushek (1986).
77. This point was made more than twenty years ago: "Are our empirical findings necessarily inconsistent with those of several authors who argue that the quality of schooling has little effect on output measures such as tests of cognitive skills? We think not. First, there is to our knowledge no precise link between test scores and earnings." (Johnson and Stafford, 1973, p. 153).

learned in school and subsequently rewarded in the labor market. And students' performance on tests while they are in school may be a poor indicator of what is retained years later, when they are in the labor market.

Second, the conclusion that school inputs do not have an effect on test scores is open to question. Many of the individual studies in the literature have low power, even though they may have power as a group. Indeed, the meta-analysis by Lawrence Hedges, Richard Laine, and Rob Greenwald suggests that school quality does affect test scores.[78] Although one can criticize the assumptions that underlie any meta-analysis, one must bear in mind that similar assumptions are implicit in other quantitative summaries of the literature. It should also be noted that a recent experiment in which students were randomly assigned to large and small classes in Tennessee found that students tended to perform better on tests if they were assigned to small classes.[79]

Third, because educational attainment appears to be related to school quality, the type of selection issues that arise in the literature on earnings may also arise in the literature on test scores. In particular, marginal students who benefit most from improved school quality may be less likely to drop out or be held back a grade. Therefore studies of the relationship between test scores and school quality that condition on grade level may be biased toward finding no effect of school quality. This issue can be investigated by implementing a reduced form model that conditions on age, but not grade level.

References

Akerhielm, Karen. 1995. "Does Class Size Matter?" *Economics of Education Review* 14 (September): 229–41.

Akin, John S., and Irwin Garfinkel. 1980. "The Quality of Education and Cohort Variation in Black-White Earnings Differentials: Comment." *American Economic Review* 70 (March): 186–91.

Angrist, Joshua D., and Alan B. Krueger. 1991. "Does Compulsory School Attendance Affect Schooling and Earnings?" *Quarterly Journal of Economics* 106 (November): 979–1014.

Ashenfelter, Orley, and Alan B. Krueger. 1994. "Estimates of the Economic

78. Hedges, Laine, and Greenwald (1993).
79. See Mosteller (1995).

Return to Schooling from a New Sample of Twins." *American Economic Review* 84 (December): 1157–73.

Becker, Gary S. 1967. *Human Capital and the Personal Distribution of Income: An Analytical Approach.* Institute of Public Administration and Department of Economics, University of Michigan.

Behrman, Jere R., and Nancy Birdsall. 1983. "The Quality of Schooling: Quantity Alone Is Misleading." *American Economic Review* 73 (December): 928–46.

Behrman, Jere R., and others. 1980. *Socioeconomic Success: A Study of the Effects of Genetic Endowments, Family Environment, and Schooling.* Amsterdam: North Holland.

Betts, Julian R. 1995. "Does School Quality Matter? Evidence from the National Longitudinal Survey of Youth." *Review of Economics and Statistics* 77 (May): 231–50.

Bond, Horace Mann. 1934. *The Education of the Negro in the American Social Order.* Prentice-Hall.

Boozer, Michael A. 1995. "Segregation, Dropouts, and School Quality." Unpublished paper. Princeton University (January).

Boozer, Michael A., Alan B. Krueger, and Shari Wolkon. 1992. "Race and School Quality Since *Brown* v. *Board of Education.*" *Brookings Papers on Economic Activity, Microeconomics.* 269–326.

Boozer, Michael A., and Cecilia Rouse. 1995. "Intraschool Variation in Class Size: Patterns and Implications." Unpublished paper. Princeton University.

Brattsberg, Bernt, and Dek Terrell. 1995. "U.S. Immigrants' Returns to Education and Quality of Schooling." Unpublished paper. Kansas State University (February).

Cameron, Stephen V., and James J. Heckman. 1993. "The Nonequivalence of High School Equivalents." *Journal of Labor Economics* 11 (January, part 1): 1–47.

Card, David. 1995. "Schooling, Earnings and Ability Revisited." In *Research in Labor Economics*, vol. 14, edited by Solomon Polachek, 23–48. Greenwich, Conn.: JAI Press.

Card, David, and Alan B. Krueger. 1992a. "Does School Quality Matter? Returns to Education and the Characteristics of Public Schools in the United States." *Journal of Political Economy* 100 (February): 1–40.

———. 1992b. "School Quality and Black-White Relative Earnings: A Direct Assessment." *Quarterly Journal of Economics* 107 (February): 151–200.

———. 1995. "The Economic Return to School Quality." In *Assessing Educational Practices: The Contribution of Economics*, edited by William Baumol and William Becker. Cambridge, Mass.: MIT, 161–82.

———. 1996. "Labor Market Effects of School Quality: Theory and Evidence." Working paper 5450. Cambridge, Mass.: National Bureau of Economic Research.

Fogel, Robert William, and Stanley L. Engerman. 1974. *Time on the Cross*. Little Brown.

Friedman, Milton. 1962. *Capitalism and Freedom*. University of Chicago Press.

Griliches, Zvi. 1977. "Estimating the Returns to Schooling: Some Econometric Problems." *Econometrica* 45 (January): 1–22.

Griliches, Zvi, and William M. Mason. 1972. "Education, Income, and Ability." *Journal of Political Economy* 80 (May/June, part 2): S74–S103.

Grogger, Jeff. Forthcoming. "Does School Quality Explain the Recent Black/White Wage Trend?" *Journal of Labor Economics*.

Hanushek, Eric A. 1974. "Efficient Estimators for Regressing Regression Coefficients." *American Statistician* 28 (May): 66–67.

———. 1986. "The Economics of Schooling: Production and Efficiency in Public Schools." *Journal of Economic Literature* 24 (September): 1141–77.

Hanushek, Eric, Steven Rivkin, and Lori Taylor. 1995. "The Identification of School Resource Effects." Unpublished paper. University of Rochester.

Harlan, Louis R. 1958. *Separate and Unequal: Public School Campaigns and Racism in the Southern Seaboard States 1901–1915*. University of North Carolina Press.

Haveman, Robert H., and Barbara L. Wolfe. 1984. "Schooling and Economic Well-Being: The Role of Non-Market Effects." *Journal of Human Resources* 19 (Summer): 377–407.

Heckman, James J., Anne Layne-Farrar, and Petra Todd. 1995. "The Schooling Quality-Earnings Relationship: Using Economic Theory to Interpret Functional Forms Consistent with the Evidence." Working Paper 5288. Cambridge Mass.: National Bureau of Economic Research.

Heckman, James J., and Solomon Polachek. 1974. "Empirical Evidence on the Functional Form of the Earnings-Schooling Relationship." *Journal of the American Statistical Association* 69 (June): 350–54.

Hedges, Lawrence V., Richard Laine, and Rob Greenwald. 1993. "Does Money Matter? A Meta-Analysis of Studies of the Effects of Differential School Inputs on Student Outcomes." *Educational Researcher* 23 (April): 5–14.

Hungerford, Thomas, and Gary Solon. 1987. "Sheepskin Effects in the Returns to Education." *Review of Economics and Statistics* 69 (February): 175–77.

Johnson, George, and Frank Stafford. 1973. "Social Returns to Quantity and Quality of Schooling." *Journal of Human Resources* 8 (Spring): 139–55.

Jud, G. Donald, and James L. Walker. 1977. "Discrimination by Race and Class and the Impact of School Quality." *Social Science Quarterly* 57 (March): 731–49.

Lang, Kevin. 1993. "Ability Bias, Discount Rate Bias and the Return to Education." Unpublished paper. Boston University.

Levy, Frank, and Richard J. Murnane. 1992. "U.S. Earnings Levels and Earnings Inequality: A Review of Recent Trends and Proposed Explanations." *Journal of Economic Literature* 30 (September): 1333–81.

Link, Charles R., Edward C. Ratledge, and Kenneth A. Lewis. 1980. "The Quality of Education and Cohort Variation in Black-White Earnings Differentials: Reply." *American Economic Review* 70 (March): 196–203.

Margo, Robert A. 1990. *Race and Schooling in the South, 1880–1950: An Economic History*. University of Chicago Press.

Miller, Paul, Charles Mulvey, and Nick Martin. 1995. "What Do Twins Studies Reveal about the Economic Returns to Education? A Comparison of Australian and U.S. Findings." *American Economic Review* 85 (June): 586–99.

Mincer, Jacob. 1974. *Schooling, Experience, and Earnings*. New York: National Bureau of Economic Research.

Morgan, James, and Ismail Sirageldin. 1968. "A Note on the Quality Dimension in Education." *Journal of Political Economy* 76 (September/October): 1069–77.

Morgenstern, Richard D. 1973. "Direct and Indirect Effects on Earnings of Schooling and Socio-Economic Background." *Review of Economics and Statistics* 55 (May): 225–33.

Mosteller, Fredrick. 1995. "The Tennessee Study of Class Size in the Early School Grades." *Critical Issues for Children and Youths* 5 (Summer/Fall): 113–27.

Murnane, Richard J., John B. Willett, and Frank Levy. 1995. "The Growing Importance of Cognitive Skills in Wage Determination." *Review of Economics and Statistics* 77 (May): 251–66.

Murray, Sheila E., William N. Evans, and Robert M. Schwab. 1995. "The Effects of School Resources on High School Completion: Evidence from Panel Data." Unpublished paper. University of Maryland.

Park, Jin Heum. 1994. "Returns to Schooling: A Peculiar Deviation from Linearity." Unpublished paper. Princeton University.

Ribar, David C. 1994. "Teenage Fertility and High School Completion." *Review of Economics and Statistics* 76 (August): 413–24.

Ribich, Thomas I., and James L. Murphy. 1975. "The Economic Returns to Increased Educational Spending." *Journal of Human Resources* 10 (Winter): 56–77.

Rizzuto, Ronald, and Paul Wachtel. 1980. "Further Evidence on the Returns to School Quality." *Journal of Human Resources* 15 (Spring): 240–54.

Saiger, Aaron, and Timothy Irwin. 1995. "Does School Quality Matter? Evidence from the National Longitudinal Survey of Youth: A Comment." Unpublished paper. Princeton University.

Spence, Michael. 1973. "Job Market Signaling," *Quarterly Journal of Economics* 87 (August): 355–74.

Tremblay, Carol H. 1986. "The Impact of School and College Expenditures on the Wages of Southern and Non-Southern Workers." *Journal of Labor Research* 7 (Spring): 201–11.

Wachtel, Paul. 1975. "The Returns to Investment in Higher Education: Another

View." In *Education, Income, and Human Behavior,* edited by F. Thomas Juster, 151–70. McGraw-Hill.

———. 1976. "The Effect on Earnings of School and College Investment Expenditures." *Review of Economics and Statistics* 58 (August): 326–31.

Willis, Robert J. 1986. "Wage Determinants: A Survey and Re-interpretation of Human Capital Earnings Functions." In *Handbook of Labor Economics,* vol. 1, edited by Orley Ashenfelter and Richard Layard. New York: North Holland.

Willis, Robert J., and Sherwin Rosen. 1979. "Education and Self-Selection." *Journal of Political Economy* 87, part 2 (October): S7–36.

CHAPTER 6

Is There a Link between School Inputs and Earnings? Fresh Scrutiny of an Old Literature

Julian R. Betts

A WIDESPREAD perception exists that American public schools are not providing students with the skills they need to compete in an increasingly competitive economy. For instance, the influential publication *A Nation at Risk* paints an alarming picture of the skills acquired by the typical American student while at school.[1] Indeed, Eric Hanushek establishes that scores on standardized tests such as the Scholastic Aptitude Test have typically stagnated or fallen during the last twenty-five years.[2] John Bishop shows that these declines in test scores have significantly affected the overall productivity of the American economy.[3] Against this backdrop of stagnating educational achievement, Hanushek notes that real spending per student in American public schools has more than doubled during the last twenty-five years.

That academic performance has not improved during a period when spending per pupil has grown dramatically suggests two possible explanations. The first is that widespread inefficiency in public schools has limited the effectiveness of educational spending. The second is that socioeconomic trends in the broader society, such as the rising incidence

---

1. National Commission on Excellence in Education (1983).
2. Hanushek (1986, 1989, 1991). Some authors have claimed that the fall in test scores merely reflects selectivity bias: as the proportion of students taking these tests has risen, the average "quality" of test writers has fallen. But Murray and Herrnstein (1991) show that demographic trends cannot explain the decline in test scores because in every decade they move in the wrong direction. For instance, during the period in which Scholastic Aptitude Test (SAT) scores dropped, from the mid-1960s through the early 1980s, the proportion of the eighteen-year-old population taking the test actually dropped slightly. Murray and Herrnstein argue that the declining quality of the college-bound track of high school education must bear some of the blame for the decline in test scores in the 1970s.
3. Bishop (1989).

of single-parent families and children raised in poverty, may have increasingly hampered students' achievement over the years.

From the point of view of the education policymaker, little can be done within schools to counteract adverse socioeconomic trends, especially given the fiscal restraints currently being imposed on most public institutions. But much could be done to reorganize the way in which school systems spend. This raises a series of crucial questions. First, does educational spending have a large effect on student outcomes? Second, which types of school inputs are most influential in determining student success? Do factors other than spending influence the productivity of schools?

A related question concerns how best to measure student performance. Most of the literature on school quality has attempted to measure student outcomes in terms of test scores or gains in test scores. As I argue later, data sets that provide test scores do confer several unique benefits. However, it is important to supplement this work with research that examines the long-term effects of schooling. From an economist's perspective, the best measure of student performance is some measure of income, which is more closely linked to a person's welfare than are test scores per se.

The goal of this chapter is to provide a detailed review of the literature on the link between school resources and students' success after leaving school. I examine two outcome measures: earnings and educational attainment. The review suggests an unsettled literature, in which some authors find strong effects of school inputs while other authors find no significant link at all. Because of the heterogeneous nature of past results, I endeavor to find patterns that distinguish the studies that suggest that school expenditures are not very productive from those that find that they are productive. In the first section, several striking patterns emerge:

—Most of the studies that find no link or a weak link between school inputs and student outcomes measure school inputs at the level of the actual school attended; studies that do find a strong effect typically measure school resources at the level of the state.

—Studies that find that school inputs have a strong impact tend to examine workers schooled before the 1960s. The opposite holds for studies that find no impact.

—Studies that find no significant link tend to examine workers who are in their early thirties or their twenties at the time earnings are observed.

I then examine the rate of return to spending on school inputs and discuss five sets of hypotheses that might explain the observed patterns, and the evidence available to date on each of the hypotheses.

In the second section I examine the much smaller literature on the link between school inputs and educational attainment. Highly similar results appear in this literature: only some studies find a significant positive link between school inputs and educational attainment. Furthermore, studies that measure inputs at the school actually attended typically find the weakest results. In the final sections I suggest possible directions for future research and briefly summarize and interpret the results.

The Direct Impact of School Inputs on Earnings

In this section I first examine the body of research that measures the direct impact of school expenditures on earnings, holding constant the person's level of education. I then consider the rate of return to spending on school inputs. Finally, I discuss five sets of hypotheses that might explain the observed patterns.

Basic Results and Patterns in the Literature

In the late 1960s Finis Welch and James Morgan and Ismail Sirageldin did pioneering work on the question of school quality and earnings.[4] Since then, twenty-one other studies have examined the issue. Though this number may sound large, it is important to realize that many studies replicate earlier work in that they use the same data sources for information on school inputs. For example, six of the twenty-three studies use the National Longitudinal Survey of Young Men (NLS-YM) to test for a link between expenditures at the level of the school district and the earnings of young males; and nine of the twenty-three studies use state-level information on school inputs from the *Biennial Survey of Education.* The studies do vary in method and in periods of time covered, but clearly they should not be treated as statistically independent studies.

Table 6-1 describes the results of the studies, showing the source of the data on school inputs in each case. Bear in mind that fifteen of the twenty-three studies use just two data sources for school resources. The numbers in the table are the percentage of earnings regressions in the

4. Welch (1966); Morgan and Sirageldin (1968).

Table 6-1. *Percentage of Wage Regressions with Significant Results at 5 Percent, by Author and Data Source*

Study	Expenditure per pupil	Teacher-pupil ratio	Teacher education	Teacher salary	Teacher experience	Length school year	Books per student
Akin and Garfinkel (1977)	75		100				
Card and Krueger (1992a)		92		79	0	46	
Card and Krueger (1992b)		47		67		17	
Johnson and Stafford (1973)	75						
Morgan and Sirageldin (1969)	100						
Morgenstern (1973)	40	0		0			
Nechyba (1990)	100						
Rizzuto and Wachtel (1980)	95	25		100		100	
Welch (1966)	0	−67		25			
Average Biennial Survey (state)	**69**	**19**	**100**	**54**	**0**	**54**	
Wachtel (1975)	100	0					
Wachtel (1976)	67						
Average Biennial Survey (district)	**83**	**0**		**100**		**100**	
Jud and Walker (1977)	0						
Link and Ratledge (1975b)	100						
Link and Ratledge (1975a)	94						
Link, Ratledge, and Lewis (1976)	100						
Link, Ratledge, and Lewis (1980)	83						
Tremblay (1986)	50						
Average NLS-YM (district)	**71**						

Ribich and Murphy (1975)	0				
Project Talent (district)	0				
Kohen (1971)				0	0
Parnes and Kohen (1975)				0	0
NLS-YM-(school)[a]				0	0
Wachtel (1975)	0		100		
NBER-Thorndike (school level)[b]	0		100		
Betts (1995)		0	0	−4	
NLSY (school)		0	0	−4	0
Grogger (forthcoming)		0	0		0
HSB (school)[d]		0	0		
Altonji (1988)			33		
Grogger (forthcoming)	−50	−50	75		
Average NLS 72 (school)[e]	−50	−50	54		
Means across data sources	45	−5	51	38	0
Means by level of aggregation					
State	69	19	100	54	0
District	51	0	39	100	
School	0	−13		−2	

Source: Author's calculations.

a. NLS-YM: National Longitudinal Survey of Young Men.

b. NBER-Thorndike: National Bureau of Economic Research–Thorndike data set.

c. NLSY: National Longitudinal Survey of Youth.

d. HSB: High School and Beyond.

e. NLS 72: National Longitudinal Study of the High School Class of 1972.

given study which find that the stated school input is statistically significant at 5 percent or less when education is controlled for. (The majority of studies control for education in all specifications.)[5] Several numbers in the table are negative, indicating that the only significant coefficients were negative.

The most commonly used measure of school inputs is spending per student. The studies that measure spending by state averages almost always find a positive association between educational expenditures and average earnings. Paul Wachtel uses *the Biennial Survey of Education*—the same data source as the state-level studies—but aggregated only to the level of the school district.[6] He obtains similar results. Other studies using school district data based on the NLS-YM find positive results, but not nearly as uniformly. Thomas Ribich and James Murphy, using Project Talent data, find no significant link.[7] Wachtel, in his 1975 study, presents the only evidence on the link between total expenditures at the actual school attended and earnings and finds no significant link.

Because many studies in this table replicate earlier work, it is important to weight the studies appropriately. Thus below each set of studies that use the same data source for school inputs there appears in bold face a simple average of the percentage of regressions that were significant at 5 percent for the group. Toward the bottom of the table, in the row labeled means across data sources, an average of these mean percentages is listed. Thus for school expenditures, the average percent "score" across the various sources of school data is 45 percent.

In an attempt to determine whether the level of aggregation influences the results, the bottom of the table reports the average percentage of regressions giving significant results, based on the level of aggregation for the school inputs. An interesting pattern results: although 69 percent of the state-level regressions and 51 percent of the district-level studies give positive and significant results, the sole school-level study finds no significant link.[8] One should be cautious about identifying a pattern based on one school-level study. But as is shown later, for every measure of school resources, data sets that measure actual school inputs produce

5. In some cases authors mention the results of regressions in the text only. Where there was no ambiguity as to the type of regression run and the results, these are included in the table.
6. Wachtel (1975, 1976).
7. Ribich and Murphy (1975).
8. The school-level study is Wachtel (1975).

the weakest evidence of a significant link between spending and student outcomes.

Richard Murnane and others argue that it is not enough simply to test for a link between educational spending and student performance: "Much of the debate about school expenditures has been sterile because it ignores *how* dollars are used. Researchers have not carefully analyzed how spending money in one way or another does or does not affect students' experiences."[9] Indeed, a school administrator who has a fixed budget would probably be more concerned about *which* types of spending were more effective than about the overall impact of the level of spending. Similarly, a policymaker would probably want to be reassured that observed correlations between school expenditures and students' subsequent earnings reflected a causal relation from spending to outcomes, rather than a spurious correlation or even a reverse causation. To ease both these concerns, it makes sense to study whether and how specific types of school expenditures affect earnings. The remaining columns in table 6-1 summarize the state of knowledge about such relations.

As the table makes clear, when researchers have attempted to identify the specific components of total educational spending that most influence earnings, most studies have found either no link or a positive link that is not robust to changes in specification or subsample. The school input for which there is the strongest evidence of a positive effect is the teacher's level of education. But even here, the average percentage of regressions that are significant, when averaged across data sources, is only 51 percent. Slightly more than one-third of the regressions find a positive and significant link between earnings and teacher salary and length of the school year. Neither of the studies that examine the impact of library resources finds a significant effect.

Perhaps most disheartening is that, of the eleven studies that test for a relation between the teacher-pupil ratio and earnings, only one finds a positive and significant link in 50 percent or more of the regressions reported.[10] Eight of the eleven studies reported an insignificant (or negative and significant) relationship between the teacher-pupil ratio and earnings in every specification.[11]

9. Murnane and others (1991, p. 7).
10. Card and Krueger (1992a).
11. Some studies use class size rather than the teacher-pupil ratio as a regressor. Table 6-1 assumes that, for instance, a negative coefficient on class size indicates that the teacher-pupil coefficient would be positive.

The bottom of the table shows the breakdown of results by level of aggregation of the school inputs. The aforementioned pattern appears for every type of school input: inputs that seem effective when measured at the state level prove to be insignificantly related to earnings when the input is measured for the actual school attended.[12] Indeed, across five microeconomic data sets—the NLS-YM, the National Longitudinal Study of the High School Class of 1972 (NLS72), the National Bureau of Economic Research (NBER)-Thorndike data, and the more recent National Longitudinal Survey of Youth (NLSY), and High School and Beyond (HSB), most school inputs are insignificantly different from zero in every specification reported.[13] The only specific school input for which there is much evidence from school-level data of any sort of positive relation is, as in other chapters, teacher education, for which 39 percent of regressions based on school-level data sources show a significant positive relation.

It is important to realize that the school-level studies do not claim that all schools are equally good.[14] What the studies typically find is that schools differ substantially in quality but that standard measures of school resources do not capture these differences.

In figure 6-1 each study in table 6-1 is put into one of three categories, depending on whether it finds that school inputs are statistically significant, significant only in some specifications, or insignificant.[15] For each study, the approximate period during which workers were enrolled in grades 1 through 12 is plotted. In addition, the figure groups school-level studies in the upper panel, studies that use district-level measures of

12. The district-level results for these specific inputs, which in each case derive from Wachtel's (1975) analysis of data from the *Biennial Survey of Education*, typically but not always mirror the results obtained using *Biennial Survey of Education* data at the state level.

13. The NLSY is a nationally representative data set for which school data were collected in 1979; the HSB began in 1980.

14. See, for example, Betts (1995) and Grogger (forthcoming) for evidence that school fixed effects in earnings regressions are highly statistically significant. Murnane (1975) shows that teachers differ significantly in terms of the rate at which their students improve in standardized tests.

15. To allocate studies into these three groups the average of the percentages reported in table 6-1 was taken across all school inputs examined in a given study. Studies with an average of 66.6 percent or higher were labeled "significant," those with an average between 33.3 percent and 66.6 percent "sometimes significant," and those with an average below 33.3 percent "insignificant." The one borderline case was Card and Krueger (1992a), for which the raw average was 63 percent. I allocated this paper to the significant category because it would have easily fit into this category if not for an insignificant result on the impact of teacher experience.

Figure 6-1. *Classification of Studies by Significance of School Inputs and Years in Which Students Received Grade 1–12 Education*[a]

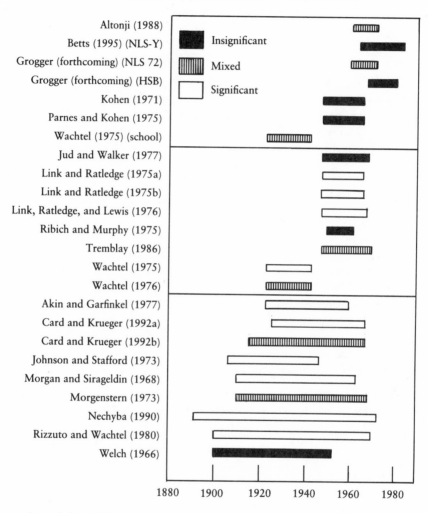

Source: Author's calculations

a. School-level studies are in the top panel; those that use district-level measures are in the middle panel; those that use state-level measures are in the bottom panel.

school inputs in the middle panel, and those that use state-level measures of school inputs in the bottom panel.

The figure illustrates two patterns in the literature. First, as mentioned before, the less aggregated data sources tend to reveal no or weak relations between inputs and earnings. Second, the figure suggests that most of the studies that do find a positive and significant link between inputs and earnings are based on workers who attended grade school between 1900 and 1960. All but one of the studies that fail to find a significant link between spending and outcomes examine workers who obtained their grade school education between the mid-1950s and the early 1980s. A possibly related pattern concerns the age at which workers' earnings are measured. Most of the school-level studies, which uniformly find no effects or mixed effects of school inputs on earnings, measure earnings for workers aged thirty-two or under. The major exception is Wachtel, who reports results for workers in the National Bureau of Economic Research-Thorndike data set who were between thirty and fifty-two when earnings were recorded.[16]

The Internal Rate of Return to School Expenditures

Besides examining the question whether there is a significant link between school resources and earnings, it is also important to estimate the economic returns to school expenditures based on the coefficient estimates. This subsection offers such calculations. First, it presents estimated elasticities of earnings with respect to various measures of school resources. Second, it converts these elasticities into internal rates of return for spending per pupil and for the most commonly used measure of specific school inputs, which is class size. One conclusion that emerges is that the estimated internal rate of return to educational expenditures varies considerably by the level of aggregation of the study, with school-level analyses typically yielding lower estimates of elasticities than studies that use state averages as proxies. A second significant finding is that the rates of return are typically positive but very small. Under reasonable assumptions about discount rates, the rate of return to additional spending on school resources is near or even below zero. In stark contrast, spending on additional years of education has a dramatically higher rate of return.

ELASTICITIES. Table 6-2 presents estimated elasticities and standard errors for overall spending per student. Here only state-level and district-level analyses are available.[17] The elasticity of earnings with respect to

16. Wachtel (1975).
17. This and subsequent tables note cases where elasticities could not be calculated with the notation n.a. One common problem was that in some cases authors reported (typically statistically insignificant) results in the text without stating coefficient estimates. Occasionally a lack of information on variable means also prevented calculation of elastic-

Table 6-2. *Estimates of Elasticity and Standard Error of Earnings with Respect to Spending per Pupil, by Author and Data Source*

Study	Input coefficient	Input* ED coefficient	Elasticity	Standard error
Akin and Garfinkel (1977) (blacks)	0.1528		0.1528	0.0599
Akin and Garfinkel (1977) (whites)	0.1676		0.1676	0.1035
Johnson and Stafford (1973)			0.1980	0.0510
Morgan and Sirageldin (1968)	0.0024		0.2688	0.0504
Morgenstern (1973) (whites)	0.12		0.0362	0.1688
Morgenstern (1973) (blacks)	0.23		0.0638	0.0321
Nechyba (1990)			n.a.	n.a.
Rizzuto and Wachtel (1980) (70 whites)			0.0772	0.0098
Rizzuto and Wachtel (1980) (60 whites)			0.1166	0.0078
Rizzuto and Wachtel (1980) (70 blacks)			0.1085	0.0318
Rizzuto and Wachtel (1980) (60 blacks)			0.0919	0.0302
Welch (1966)			n.a.	n.a.
Average Biennial Survey (state)			**0.1281**	**0.0545**
Wachtel (1975)	1.8377		0.1966	0.0304
Wachtel (1976) (1955 earnings)[b]	0.2908		0.0849	0.0286
Wachtel (1976) (1969 earnings)	0.6835		0.1996	0.0352
Average Biennial Survey (district)			**0.1604**	**0.0314**
Jud and Walker (1977)[c]	0.57		0.0504	0.504
Link and Ratledge (1975b)			0.1762	0.0503
Link and Ratledge (1975a)[c]	0.95		0.1223	0.0437
Link, Ratledge, and Lewis (1976)			n.a.	n.a.
Link, Ratledge, and Lewis (1980) (whites)		0.0102	0.1275	0.0288
Link, Ratledge, and Lewis (1980) (blacks)		0.0159	0.1717	0.0626
Tremblay (1986) (South)		0.0101	0.1212	0.0602
Tremblay (1986) (North)		0.003	0.0360	0.0486
Average NLS-YM (district)			**0.1151**	**0.0492**
Ribich and Murphy (1975)	2.18		0.0128	0.0146
Project Talent (district)			**0.0128**	**0.0146**
Wachtel (1975) (school level)			n.a.	n.a.
NBER-Thorndike (school)			**n.a.**	**n.a.**
Means across data sources			0.1041	0.0374
Means by level of aggregation				
State			0.1281	0.0545
District			0.0961	0.0317

Source: Author's calculations.
n.a. Not able to calculate. See note 17 in text.
a. *ED* is years of schooling.
b. The standard error for the 1955 earnings model of Wachtel (1976) corrects for a typographical error in that paper which labels the standard error incorrectly as *t* statistics.
c. The mean expenditure per pupil used in calculating elasticities for Jud and Walker (1977) and Link and Ratledge (1975a) is $571, which was calculated by the author from the full NLS-YM sample.

spending per pupil varies widely across studies, from 0.01 to 0.27, with a mean for the state-level and district-level studies of 0.128 and 0.096.[18]

Table 6-3 presents similar results for studies that examine the teacher-pupil ratio.[19] A strong pattern emerges: the lower the level of aggregation at which the school input is measured, the lower the average elasticity. In the school-level analyses by Jeff Grogger and myself, the mean elasticity is slightly negative but insignificant.

It is worthwhile to convert the elasticity of earnings with respect to the teacher-pupil ratio, η, into σ, the elasticity that measures the percent increase in earnings that results from a given percent increase in spending aimed at reducing class size. Classroom expenditures typically account for about 60 percent of total educational expenditures, with overhead and administrative costs taking up much of the remaining costs.[20] This

---

ities. The first of these problems is likely to bias the mean estimated elasticities upward.

Authors use various specifications of the earnings-spending relationship, such as log-log or log-linear models, in which spending per pupil may be interacted with education or entered on its own. Coefficients are shown in the table to guide the reader toward the model(s) chosen from each study. In the case of studies that provide multiple specifications, the model selected is typically the one with the fullest set of background controls, including education. In later tables that list elasticities for other school inputs, if an author estimates the impact of several inputs, the specification selected preferably includes only the given measure of school input, so as to reduce potential multicollinearity problems.

18. It is important to recognize that the mean and the mean standard error printed at the bottom of the table do not provide a test of the hypothesis that school spending has no effect on earnings. The standard error of the mean will be smaller than the mean standard error, since the variance of the mean will equal $(1/n^2)$ times the sum of variances and covariances. But since many of the studies use the same sample of workers (in particular, all of the NLS-YM studies), many of the covariance terms will be positive and large. Some of the state-level studies also draw from the same sample of workers. For instance, Welch (1966), Rizzuto and Wachtel (1980), Card and Krueger (1992a, 1992b), and Nechyba (1990) all draw data from the decennial censuses, and there is some overlap between the census years, and hence in the sample of workers, used in some of these studies. In addition, Morgan and Sirageldin (1968) and Johnson and Stafford (1973) use the same data source. There is a second reason why the covariance terms are likely to be positive. Even in the state-level studies that use entirely different samples of workers, the estimated elasticities are likely to be positively correlated across studies due to measurement error in the state-level data. Since all of the state-level studies take their data on school resources from the *Biennial Survey of Education*, and since these data are likely to have errors, the coefficient estimates will be positively correlated even if different studies use different samples of workers. It is quite likely that the *Biennial Survey of Education* data contain measurement error. For instance, the survey contains scant information on any variation in how data were gathered in different states or on how individual states might have changed variable definitions or data-gathering methods over the years.

19. For studies that use class size as the independent variable, the negative of the estimated elasticity is used as an estimate of the elasticity of earnings with respect to the teacher-pupil ratio.

20. For instance, in 1987–88 instructional expenditures accounted for 61.7 percent of

Table 6-3. *Estimates of Elasticity and Standard Error of Earnings with Respect to the Teacher-Pupil Ratio, by Author and Data Source*[a]

Study	Input coefficient	Elasticity	Standard error
Card and Krueger (1992a)	− 0.0042	0.112	0.016
Card and Krueger (1992b)	− 0.0028	0.086	0.031
Morgenstern (1973)		n.a.	n.a.
Rizzuto and Wachtel (1980)		n.a.	n.a.
Welch (1966)		n.a.	n.a.
Average Biennial Survey (state)		**0.099**	**0.023**
Wachtel (1975)	0.7806	0.024	n.a.
Average Biennial Survey (district)		**0.024**	**n.a.**
Kohen (1971)		n.a.	n.a.
Parnes and Kohen (1971)		n.a.	n.a.
NLS-YM (school)		**n.a.**	**n.a.**
Betts (1995)	0.2503	0.014	0.025
NLSY (school)		**0.014**	**0.025**
Grogger (forthcoming)	− 0.0031	− 0.059	0.036
HSB (school)		**− 0.059**	**0.036**
Grogger (forthcoming)	− 0.0033	− 0.066	0.039
Average NLS 72 (school)		**− 0.066**	**0.039**
Means across data sources		0.002	0.030
Means by level of aggregation			
State		0.099	0.023
District		0.024	n.a.
School		− 0.037	0.033

Source: Author's calculations.
n.a. Not able to calculate. See note 17 in text.
a. Several authors use class size, the reciprocal of the teacher-pupil ratio, as a regressor. Elasticities in the table are signed such that a positive sign indicates that a higher teacher-pupil ratio raises earnings.

might imply that $\sigma = \eta/0.6$. But such a conversion is apt to overstate the impact of a dollar spent on reducing class size, because it is unlikely that policymakers could simply reduce class sizes without affecting overhead and capital expenditures.[21] On the other extreme, it is probably unrealistic to assume that all noninstructional costs vary directly with the number of classrooms. Therefore, I take a middle ground, assuming

total current expenditures on public K–12 education. *Digest of Education Statistics* (1991, p. 154).

21. In early 1994 the San Diego Unified School District proposed reducing the maximum class size for children in grades 1 and 2 to twenty-five students. Teachers opposed the move, because in several schools the action would have required eliminating either the school library or computer room to create a new classroom. This is an example of how decreasing class size can increase schools' long-term capital needs. See Sharon L. Jones, "Teachers Flay Policy; Blacks Charge Racism," *San Diego Union Tribune*, April 6, 1994, pp. B1, B4.

Table 6-4. Estimates of Elasticity and Standard Error of Earnings with Respect to Teachers' Education, by Author and Data Source[a]

Study	Input coefficient	Input* ED coefficient[b]	Elasticity	Standard error
Card and Krueger (1992a)		0.0038	0.2432	0.0832
Average Biennial Survey (state)			0.2432	0.0832
Wachtel (1975) (school-level)	0.0023		0.0738	n.a.
NBER-Thorndike (school)	0.0023		0.0738	n.a.
Betts (1995)	5.41E-05		0.0025	0.0155
NLSY (school)			0.0025	0.0155
Grogger (forthcoming)	0.006		0.0079	0.0264
HSB (school)			0.0079	0.0264
Altonji (1988)	0.0007		0.0284	0.0244
Grogger (forthcoming)	0.042		0.0487	0.0197
Average NLS 72 (school)			0.0386	0.0220
Means across data sources			0.0732	n.a.
Means by level of aggregation				
State			0.2432	0.0832
School			0.0307	n.a.

Source: Author's calculations.
n.a. Not able to calculate. See note 17 in text.
a. See text for important differences in specification between studies and assumptions used to calculate elasticities. The mean standard error across the three school-level studies for which standard errors could be calculated is 0.0213.
b. ED is years of schooling.

that expenditures related to class size affect 80 percent of total educational spending. Thus the elasticity of earnings with respect to the teacher-pupil ratio can be converted into the elasticity with respect to spending by dividing by 0.8. The resulting elasticity based on state-level, district-level, and school-level studies is 0.12, 0.03, and -0.05, respectively. If one uses the mean standard error as an estimate of the standard error of the mean, the upper bound on the 95 percent confidence interval for the mean of the school-level estimates is only 0.03. (The true upper bound is likely to be less, since the three school-level studies use different data sources and hence the covariance between the estimates is likely to be low.)

Table 6-4 presents estimated elasticities of earnings with respect to teacher education. Several assumptions had to be made to obtain elasticities for David Card and Alan Krueger's and Grogger's studies.[22] In

22. Card and Krueger (1992a); Grogger (forthcoming). Specifically, the estimated elasticity from the Card and Krueger study requires an assumption about the threshold at which the returns to education become positive. Following Card and Krueger (p. 20) I assume a threshold of eight years. In addition, I assume that the average years of schooling of teachers was sixteen. Grogger's regressor is a dummy variable for whether 30 percent or more of the school's teachers had advanced degrees. I assume that the mean percentage

addition, Card and Krueger's study is not comparable with the school-level studies: the former uses teachers' mean years of schooling as a regressor, while the latter studies use the percentage of teachers with a master's degree or higher. A rough comparison can be made by calculating the effect of increasing the percentage of teachers with master's degrees from 50 percent (the typical value in the 1980s, as shown by Betts)[23] to 55 percent. This would increase the average years of schooling of teachers from about 17 to 17.1 if teachers without a master's degree hold a bachelor's degree. The result would be an increase in earnings of 0.1 percent, based on the Card and Krueger estimate. The mean effect based on the school-level studies of increasing the number of teachers with a master's degree from 50 percent to 55 percent would be a 0.3 percent wage gain. When one takes the average elasticity of the school-level studies after excluding Wachtel's estimate, which examines workers who attended high school in the first half of the century, the predicted wage gain drops to just 0.16 percent. In the estimates based on the most recent samples, the NLSY and HSB, in which workers attended high school in the mid-1970s through the early 1980s, the predicted wage gain drops to 0.05 percent.

On the basis of a comparison of these results with those on the level of statistical significance from table 6-1, it would appear that the impact of teacher education on earnings is significant and quite large on cohorts educated in the first half of the century, only weakly significant but quite large on a sample of workers educated from the mid-1950s through 1972 (see the studies using the NLS 72), and statistically insignificant and very small for workers who graduated between the late 1970s and the early 1980s.[24] However, given the large number of assumptions necessary to derive the elasticities, these results should be treated cautiously.

---

of such teachers in schools under the 30 percent limit was 15 percent, and that the mean percentage in schools above the limit was 50 percent. An estimate of the mean percentage of teachers with a master's degree is also needed to calculate the elasticities. For the NLS72 I used the value reported for this data set by Altonji (1988); for the HSB data set I used the mean reported by Betts (1995) from the NLSY. (The data on schools in the NLSY were gathered in 1979, the year before the HSB study began.)

23. Betts (1995, p. 248).

24. To estimate the elasticity of earnings with respect to spending on teacher education, information is needed on the wage premium associated with a master's degree in the teaching profession. Accordingly, I ran a standard log wage regression for teachers in the March 1993 Current Population Survey tape, and found roughly a 17 percent wage premium. Assuming that teachers' salaries account for 60 percent of educational spending, and using the estimated wage gain of 0.1 percent based on the Card and Krueger estimate, the implication is that an elasticity of earnings with respect to spending on the percentage

Table 6-5. *Estimates of Elasticity and Standard Error of Earnings with Respect to Teachers' Salary or Relative Salary, by Author and Data Source*

Study	Input coefficient	Elasticity	Standard error
Card and Krueger (1992a)	0.0477	0.0460	0.0066
Card and Krueger (1992b)	0.02	0.1584	0.1663
Morgenstern (1973)		n.a.	n.a.
Rizzuto and Wachtel (1980)		n.a.	n.a.
Welch (1966)		n.a.	n.a.
Average Biennial Survey (state)		**0.1022**	**0.0864**
Wachtel (1975)	0.1131	0.2239	n.a.
Average Biennial Survey (district)		**0.2239**	**n.a.**
Kohen (1971)		n.a.	n.a.
Parnes and Kohen (1971)		n.a.	n.a.
NLS-YM (school)		**n.a.**	**n.a.**
Betts (1995)	−0.0396	−0.0338	0.3202
NLSY (school)		**−0.0338**	**0.3202**
Means across data sources		0.0974	n.a.
Means by level of aggregation			
State		0.1022	0.0864
District		0.2239	n.a.
School		−0.0338	0.3202

Source: Author's calculations.
n.a. Not able to calculate. See note 17 in text.

The other two school inputs that have been examined extensively are teacher salary and length of the school year. Results are shown in tables 6-5 and 6-6. Again, the same pattern emerges: the elasticities are much smaller in the school-level studies than in the studies that use state averages as a proxy. The average elasticities of earnings with respect to the given inputs for state-level and school-level studies are 0.10 and −0.03 for teacher salary, and 0.15 and 0.02 for the length of the school year.[25]

THE RATE OF RETURN TO SCHOOL SPENDING. What then is the rate of return to expenditures on school quality? This subsection studies that important question. The calculations are presented separately for the two

---

of teachers with master's degrees is roughly 0.2. Given the assumptions necessary to arrive at this result, the true confidence interval for the estimate is probably rather high.

25. As discussed later, the school-level studies of these two variables produce large standard errors, probably because of the small degree of variation in these inputs in more recent data sets. But it is still noteworthy that the same pattern of lower elasticities and lower significance in the school-level studies carries over to these inputs.

Table 6-6. *Estimates of Elasticity and Standard Error of Earnings with Respect to Length of the School Year, by Author and Data Source*

Study	Input coefficient	Elasticity	Standard error
Card and Krueger (1992a)	0.0012	0.2101	0.0263
Card and Krueger (1992b)	0.00056	0.0953	0.0766
Rizzuto and Wachtel (1980)		n.a.	n.a.
Average Biennial Survey (state)		**0.1527**	**0.0514**
Wachtel (1975)	0.0048	0.8746	n.a.
Average Biennial Survey (district)		**0.8746**	**n.a**
Grogger (forthcoming)	− 0.001	− 0.0360	0.2880
HSB (school)		**−0.0360**	**0.2880**
Grogger (forthcoming)	0.002	0.0738	0.1845
Average NLS 72 (school)		**0.0738**	**0.1845**
Means across data soures		0.2663	0.1746
Means by level of aggregation			
State		0.1527	0.0514
District		0.8746	n.a.
School		0.0189	0.2363

Source: Author's calculations.
n.a. Not able to calculate. See note 17 in text.

most commonly used measures of school inputs: overall expenditure per pupil and the teacher-pupil ratio.

It is important to discount future costs and benefits when calculating the net benefits from spending on a given school input, because all the costs are incurred in the early years of a person's life, while the economic benefits manifest themselves only much later as a student leaves school and enters the work force. The following calculations discount all costs and benefits to the year in which a student is in kindergarten. I assume that a 1 percent increase in spending per student is made in every school year between kindergarten and grade 12. To calculate the resulting increase in the discounted value of lifetime earnings, I multiply the predicted percent wage gain by the discounted value of earnings for the average American male worker between the ages of nineteen and sixty-four. The calculation of the present discounted value of earnings uses the actual profile of earnings by age for male American workers, obtained using weighted earnings data from the March 1993 Current Population Survey (CPS) tape. This tape contains information on annual earnings in 1992. The average annual earnings of male workers obtained from the CPS, taken as a simple mean across all ages from nineteen to sixty-four, was $22,737.[26]

26. Male workers are chosen, since the studies in table 6-1 examine earnings of men only.

Table 6-7. *Internal Rate of Return and Ratio of Net Benefits to Costs from Increasing Given Type of School Expenditure, Calculated from Average Elasticities of Earnings with Respect to School Inputs and Average Male Wage Profiles, 1992*[a]

Discount rate (percent)	Spending per pupil		Teacher-pupil ratio	
	State-level studies	District-level studies	State-level studies	All studies
0	1.061	0.546	0.993	−0.517
1	0.531	0.149	0.481	−0.641
2	0.153	−0.135	0.115	−0.730
3	−0.119	−0.339	−0.148	−0.794
4	−0.319	−0.489	−0.341	−0.840
5	−0.467	−0.600	−0.484	−0.875
6	−0.577	−0.683	−0.591	−0.901
Internal rate of return (percent)	2.55	1.45	2.35	n.a.

Source: Author's calculations
n.a. Not able to calculate.
a. A negative ratio indicates that the present value of the costs of the given investment exceeds the present value of the benefits. Internal rates of return in this and the following tables are calculated to within ± 0.05 percent.

Table 6-7 presents, in present value terms, the *net* return (in terms of added wages less costs) as a proportion of the cost of the given type of school spending for various rates of discount. Thus a negative value indicates that at the specified rate of discount, the costs of increased spending outweigh the benefits.[27] The first two columns show the returns to increased spending per student, calculated using the average elasticity from state-level and district-level analyses, respectively, as shown in table 6-2. The last two columns show the returns to spending that are targeted toward increasing the teacher-pupil ratio, assuming as before that 20 percent of overall educational spending is overhead that is independent of class size. These columns list the estimated returns using the average elasticity from the state-level analyses and the average elasticity based on all data sources.[28] The bottom row of the table shows the internal rate of return to spending of the given type, that is, the rate of discount at which the spending produces a zero net return.

The table makes clear that even under the most optimistic assumptions, the returns to additional spending per pupil are fairly modest. The

27. To give an example, based on state-level studies, the first column suggests that if one discounts future costs and benefits at a rate of 2 percent, a dollar allocated to increased spending per pupil leads to a net return (after costs) of 15.3 cents.
28. The estimated returns based on school-level analyses are in fact negative at all positive discount rates.

same can be said for spending aimed specifically at reducing class size. In fact, even at reasonably low discount rates, the rate of return is negative. The internal rate of return to overall spending is 2.55 percent based on state-level analyses, and even lower at 1.45 percent in district-level analyses. The internal rate of return to spending on class size is 2.35 percent in the state-level studies. In the school-level studies the rate of return to spending on class size is negative even when future gains to wages are not discounted at all. The average across all studies, as shown in the table, points to the same pessimistic conclusion.

The above estimates assume that better schools increase earnings, but leave fringe benefits unchanged. It is possible that better schooling leads to higher fringe benefits as well. Ronald Ehrenberg and Robert Smith report that in 1986 fringe benefits accounted for 28.3 percent of total compensation. However, they state that many components of these benefits do not increase with incremental increases in earnings. These quasi-fixed components include medical and life insurance, which composed 6.3 percent of total compensation, and miscellaneous retirement costs, including insurance annuities and administration (1.4 percent).[29] This leaves 20.6 percent of total compensation in the form of fringe benefits that might vary with earnings. Thus it is useful to reestimate the internal rate of return to school spending on the assumption that any increase in wages also leads to a proportional increase in these benefits.[30] Each of these new internal rates of return was 0.9 to 1.0 percent higher than those reported in table 6-7. The exception was the teacher-pupil ratio, for which, based on all studies, it continues to be true that the costs outweigh the costs at any nonnegative discount rate.

These estimates are probably upper bounds: other components of fringe benefits which Ehrenberg and Smith label as quasi-fixed were treated as variable in the above calculations. These include unemployment insurance and miscellaneous benefits such as free meals, which together total 1.6 percent of total compensation. Perhaps more important, it was assumed that fringe benefits in the form of employers' contributions to social security, which accounted for 4.4 percent of total compensation in 1986, are returned to the worker after retirement.[31] This assumption ignores the fact, illustrated in the work of George Borjas,

29. Ehrenberg and Smith (1991, pp. 144–46). I thank John Bishop and Alan Krueger for suggesting this extension.
30. This was done by multiplying earnings each year by [1 + (20.6/71.7)] = 1.287, where 71.7 represents the share of earnings in overall compensation.
31. Ehrenberg and Smith (1991, pp. 144–46).

that a typical worker is likely to receive only a small fraction of his or her employer's social security contributions after retirement.[32]

The sensitivity of the estimated payback to spending per pupil begs the question of how to choose an appropriate rate of discount. Consider, first, whether individuals would be willing to finance additional school spending out of their own pocket, given the returns that they would earn after graduating. Emily Lawrance estimates that people's rate of time preference lies between 12 percent and 19 percent.[33] Such people would never want to invest in extra spending per pupil if they had to bear the costs. A government planner, on the other hand, might use the real rate of interest. Between 1984 and 1993 the average real interest rate was 4.5 percent; between 1989 and 1993 the average was 3.2 percent.[34] At either rate the costs of increasing spending per pupil exceed the benefits. The exceptions are the state-level internal rates of return for spending per pupil and spending on the teacher-pupil ratio, in which it is assumed that educational spending increases fringe benefits, thus raising the internal rates of return to 3.45 percent and 3.35 percent. These returns are marginally above the 3.2 percent average real interest rate between 1989 and 1993. But at the higher rate prevailing between 1984 and 1993 additional school spending would not be viable.

Unfortunately, even these modest estimates of the returns to school spending may be overoptimistic. The reason is that they calculate the benefits of increased spending as a percent increase in the wages earned by men.[35] Since men constitute only half the population attending school, and since women have a weaker attachment to the labor force than do men, the overall gain in earnings for the whole population could be considerably lower than stated in table 6-7. Accordingly, table 6-8 repeats the analysis in table 6-7 but uses the average earnings of *all* people between the ages of nineteen and sixty-four, rather than just men. The average earnings across each age group are $17,252, which is only 76 percent of the male-only average. The internal rate of return in the state-level studies of spending per pupil and spending on the teacher-pupil ratio drops to a mere 1.5.[36] These estimates are relatively small.

---

32. Borjas (1996, pp. 160–61).

33. Lawrance (1991, p. 54).

34. These interest rates are based on government data on the personal consumption expenditure price index and the yield on ten-year treasury bonds.

35. I am indebted to Jeff Grogger for this point.

36. Of course, an important assumption in this analysis is that the elasticity of women's earnings with respect to spending per pupil equals that for men. An examination of the

Table 6-8. *Internal Rate of Return and Ratio of Net Benefits to Costs from Increasing Given Type of School Expenditure, Calculated from Average Elasticities of Earnings with Respect to School Inputs and Average Wage Profiles of All Workers, 1992*[a]

	Spending per pupil		Teacher-pupil ratio	
Discount rate (percent)	State-level studies	District-level studies	State-level studies	All studies
0	0.564	0.173	0.512	−0.634
1	0.169	−0.123	0.131	−0.726
2	−0.114	−0.335	−0.143	−0.792
3	−0.319	−0.489	−0.341	−0.841
4	−0.470	−0.602	−0.487	−0.876
5	−0.582	−0.687	−0.596	−0.902
6	−0.667	−0.750	−0.678	−0.922
Internal rate of return (percent)	1.55	0.55	1.45	n.a.

Source: Author's calculations.
n.a. Not able to calculate.
a. A negative ratio indicates that the present value of the costs of the given investment exceeds the present value of the benefits.

It is useful to compare the rates of return of increased spending per pupil with the rates of return from an extra year of education. Table 6-9 provides such a comparison. Results on spending per pupil from the state-level data (for males) are reproduced in column 1. The remaining columns estimate the net social return to spending on one extra year of education. I assume that an extra year of schooling increases a worker's wages by 7.5 percent, which is the return that cross-sectional studies typically estimate. To calculate the benefits of one year of schooling, I thus calculate the present value of a 7.5 percent increase in the wage profile of American men who hold a high school diploma or less, again based on the March 1993 CPS. Column 2 shows the net return to finishing grade 12 for an eighteen-year-old student who has finished grade 11. The cost of this extra year of education is wages forgone plus $5,000, which approximates average spending per pupil in public schools.[37] Column 3 instead estimates the social return to enrolling a nineteen-year-old

---

school spending-earnings link for women would fill a large hole in our knowledge. In table 6-8, as in the previous table, if one factors in fringe benefits, the internal rates of return rise by about 0.9 percent, while the rate of return based on the average of all studies of the teacher-pupil ratio remains negative at all non-negative interest rates.

37. In 1990–91 in American public schools total spending per pupil was $5,320, while current expenditure was $4,847 per pupil. *Digest of Education Statistics* (1991, p. 155).

Table 6-9. *Internal Rate of Return and Ratio of Net Benefit to Cost for Spending per Pupil versus Spending on One Additional Year of Schooling*[a]

Discount rate (percent)	Spending per pupil (1)	Extra education	
		Grade 12 (2)	One year at college (3)
0	1.061	4.907	2.598
1	0.531	3.700	1.885
2	0.153	2.799	1.348
3	−0.119	2.118	0.939
4	−0.319	1.595	0.624
5	−0.467	1.189	0.378
6	−0.577	0.8705	0.183
Internal rate of return (percent)	2.55	10.95	7.25

Source: Author's calculations.
a. Male wage profiles in 1992 are used for these calculations. All figures are discounted to the year in which the student is in kindergarten. College cost is based on average spending per student at all postsecondary institutions.

high school graduate in college for one year. The costs are the opportunity cost (the average wages of a nineteen-year-old) plus the average cost of a year of college education. In 1991 the average college expenditure per student (at all levels, both public and private) was $7,949.[38]

The results are striking. At a discount rate of 3 percent, money targeted to increasing spending per pupil earns less than a zero rate of return. In contrast, spending to keep the student in high school one extra year returns $3.12 for every $1.00 invested, for a net return of $2.12. The estimates for one year at college are also positive and large. The internal rate of return for spending on one extra year of education is far higher than that for spending per pupil. In the case of spending on one extra year of high school, the internal rate of return is over four times as high.[39]

The fact that the returns to an extra year of schooling are so much higher than the returns to further increases in spending per pupil is

38. This figure was calculated by dividing total "educational and general" current fund expenditures of American postsecondary institutions in 1991 by enrollment levels. Bureau of the Census (1994, pp. 187, 192). As such, the figure probably overstates the costs to society of enrolling one student in a college, since it includes expenses such as research, plant operation and general institutional support, some of which sustain the nonteaching endeavors of colleges. Thus the estimated rate of social return to college in table 6-9 probably underestimates the true social returns.

39. When the internal rates of return to an extra year of high school or college were recalculated adding fringe benefits, the internal rates of return rose to 12.15 percent and 8.15 percent respectively.

perhaps the most important finding of the chapter. Indeed, when one estimates the present discounted value of spending on reducing class size, based on all studies, the return is negative at even a zero rate of discount. This compares with a return of approximately ten percent for policies designed to increase years of education, such as increases in the school-leaving age.

Five Hypotheses to Explain the Observed Patterns

The three most important observed patterns from the above review are that school inputs are less strongly linked to earnings in studies that measure the resources of the school actually attended, as well as in studies of more recently educated workers and of workers who are thirty-two or under at the time of the wage observation. We now examine five hypotheses for these patterns.

Structural Change

As seen in figure 6-1, the studies that show the strongest evidence that school spending affects students' subsequent earnings tend to examine workers educated between 1900 and 1960, whereas the studies showing no effect typically examine workers who attended school more recently. One potential explanation is that public education has undergone a structural change in the last thirty years. This section discusses three potential sources of such a structural change.

Diminishing returns to school inputs. Perhaps the most obvious explanation for why only those school expenditures incurred in the first half of the century appear to be strongly positively correlated with earnings is that the education production function, like all well-behaved production functions, is subject to diminishing returns. If labor-market success depends on several inputs, including not only school inputs but also family inputs and peer group inputs, and if these inputs remained constant while real spending per pupil doubled over the last twenty-five years, the effectiveness of public school spending should have declined.

Many studies in the 1970s and 1980s explicitly addressed this issue. By specifying a log-log specification for wages w as a function of spending per pupil Q, that is,

$$(6\text{-}1) \qquad \ln(w) = c + \alpha \ln Q + X\Gamma + error,$$

where X is a vector of other variables including family background, and Γ is a vector of coefficients, diminishing returns would be signified by an estimate of the parameter α less than one. Most authors have found exactly this. For instance, George Johnson and Frank Stafford estimate α to be 0.198; using a similar specification, John Akin and Irwin Garfinkel find values for α of 0.167 and 0.153 for white and black males, respectively.[40] These results suggest sharply diminishing returns to school expenditures. However, one must be careful to recognize that these estimates assume a very specific functional form in which school expenditures Q are separable from other inputs:

$$(6\text{-}2) \qquad\qquad w = Q^{\alpha} \exp(X\Gamma).$$

It is important to consider whether other specifications yield similar results. Johnson and Stafford do estimate a model in which the log of Q is replaced by a quadratic function of Q. In this specification they find log earnings to be a concave function of expenditures, which supports the idea of diminishing returns.

Perhaps a more convincing way of testing for diminishing returns is to test for declining productivity of school inputs over time, given the sizable increases in school expenditures during the last half-century. Card and Krueger analyze the correlation between the earnings of white males in 1979 and the level of various school inputs during the decades during which these workers attended grade school, which spans the period from approximately 1926 through 1966. Both Grogger and I test for diminishing returns in the results presented by Card and Krueger.[41] Grogger concludes that the impact of school inputs on earnings has declined as the level of school inputs has risen. My study also reports evidence that the Card and Krueger data display diminishing returns. However, it notes that the results are not very robust to specification. This may imply either that there are not diminishing returns, or simply that with only 147 state-cohort observations, this data set may be too small to produce precise estimates of a quadratic relationship.

As mentioned, most of the studies that measure inputs at the school level find no significant link between inputs and earnings. Unfortunately, these studies rarely if ever model log earnings as a function of both school inputs and their squares.[42]

40. Johnson and Stafford (1973); Akin and Garfinkel (1977).
41. Card and Krueger (1992a); Grogger (forthcoming); Betts (1995).
42. Betts (1995) does report such estimates using the NLSY but finds that none of the school inputs became significant in such specifications.

On a related note, the literature needs to acknowledge that the level of school inputs has changed over time. If an empirical model based on historical data assumes that log earnings are a *linear* function of a given school input, then one should not apply the historical elasticity of earnings with respect to the input without adjusting for the fact that the input level has changed over time. This criticism does not apply strongly to the studies of spending per pupil, many of which use a log-log specification. Similarly, it may not be particularly harmful to apply historical elasticities of earnings with respect to teacher salaries to today, since, as Hanushek has noted, teacher salaries have remained fairly stable over the last few decades.[43] It appears that this problem may be most acute in the studies of class size or the teacher-pupil ratio. Average class size in the 1979 NLSY sample of high schools analyzed by Betts was 17.9, as against 26.5 to 32.6 in the state-level and district-level studies examined in table 6-3. When the elasticities are recalculated using the modern class size, the average state-level elasticity in table 6-3 declines from 0.0991 to 0.0628. The internal rate of return to an elasticity of this size is only 0.5 percent, based on the earlier analysis of earnings of men.[44]

Given that the existence of diminishing returns would do much to reconcile the diverse results in the literature, more research is needed in this area, especially using school-level data sets. Authors might also want to consider alternative specifications of nonlinear effects of school inputs, such as splines.[45]

In summary, there does exist evidence of diminishing returns to school inputs, which would help to explain why most of the studies that find strong effects of school resources examine schooling in the first half of the century. But the evidence at present is too weak to draw definitive conclusions.

The bureaucratization of public education. One potential explanation for why school inputs appear to matter less for people educated after the

---

43. Hanushek (1986).

44. In contrast, the district-level elasticity from Wachtel (1975) rises from 0.0240 to 0.0437, since Wachtel uses the inverse of class size as his regressor. One retort to the logic in this paragraph is that one cannot employ the log-linear specification used in most of the studies to extrapolate to today's class sizes. If that were true, then there would be a nonlinearity in the returns to class size, which would create aggregation bias in the district-level and state-level studies. I discuss this potential problem later.

45. A recent example of this technique from the test score literature is provided by Ferguson (1991), who examines the link between test scores and school inputs across Texas school districts. He finds that the student-teacher ratio has no impact on test scores for values below eighteen, but a significant negative effect above this value.

1950s is a change that has occurred in the way in which public education is administered. Over the last fifty years enrollment at the average school has risen. As recently as 1951, 50,742 of the nation's 123,763 public elementary schools were still one-teacher schools.[46] Similarly, the number of students per school district has risen over time: the number of school districts has plummeted over the decades, even while enrollment mushroomed. Figure 6-2 illustrates this strong centralizing trend, which no doubt in part reflects the consolidation of rural school districts as the one-room schoolhouse slowly disappeared. (By 1967 there were only 4,146 one-teacher elementary schools left.)[47]

The size of the school and the school district could both affect the productivity of schools. On the one hand, economies of scale encourage larger schools and, possibly, school systems. Welch quotes the authors of the *Rural School Survey*, who state that small rural schools were likely to be inefficient because the small enrollment meant that teachers could not specialize in the subjects taught, or, presumably, even in the grade levels taught.[48] On the other hand, three arguments suggest that large schools and school districts might hurt the quality of education. First, consider the number of principal-agent problems that exist in education: incentives must be structured correctly between parents and schools, principals and teachers, and teachers and students. It is likely that these problems will be exacerbated in large schools or districts, where teachers and students become anonymous faces in the hallway. Second, larger school systems might be less efficient owing to diseconomies of scale caused by increasing administrative burdens in larger systems. Third, simple ideas of competition suggest that if parents have little choice over what school or school district in which to enroll their child, the quality of the education is likely to be lower.

Consider first the question of school size. Two recent school-level studies report that school size is the one school trait that is significantly and systematically related to students' later earnings.[49] However, the elasticities of earnings with respect to school size are only 0.045 in the case of Betts's analysis of the NLSY, 0.043 in the case of Grogger's analysis of the HSB data set, and 0.019 in his analysis of the NLS72 data set. Within the range of high school sizes observed over the last two

---

46. *Biennial Survey of Education* (1950–52, pp. 4–5).
47. *Digest of Education Statistics* (1970, p. 7).
48. Welch (1966).
49. Betts (1995); Grogger (forthcoming).

Figure 6-2. *Number of School Districts in the United States, 1940–90*

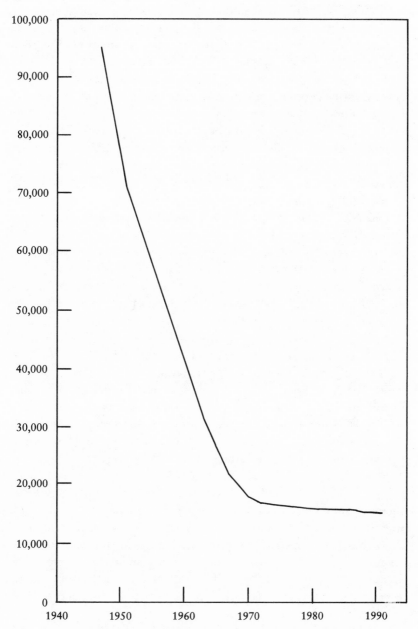

decades, there appears to be a small (but positive) effect of school size on students' subsequent earnings.

Caroline Hoxby presents interesting evidence on the effect of school district size.[50] She hypothesizes that the level of concentration of school districts will be negatively related to student outcomes: in cities with only a few school districts, schools will experience less competition for students from neighboring districts. By combining earnings data from the NLSY with standard metropolitan statistical area (SMSA)–level information on the concentration of school districts, and SMSA-level measures of school inputs, she finds that most of the school inputs do not significantly influence earnings, but that, as hypothesized, a higher degree of concentration among school districts is associated with significantly lower earnings for workers.

Finally, some indirect evidence on the influence of bureaucracies in public education is available. Gary Anderson, William Shugart, and Robert Tollison use a 1984 cross section to show that test scores are lower in states with larger educational bureaucracies.[51] There is also some evidence that school administrators believe administrative burdens are rising. For instance, in a 1987 survey of high school principals, 69 percent reported that *new* state guidelines and requirements were hindering efficiency at their schools.[52]

Thus available evidence suggests that larger schools are associated with slightly higher earnings for graduates, but there is also some evidence that the size of the education bureaucracy and the size of the school district might be negatively related to students' earnings after leaving school. The precipitous centralization of the nation's school districts over the last thirty-five years might thus be causally related to the weak links between school inputs and earnings observed for recent graduates.

The unionization of public school teachers. The impact of unions on the productivity of employers is theoretically uncertain. Consider the literature on unions in the private sector. Traditional models argue that unions decrease firms' productivity by capturing rents, or quasi rents, through practices such as featherbedding. Opposing this point of view is Albert Hirschman's exit-voice model, which implies that unions can increase productivity by giving workers a channel through which they can express grievances or suggestions without fear of retribution.[53] The em-

50. Hoxby (1994a).
51. Anderson, Shugart, and Tollison (1991).
52. *Digest of Education Statistics* (1991, p. 92).
53. Hirschman (1971).

pirical work by Richard Freeman and James Medoff lends some credence to this point of view.[54]

What then is the impact of teacher unionization on the efficiency of public schools? Teacher unionization certainly grew most quickly starting in the early 1960s, the approximate point at which this survey suggests a structural change may have occurred in the effect of school inputs on earnings. Hoxby documents that between 1960 and 1984 membership in the two leading teacher unions almost tripled, and that between 1978 and 1984 the proportion of teachers who were unionized rose from 55 percent to 65 percent.[55]

The bulk of the literature on teacher unionization examines the impact of unions on student test scores. Perhaps the most detailed test-score study is provided by Randall Eberts and Joe Stone. Using a random sample obtained in the late 1970s, they study gains in math test scores for 14,000 students in grade 4 as a function of school inputs and teacher unionization. They find that unionized schools produce about the same growth in math achievement as do nonunionized schools, but at a 15 percent higher cost. The implication is that unions reduce the efficiency of public schools.[56]

Hoxby presents the first available evidence on whether teacher unionization affects educational attainment or earnings of students after they leave school. Using the HSB data set, Hoxby replicates the findings by Grogger that in the HSB most school inputs are not significantly related to students' earnings five years after graduation.[57] But, when she adds interactions between the school inputs and an instrumented value for whether the school's teachers were unionized, several of the school inputs become significant. Typically, she observes that a given school input becomes positively related to earnings in nonunionized schools but is insignificantly related to earnings in unionized schools. A major exception to this pattern is spending per pupil, which remains insignificantly

54. Freeman and Medoff (1984).

55. Hoxby (1994b, tables 1 and 2). Between 1960 and 1984 the total number of public school teachers rose by approximately 55 percent

56. Eberts and Stone (1984). There exist several other studies on unionization and test scores. For instance, Grimes and Register (1990, 1991) find that students in unionized schools have higher test scores, whereas Kurth (1987) finds that unionization is negatively linked to test scores. These results are somewhat less convincing than those by Eberts and Stone, either because the study models test scores without conditioning on lagged test scores, which is necessary to control for unobserved prior inputs, or because the study aggregates beyond the level of the school or school district.

57. Hoxby (1994b); Grogger (forthcoming).

related to students' earnings in either specification. Similar patterns emerge when students' educational attainment is modeled. Finally, Hoxby, like Eberts and Stone, finds that unionized schools tend to spend more.

Thus available evidence suggests that unionization among teachers lowers the efficiency of public schools. Perhaps the main problem afflicting this literature is the potential for reverse causation: are teachers more likely to unionize schools that they believe to be inefficient? If so, unionization could be a positive predictor of spending per pupil and a negative predictor of student outcomes, as observed.

DOES MEASURED SCHOOL QUALITY MATTER ONLY FOR OLDER WORKERS? Figure 6-1 demonstrates that most of the studies that conclude that school inputs "do not matter" use data on workers educated during the past four decades. Although the preceding section discusses the possibility that this pattern reflects a structural change, an alternative interpretation is that school inputs do affect workers' earnings, but only as workers become older and settle into careers. Most of the school-level studies that fail to find an effect of school inputs examine workers who not only were educated recently but also were aged thirty-two or younger at the time that earnings were measured.[58]

Wachtel provides the only strong evidence in favor of the hypothesis that the school-quality effect is age dependent. Using the NBER-Thorndike data set, he regresses the earnings of workers in both 1955 and 1969 on district-level spending per pupil. He finds that the spending coefficient in 1955, when workers in the sample were aged thirty to thirty-eight, was less than half the value of the coefficient obtained for the 1969 regression, though it was still significant.[59]

In contrast, my study isolates wages observations in the NLSY sample for workers with at least three or six full years of work experience before the start of the given year, and finds that in this sample no measures of school inputs become statistically significant.[60] In a second study, I reanalyze census wage data and state-level school resource data, using workers aged 20–59 instead of 30–59. This study explicitly tests for age

58. There is one important exception to this pattern. Wachtel (1975) examines earnings of workers aged forty-four to fifty-two as a function of inputs at the school level. Expenditures per pupil were not significant, but teacher education was. However, in the case of the latter regression, data were available for only 13.2 percent of the sample.

59. Wachtel (1976, pp. 328–30).

60. Betts (1995).

dependence using pooled 1970 and 1980 census wage data. It revealed little evidence that the impact of school resources is lower for workers in their twenties than it is for older workers.[61] Similarly, Grogger compares the final wage observation of the NLS72, taken in 1986, with the wage observation from 1979.[62] The coefficients on class size and term length change in a direction suggesting that school inputs become *less* important as workers age. The coefficient on a dummy variable for teacher education changes in opposite directions in two different specifications.

In summary, only one study suggests that school inputs have a greater influence on earnings for older workers than younger workers. Evidence from 1970 and 1980 census data and from two other more recent data sets suggests that there is no age effect.

DOES SCHOOL QUALITY MATTER ONLY AT EARLIER GRADE LEVELS?
Without exception the studies that measure school inputs at the level of the school actually attended obtain data for high schools only. It may be that the reason these papers find so little effect of school inputs on subsequent earnings is that school resources matter most when students are in earlier grades, where work habits and mastery of the three Rs are imparted.

A rebuttal to this hypothesis is that school resources at the high school level should be highly correlated with resources in earlier grades. Perhaps the most important issue is whether school-level data sets are contaminated by students who move from one school district to another, thereby reducing the correlation between high school traits and primary school traits. With this in mind, in my 1995 paper I exclude from the sample students who had moved to the given city within three years, or in another specification, six years, of the year in which the survey of schools was performed.[63] Despite removing these students, I find that the school inputs remained statistically insignificant in the subsample.

The test score literature also offers evidence on whether school inputs matter more in earlier grades. The Coleman report finds that school

---

61. Betts (1994a). This paper also reanalyzes the NLSY sample used in Betts (1995) in several ways. To predict these workers' relative earnings when they enter their prime earning years, I match the occupation held by each worker in 1989 to estimated coefficients of (three-digit) occupation dummies from a log wage regression for white males aged forty to fifty-five in the 1980 census. Using these values as a proxy for later earnings, I find that the impact of school inputs remains insignificant.
62. Grogger (forthcoming).
63. Betts (1995).

inputs were not strongly related to test scores at any grade level.[64] Many other researchers find similar results.[65]

The idea that school inputs may be more important in the early years of schooling certainly deserves more study. But on the whole the evidence available at present, along with the likelihood that secondary and primary school inputs are highly correlated for most people, suggests that this hypothesis is at best of limited importance in explaining why the school-level studies find no link between school resources and earnings.

MEASUREMENT ERROR AND LACK OF POWER IN THE SCHOOL-LEVEL STUDIES? Since the state-level and school-level studies give such different results, this subsection and the following one examine econometric issues that may explain the differences. Several potential problems beset the school-level analyses. First, it is possible that the school-level studies lack power. Second, it is conceivable that measurement error has biased the coefficients on the school inputs toward zero.

The power of tests for the effectiveness of school inputs may be low in the school-level studies for two reasons. First, the sample size is small relative to the data sets based on census data: hundreds of thousands of wage observations in the census as against anywhere from one thousand to just over ten thousand in the school-level analyses. Second, it is well known that interstate differences in school inputs have largely disappeared over the past half-century. This implies that even if a relation does exist between school resources and wages, it would be harder to detect with the recent school-level studies, because of a lack of variation in the school inputs.[66]

Neither of these arguments appears to be compelling. Two of the factors that are positively related to the power of a test are the sample size and the inverse of the variance of the data generation process (dgp), under the assumption that the dgp is fixed.[67] Consider the census-level studies, which have many observations on wages that are then regressed on 50 to 150 observations of state-level school inputs (depending on the

---

64. Coleman and others (1966).

65. One exception is the work by Ferguson (1991), who finds that a student-teacher ratio above eighteen is associated with lower test scores among students in grades 1 through 7. But he finds no significant link in the upper grades.

66. See Betts (1995) for evidence on convergence over time in interstate differences in class size and teacher salaries.

67. Davidson and MacKinnon (1993, chap. 12). The dgp refers to the underlying "true model" which has generated the data.

number of cohorts and states in the study). To a first-order approxima-
tion they are equivalent to regressing *mean* wages for people from a given
state of birth and birth-year cohort on mean personal traits and mean
school quality in the state. (The results will be consistent if the models
meet the linearity conditions necessary to avoid aggregation bias, which
is an implicit assumption in these studies.) Thus the use of census data
increases the power of the test, because the use of *average wages* reduces
the variance of the dgp. But on the other hand, the true number of
observations in these studies is the number of observations on school
quality. This number is very small in the census-level studies. For
instance, there are 147 observations on school inputs in Card and
Krueger.[68]

The school-level studies, in contrast, will have a higher variance of the
dgp, which will decrease power. But they also typically have a greater
number of observations on school quality than the studies that measure
school inputs by state. For instance, my NLSY sample contains 600 to
700 observations on school quality, more than four times the number in
most state-level analyses. Similarly, Grogger's analyses of HSB and of
NLS72 data contain information on approximately 750 and 800 schools,
respectively.[69]

The second reason why school-level analyses, such as those by Andrew
Kohen, Joseph Altonji, Betts, and Grogger, may have low power is that
by the 1960s and 1970s, when most of the people in these samples
attended school, interstate differences in school inputs had largely converged.[70] This criticism seems possible in two cases: my study reports
that the ratio of the ninetieth to tenth percentile values of teachers'
relative salary was only 1.33 in his sample. Grogger reports that in both
his data sets the standard deviation of term length was only one to two
weeks. For the other measures of school inputs in these studies, such as
class size and levels of teacher education, the interschool variation was
considerable. Both Grogger and I point out, for instance, that the interschool variations in class size in our data sets are considerably larger
than the *interstate* variations in class size in the early years of the century.

Do the school-level studies in fact lack power? I address this question by running a power analysis in which the coefficients on the class

68. Card and Krueger (1992a). The foregoing exposition is not strictly correct, because
by taking averages one would lose some efficiency, although the estimated coefficients
should be consistent if there is no aggregation bias.

69. Personal communication from Jeff Grogger, 1994.

70. Kohen (1971); Altonji (1988); Betts (1995); Grogger (forthcoming).

size and teacher salary variables are set so that the wage elasticity equals the values reported by Card and Krueger.[71] The latter do not report an elasticity for the effect of teachers' holding a master's degree, so I assign an elasticity midway between those of class size and teachers' relative salary. If the NLSY data set has low power, then in this exercise the *t*-statistics will be below 2. The actual *t*-statistics that would be obtained if these elasticities described the dgp were 7.37 for class size, 9.01 for teacher education, and 1.44 for teacher salary. Thus the NLSY contains ample power to reject the hypothesis that the first two school inputs do not matter. The low *t*-statistic on the salary variable, though larger than the value obtained using the actual data, suggests that there may be too little variation in this input to detect an effect unless it is very strong.

In summary, the school-level analyses based on recent data sets may have insufficient power to detect an effect of term length or teacher salary unless it is very strong. But they appear to have very high power in tests of the effect of teacher education and class size.

A second possible criticism of the school-level studies is that the school inputs are measured with error, so that their coefficients will be biased toward zero. State-level analyses might reduce this problem, since they use an average taken across schools. One can test this hypothesis directly by rerunning the school-level analyses using two stage least squares (2SLS), with state-level school resources serving as instruments for the school-level variables. Both Grogger and I take this step and find that the instrumented school inputs remain insignificant. This finding reduces the plausibility of the existence of significant measurement error.[72]

To conclude, two possible criticisms of the school-level analyses are that they lack power and that they are biased because of measurement error. Evidence to date suggests that the data sets have high power in tests of the effect of class size and teachers' level of education, but lower power in tests of the effect of term length and teacher salary. Tests for measurement error have rejected this explanation for why the school-level studies find no significant link between school inputs and earnings.

71. Betts (1995); Card and Krueger (1992a).

72. Betts (1995) also tries inserting the state-level measures of the teacher-pupil ratio and teacher relative salary directly into the earnings regression. The regression with state-level teacher-pupil ratio yields a significant coefficient. Since the 2SLS regression using this as an instrument did not yield a significant coefficient, the implication is that the part of the state-level variable that is correlated with earnings is orthogonal to the teacher-pupil ratio at the actual high school attended.

AGGREGATION BIAS AND OMITTED VARIABLE BIAS IN THE STATE-LEVEL STUDIES? The state-level studies regress a measure of earnings on personal characteristics and one or more measures of public school resources aggregated to the level of the state. Doing so can lead to several econometric problems.

First, aggregation bias may have contaminated these estimates. In general, if the true process that generates wages depends on some variable, x, measuring school resources, one can regress individual wages on the state average for x and obtain a consistent estimate of the effect of x if and only if the relation between w and x is linear. This is an important assumption that has rarely been tested in the literature. (School-level studies have usually not tested nonlinear models, probably because even the simple linear specification yields insignificant coefficients.)

Second, some of the state-level studies do not control well for other state characteristics that might influence a person's later earnings. As Murnane points out, this method creates potential for omitted variable bias: if some state-averaged characteristics, such as income, wealth, demographic composition, and political persuasions, influence subsequent earnings of students, and if these traits are correlated with school expenditures, the estimated effects of school expenditures will be biased.[73]

Card and Krueger arguably do the best job of combating this problem, by including dummy variables for state of birth in the earnings equation.[74] But even this precaution leaves open the possibility that some omitted time-varying state characteristic is biasing the estimated returns to school inputs.

Third, a problem related to the previous one affects the studies that have examined wages of workers in decennial census data. Census data contain good information on personal traits but omit important measures of family background such as parents' education and income. Suppose that parents' education (or income) is positively linked to one's earnings and that better-educated parents tend to live in states that spend more on public schools. The result of this will be an *upward* bias on the estimated returns to school expenditures. Such a bias could explain the divergence between the state-level studies and the studies that measure inputs at the school level (and that typically, at least in some specifications, also control for family background). Note that Ronald Rizzuto and Paul Wachtel report that when they repeated state-level regressions

73. Murnane (1991).
74. Card and Krueger (1992a).

of log earnings on the log of spending per student but added income per capita in the state of birth as an extra regressor, the coefficients for spending per pupil became insignificant in their 1970 sample (but not in their 1960 sample).[75] Similarly, Akin and Garfinkel report that the link between white male earnings and spending per pupil becomes insignificant with the addition of income per capita as a regressor.[76] These findings may be examples of omitted variable bias of the sort hypothesized.

Fourth, a problem that also affects the census studies is that census data do not contain information on the state in which a person was educated. Instead, researchers are forced to use the person's state of birth and to make the assumption that the person was educated in the state of birth. Given that Americans have a high propensity to migrate, this assumption deserves scrutiny. Suppose, first, that interstate migration is a totally random process. If that were the case, one would have a classic case of measurement error, in which the estimated elasticities from these studies would be biased toward zero. The alternative is that the migration of a person from one state to another is an endogenous function of observed and unobserved personal and state traits. In this case the estimated coefficients will be biased estimates of the true returns to school spending.

Card and Krueger discuss this problem, and provide a rough estimate of the size and direction of the migration bias. They estimate that the estimated returns to school spending may be 5 to 15 percent higher once one corrects for interstate migration.[77]

An ongoing research project by James Heckman, Anne Layne-Farrar, and Petra Todd, a summary of which appears in the next chapter, tests the robustness of studies that combine census data with state-level information on school inputs. The authors explicitly test the assumption in these studies that interstate migration is random, and decisively reject it. This finding implies that studies which have used census data combined with state-level measures of school inputs are likely to be biased. The problem is probably most severe in studies that add dummy variables for state or region of residence interacted with years of education, since in this specification the impact of school resources is identified solely by workers who migrate from their state of birth.

Fifth, it is possible that the state average of a school input is a biased

75. Rizzuto and Wachtel (1980).
76. Akin and Garfinkel (1977).
77. Card and Krueger (1992a, pp. 28–29).

estimate of inputs at the actual school attended by the individual because of large variations in school expenditures within each state. These variations reflect the historical reliance of school funding on local property taxes, and thus cut across socioeconomic groups. In particular, it may be important to control for interracial differences in school spending. For example, Johnson and Stafford study a sample of white males, but their measure of school quality is an average for all schools in the state, not the average for the schools actually attended by whites.[78] Since they examine people who obtained schooling in the first half of the century, a period when school resources varied dramatically between the black and white student populations and when relative school resources also changed dramatically over time, bias is likely. Similar problems occur in other studies.[79] Some studies minimize this problem either by using race-specific estimates of school resources or by pooling wage observations across races.[80]

Sixth, Heckman, Layne-Farrar, and Todd find evidence that inferences about the impact of school inputs on earnings from census data are not robust because of many other problems. Perhaps their most important finding in this regard is that once one allows for nonlinear returns to education, the impact of school resources becomes far weaker for most workers. They do this by testing the quasi-linear specification used by Card and Krueger and reject it against an alternative with graduation dummies for eight, twelve, and sixteen years of education.[81] The effects of school inputs largely disappear once one allows for nonlinear returns to education. The evidence suggests that the impact of school inputs—averaged by state of birth—is largely limited to those who graduate from college.

In summary, at least six problems potentially bias the estimated returns to school inputs in studies that use state-level estimates of school resources: (1) aggregation bias; (2) bias due to unobserved state characteristics; (3) bias due to omitted family background in studies that use census data; (4) bias due to nonrandom migration from state of birth; (5) measurement error and bias due to the use of overall state averages for school resources in regressions on subsamples (for example, by race), and (6) neglect of nonlinearities in the returns to education. The work of

78. Johnson and Stafford (1973).
79. Morgenstern (1973); Rizzuto and Wachtel (1980); Card and Krueger (1992a).
80. Morgan and Sirageldin (1968); Akin and Garfinkel (1977); Nechyba (1990); Card and Krueger (1992b).
81. Card and Krueger (1992a).

Heckman, Layne-Farrar, and Todd in this volume suggests that the returns to school spending accrue only to those who obtain a college education. Similar problems, in particular aggregation bias and nonrandom moves, may also affect some district-level analyses.

The Impact of School Inputs on Educational Attainment

Using exactly the same format as table 6-1, table 6-10 summarizes the research on the link between school resources and students' educational attainment. As with the literature on earnings, it is crucial to recognize that many studies in effect replicate earlier work, since they use the same data source for school resources.

Strikingly, the same pattern observed for studies of school resources and earnings occurs in the literature on educational attainment: in the case of every input, the evidence in favor of a positive link is strongest in the state-level data. The observed correlations weaken considerably in district-level analyses and disappear almost completely when one observes resources at the actual school attended.

Table 6-10 shows very weak support for a positive link between spending per pupil and educational attainment. Only state-level *Biennial Survey of Education* and Project Talent data point in this direction. Data from district-level *Biennial Survey of Education* information, the NLS-YM, and the NBER-Thorndike suggest no significant relation.

Of all the relations studied in the literature, the link between the teacher-pupil ratio and educational attainment is strongest, with all regressions at the district level or state level pointing toward a significant relation. However, school-level studies come to a different conclusion. Kohen finds no relation in his analysis of the NLS-YM, but that may be due to the fact that he uses an index of several inputs, including the teacher-pupil ratio.[82] Ehrenberg and Dominic Brewer find no significant relation using school-level data from High School and Beyond.[83] William Sander, who uses data for both districts and schools (since some districts contain only one high school) finds positive effects.[84] Thus, even here, the evidence of a positive significant relationship is not conclusive.

For the remaining school inputs illustrated in the table, evidence in

82. Kohen (1971).
83. Ehrenberg and Brewer (1994).
84. Sander (1993).

Table 6-10. *Percentage of Educational Attainment Regressions with Results Significant at 5 Percent, by Author and Data Source*

Study	Expenditure per pupil	Teacher-pupil ratio	Teacher education	Teacher salary	Teacher experience	Length of school year	Books per student
Akin and Garfinkel (1977)	50						
Card and Krueger (1992a)		100		100		50	
Card and Krueger (1992b)		100					
Johnson and Stafford (1973)	100						
Morgenstern (1973)	100	100		100			
Average Biennial Survey (state)	83	100		100		50	
Wachtel (1975)	0	100		0		0	
Average Biennial Survey (district)	0	100		0		0	
Jud and Walker (1977)	0						
Link and Ratledge (1975b)	0						
Average NLS-YM (district)	0						
Ribich and Murphy (1975)	83						
Project Talent (district)	83	100					
Sander (1993) (district/schools)							
Illinois schools		100		0			
Kohen (1971)		0		0			0
NLS-YM (school)		0		0			0
Wachtel (1975)	0						
NBER-Thorndike (school)	0		0				
Ehrenberg and Brewer (1994)			0		8		
HSB (school)		0	0		8		
Altonji (1988)		0	0				
Average NLS 72 (school)			0				
Means across data sources	33	60	0	25	8	25	0
Means by level of aggregation							
State	83	100		100		50	
District	28	100		0		0	
School	0	33	0	0	8		0

Source: Author's calculations.

Table 6-11. *Estimates of Increase in Educational Attainment with Respect to Spending per Pupil and Elasticity*

Study	dED/dln (Spend)[a]	Standard error	Elasticity	Standard error
Akin and Garfinkel (1977) (blacks)	0.6767	0.5371	0.0785	0.0623
Akin and Garfinkel (1977) (whites)	1.0242	0.7759	0.0867	0.0656
Johnson and Stafford (1973)	0.631	0.304	n.a.	n.a.
Morgenstern (1973) (whites)	1.1660	0.4502	0.0988	0.0382
Morgentern (1973) (blacks)	1.3884	0.2967	0.1322	0.0283
Average Biennial Survey (state)	**0.9773**	**0.4728**	**0.0990**	**0.0486**
Wachtel (1975)	0.0174	0.1633	0.0012	0.0108
Average Biennial Survey (district)	**0.0174**	**0.1633**	**0.0012**	**0.0108**
Jud and Walker (1977)[b]	> −2.075	>2.905	> −0.1716	>0.2403
Link and Ratledge (1975b)	n.a.	n.a.	n.a.	n.a.
Average NLS-YM (district)	**> −2.075**	**>2.905**	**> −0.1716**	**>0.2403**
Ribich and Murphy (1975)	0.2635	0.0796	0.0179	0.0054
Project Talent (district)	**0.2635**	**0.0796**	**0.0179**	**0.0054**
Wachtel (1975) (school level)	n.a.	n.a.	n.a.	n.a.
NBER-Thorndike (school)	**n.a.**	**n.a.**	**n.a.**	**n.a.**
Means across data sources	0.4194	0.2386	0.0394	0.0216
Means by level of aggregation				
State	0.9773	0.4728	0.0990	0.0486
District	0.1405	0.1215	0.0095	0.0081

Source: Author's calculations.
n.a. Not able to calculate.
a. *ED* is years of schooling; *Spend* is spending per pupil.
b. The means exclude the result for Jud and Walker (1977), because the elasticity could be calculated only as an inequality owing to a lack of significant digits.

favor of a link between school resources and level of education reached is either weak or nonexistent. Not a single study of the impact of teachers' level of education or books per student finds a significant link. There is some state-level evidence in support of an effect of teacher salary and length of the school year on students' educational attainment, but similar studies conducted at the level of the school district or school attended fail to find any link.

Unfortunately, it was not generally possible to convert the coefficients into elasticities or similar measures. The one exception was the results on spending per pupil. Table 6-11 displays estimates of $d(ED)/dln(Spend)$, where *ED* is years of schooling and *Spend* is spending per pupil, and the elasticities of educational attainment with respect to spending per pupil. The results in this table may be biased slightly upward because it was not possible to perform these calculation for the results of Charles Link and Edward Ratledge or for the school-level analysis of

Wachtel. (Both those sets of findings suggest no link between spending per pupil and educational attainment.)[85]

The highest estimated derivatives of years of education with respect to the natural log of spending per pupil derive from studies that use state-level data on spending. The simple mean of the five state-level estimates is 0.98. This implies that a 1 percent increase in spending per pupil increases years of education by 0.0098. Assuming a 7.5 percent increase in earnings for each extra year of education, which is what census data typically yield, I infer that a 1 percent increase in spending on a student increases his annual earnings by 0.07 percent. What is troubling about this estimate is that Wachtel, using the same data from the *Biennial Survey of Education* but at the district level, obtains a derivative that is only one-sixtieth as high.[86] The average percent gain in earnings from a 1 percent increase in spending implied using the two district-level estimates from the table (excluding the Jud and Walker result which is merely an inequality) is far lower, at only 0.01 percent.

To their credit, most of the studies on educational attainment contain rudimentary controls for family background, such as father's education. (The exceptions are the two studies that use census data, which contain no such information.) This information is important, since it is well established that family characteristics influence educational attainment.[87] Omission of these background variables could lead to omitted variable bias on the school input coefficients, which is likely to be upward. It could be argued that, in all the studies, controls for family background should be stronger.

For this reason, future research should focus on microeconomic data sets that contain good controls for both family background and the traits of the school actually attended. Perhaps the most careful effort in this direction to date is the work of Ehrenberg and Brewer.[88] As shown above, the school-level analyses suggest only a weak relation between school inputs and educational attainment at best. This literature, however, is surprisingly small relative to the literature on school inputs and earnings. A much fuller analysis of the influence of school quality on educational

85. Link and Ratledge (1975a); Wachtel (1975). The results of Jud and Walker (1977) are expressed as an inequality because the coefficient is reported as −0.00.
86. Wachtel (1975, p. 510).
87. See, for instance, Taubman (1989) for a review of the literature on the link between parental income and children's educational attainment.
88. Ehrenberg and Brewer (1994).

attainment using existing microeconomic data sets should be a top priority in future research.

Suggestions for Future Research

What are the implications for research on school quality? To minimize the prospect for omitted variable bias and other biases, it seems crucial that future work should examine school inputs at the level of the school while controlling well for family and peer group background. This recommendation is particularly important for work on educational attainment, given evidence that family background influences attainment.

Although the use of school-level data reduces the risk of mismeasurement, ideally one would like to study the link between labor-market success and the characteristics of the actual classrooms in which students study. Unfortunately, no such data sets yet exist. For this reason the test-score literature becomes all the more important: there are now several data sets available that examine changes in students' test scores over time, as well as the characteristics of the students' actual classrooms and teachers. Economists tend to be skeptical of test scores because they represent arbitrary scales. However, a recent paper by Murnane, John Willett, and Frank Levy establishes that test scores in mathematics are significantly and positively related to earnings and that this effect became stronger between the 1970s and the 1980s.[89] Grogger and Eric Eide come to the same conclusion.[90] Thus, at the very least, the test-score literature should be used as an informal cross validation of the results obtained in the literature on school quality and earnings. As shown by Hanushek, most studies in the test-score literature suggest the same conclusion as do the school-level studies of earnings reviewed here: there is not a strong link between school inputs and student success.[91]

Finally, it may be time for the school-quality literature to search for a richer paradigm. The dominant metaphor in past research has been the education production function. This phrase suggests that education is like a factory, in which the teachers' labor combines with other inputs to "add value" to students, who are intermediate inputs in the process. The strength of this metaphor is that it encourages researchers to control

---

89. Murnane, Willett, and Levy (1995).
90. Grogger and Eide (1995).
91. Hanushek (1986, 1989, 1991).

for the initial "value" of students in the labor market, by controlling for family and peer group background. It also encourages researchers to model interactions between inputs, such as that between school inputs and the students' years of education.

But education is much more than an assembly line. Given the web of principal-agent issues in public education, perhaps the literature could progress by examining more closely the human interactions within schools. From a sociological and psychological perspective, such work would involve attempting to identify the teaching methods, attitudes, and styles that characterize the best teachers. From an economic perspective, new research might study the incentives systems within schools. Some work addressing incentives issues already exists. See, for instance, the work by Hoxby and others on the effect of competition between school districts, and the role of teacher unions. Similarly, Betts shows that the amount of homework assigned by teachers is a quite significant predictor of students' gains in achievement even after controlling for standard school inputs.[92] More work in this vein could produce a better understanding of the role of standards and other incentives.

Conclusion

As reviewed by Hanushek, the literature on school inputs and test scores on the whole suggests very little linkage between school spending and student achievement.[93] A close examination of the parallel literature on earnings and school resources shows that much of this literature arrives at the same conclusion. The strongest evidence to the contrary comes from a set of studies that share three traits: they typically study the correlation between earnings and state averages of school inputs, they examine workers educated in the first half of the century, and they tend to examine wages of workers who are aged thirty or older. In contrast, many of the studies that find no link between school spending and earnings use data on the actual school attended. They also use workers who attended school in the 1960s and later and who were aged thirty-two or under when wages were observed. This second set of studies shows not only a weaker statistical link than the state-level studies but also smaller elasticities.

92. Betts (1994b).
93. Hanushek (1986, 1989, 1991).

How can one reconcile these disparate results? First, the observation that school inputs seem less effective for recently educated cohorts suggests a structural change. There exists empirical support for three sources of structural change: diminishing returns, rising bureaucratization and centralization of public education, and the rising level of teacher unionization. Second, recent evidence concerning the idea that school inputs have an effect only on older workers, based on both state-level (including census) data and school-level data, suggests that this is not an important factor. Finally, evidence about the econometric robustness of school-level and state-level studies suggests that, though problems may affect both literatures, robustness is a greater concern in the state-level studies.

In a sense, debate about the relative levels of significance and the relative size of elasticities in the state-level and school-level literatures misses a crucial point. Assume for the moment that the more optimistic state-level literature is correct. Even these studies suggest a very low or even negative rate of return to additional spending per pupil at conventional rates of discount. Indeed, perhaps the most important finding of the chapter is that spending on additional years of education appears to be a far better investment than is increasing expenditure per pupil.

What are the implications of these results for policy? A fiscal conservative might be cheered by the finding that school inputs are not statistically related to earnings in many studies. A fiscal liberal would retort that in most cases in which a coefficient is significant, its sign suggests a positive relation between school spending and subsequent earnings. A meta-analysis, though it would have to contend with the many footnoted references to insignificant results in the literature and the statistical dependencies between studies that use the same data sources, would probably show that at least some school inputs matter.

But surely nobody should be surprised to learn that schools with higher levels of inputs do no worse a job or a better job than schools with fewer inputs. The real surprise, and the central point of this chapter, is that the impact of school resources on subsequent earnings is so low. In terms of the estimated rates of return to school spending, the literature does not suggest that, on average, public school spending per pupil is too low. No doubt there exist schools in impoverished areas where increased spending is much needed. But the literature suggests that, on average, inadequate funding per pupil is not the main problem that public schools confront today. In fact, the estimated benefit-cost ratio to keeping a student in school (or college) an extra year is strikingly higher than the benefit-cost ratio of increasing spending per pupil.

Thus it appears that a further increase in school resources per pupil is not the optimal formula for increasing the earnings of workers. Rather, the better course would be to develop policies designed to encourage students to stay in school longer. Such policies might include increasing the school-leaving age, increasing standards necessary for high school graduation and for dropping out before graduation, and expanding college loan programs, all the while holding spending per pupil in public schools constant. All of these policy changes will require additional expenditures. But the evidence suggests that these investments will produce far more impressive returns than can be obtained from further increases in spending per pupil. Given the low impact of spending per pupil on outcomes, it may also be time for researchers to examine more closely nonfinancial inputs into schooling. A key issue here includes the system of incentives within which teachers and students work and learn.

Appendix A: A Response to Card and Krueger

This comment takes issue with several interpretations of the literature made in the chapter by Card and Krueger in this volume (chapter 5).

Table 5-3 in the review by Card and Krueger estimates the impact of changing class size on the returns to education, that is, the impact on $d\log(W)/dED$, with a change in class size. The three coefficient estimates reported from Betts's study in this table seemingly suggest that it is impossible to obtain narrow confidence intervals using NLSY data.[94] Unfortunately, the table does not use the correct specifications from Betts's study. For all three entries, specifications of the following form are used:

$$(6\text{-}3) \quad \log(w) = \alpha + QUAL\,\beta + X\Gamma + ED(\chi + QUAL \cdot \delta) + \epsilon,$$

where $QUAL$ is the measure of school resources, w is wages, ED is years of schooling, ϵ is an error term, and X is a set of background variables. In their table 5-3, Card and Krueger report the *partial* effect δ, rather than the actual overall impact of changing the school input on log wages, which is given by $(\beta + ED\delta)$. It is not meaningful to study one coefficient when the school resource acts through two separate coefficients.

For this reason, if one wants to estimate the impact of increasing

94. Betts (1995).

Table 6A-1. *The Impact of a 1 Percent Increase in the Pupil-Teacher Ratio on the Percentage Returns to Education in the Log Earnings Equation*[a]

Authors	Model	Without state effects	With state effects[b]
Results from Card and Krueger survey:			
Card and Krueger	Linear	−0.20	−1.37
(1992a)		(0.27)	(0.52)
Card and Krueger	Linear	−1.44	−1.25
(1992b)		(0.39)	(0.54)
Betts (1995)	OLS (white standard errors)	0.50	...
		(1.24)	
	Random effects	−4.06	...
		(1.56)	
	State average quality	5.30	...
		(6.79)	
Corrected and extended results:			
Betts (1995)	OLS (white standard errors)	−0.19	0.09
		(0.20)	(0.22)
	Random effects	0.17	0.34
		(0.40)	(0.42)
	State average quality	−2.31	...
		(1.13)	

Source: Card and Krueger (ch. 5, table 5-3) and author's calculations. For the without state effects column in the bottom panel, the OLS, random effects, and state average coefficients are from Betts (1995, table A-2, no. 2; table A-3, no. 5; table 6, no. 2), respectively.

a. This table replicates, corrects, and extends the results from Betts (1995) as presented in Card and Krueger (ch.5, table 5-3).

b. For the regressions in the bottom panel, workers born outside of the United States have been dropped from the sample used in Betts (1995).

school resources on a worker's welfare by examining only the impact on the coefficient on years of education, it would be more accurate to use coefficient estimates from a specification which does not include a levels effect:

$$(6\text{-}4) \qquad \log(w) = \alpha + X\Gamma + ED(\chi + QUAL \cdot \delta) + \epsilon.$$

Table 6A-1 repeats the results from table 5-3 in the top panel. The bottom panel reports the results from specification (6-4), where only an interaction effect is included, using the results from Betts. The column on the left indicates the corrected effects of increasing class size on the returns to education. The results look very different from those reported in the corresponding table by Card and Krueger. Both the ordinary least squares (OLS) and the generalized least squares (GLS) results give average effects of school resources which are smaller than are obtained in the state-level literature. Moreover, the point estimates of most of the results from the two papers by Card and Krueger lie outside the confidence intervals from the school-level analyses in Betts, contrary to what is presented in their table. (The confidence intervals from the correct specifications are anywhere from one fourth to one sixth as high as reported in table 5-3.) Second, Card and Krueger state that the results in Betts suggest that aggregation of class size to the state level leads to *downward* bias on the effect of reducing class size. This is because they inappropriately analyze only one part of the overall derivative of log earnings with respect to class size. Third, their statement that when Betts uses the state-level teacher-pupil ratio, smaller classes flatten the earnings-education gradient is also incorrect. The state-level estimate of model (6-4) suggests an increase in the gradient which is larger than the other state-level estimates in the table.

Since Betts uses school-level data, in this data set it is possible to allow for state-of-birth effects to control for unobserved traits of each state and at the same time include an interaction effect between education and the school input. This is a far closer parallel to the Card and Krueger specification than simply adding the school input as a levels effect. Results are shown in the second column of table 6A-1. The addition of state-of-birth dummies strengthens the conclusions. Based on Betts's NLSY sample in that study, regardless of whether one includes state-of-birth dummies both the point estimates and the entire 95 percent confidence intervals for the impact of higher class size lie well above most of the point estimates from both studies by Card and Krueger.[95]

Similarly, table 5-2 in the Card and Krueger review gives what may be an overly optimistic view of the overall elasticity of earnings with respect to class size. The table reports an elasticity from Betts of -0.043 (0.025), where the standard error is given in parentheses. The confidence interval easily encompasses the estimated elasticity of -0.074 reported by Card and Krueger.[96] This estimate from Betts is based on a reduced form which does not control for education or weeks worked. But in a reduced form which excludes education but includes actual weeks worked, the coefficient and standard error are -0.019 (0.024). The confidence interval for this estimate lies strictly above the estimated elasticity of Card and Krueger.[97]

95. Card and Krueger (1992a, 1992b).
96. Card and Krueger (1992a).
97. It should also be noted that several papers that find no or weak effects of class size on earnings are not included in table 5-2, because elasticities could not be calculated. The

In summary, the survey by Card and Krueger argues that the results obtained by Betts based on the NLSY are not informative due to large confidence intervals. The tables in their survey overstate the case considerably, because of inappropriate choice of models from Betts. In particular, the results in table 6A-1 demonstrate that when one estimates analogs to the Card and Krueger model, by adding state-of-birth effects to the NLSY data, the results are not only internally consistent but also have much smaller confidence intervals than implied in their summary.

References

Akin, John S., and Irwin Garfinkel. 1977. "School Expenditures and the Economic Returns to Schooling." *Journal of Human Resources* 12 (Fall):460–81.

Altonji, Joseph G. 1988. "The Effects of Family Background and School Characteristics on Education and Labor Market Outcomes." Northwestern University, Department of Economics.

Anderson, Gary M., William F. Shugart, and Robert D. Tollison. 1991. "Educational Achievement and the Cost of Bureaucracy." *Journal of Economic Behavior and Organization* 15 (January):29–45.

Betts, Julian R. 1994a. "Do School Resources Matter Only for Older Workers?" University of California, San Diego, Department of Economics.

———. 1994b. "The Role of Homework in Improving School Quality." University of California, San Diego, Department of Economics.

———. 1995. "Does School Quality Matter? Evidence from the National Longitudinal Survey of Youth." *Review of Economics and Statistics* 77 (May):231–50.

Biennial Survey of Education in the United States. Various years. Office of Education, Federal Security Agency.

Bishop, John H. 1989. "Is the Test Score Decline Responsible for the Productivity Growth Decline?" *American Economic Review* 79 (March):178–97.

Borjas, George J. 1996. *Labor Economics.* McGraw-Hill.

Bureau of the Census. 1994. *Statistical Abstract of the United States, 1994.* 114th ed. Department of Commerce.

Card, David, and Alan B. Krueger. 1992a. "Does School Quality Matter? Returns to Education and the Characteristics of Public Schools in the United States." *Journal of Political Economy* 100 (February):1–40.

———. 1992b. "School Quality and Black-White Relative Earnings: A Direct Assessment." *Quarterly Journal of Economics* 107 (February):151–200.

---

overall case that smaller classes significantly increase earnings is thus weaker than is apparent in their table.

Coleman, James S., and others. 1966. *Equality of Educational Opportunity.* Government Printing Office.

Davidson, Russell, and James G. MacKinnon. 1993. *Estimation and Inference in Econometrics.* Oxford University Press.

Digest of Educational Statistics. Various years. National Center for Education Statistics.

Eberts, Randall W., and Joe A. Stone. 1984. *Unions and Public Schools: The Effect of Collective Bargaining on American Education.* Lexington, Mass.: Lexington Books.

Ehrenberg, Ronald G., and Dominic J. Brewer. 1994. "Do School and Teacher Characteristics Matter? Evidence from High School and Beyond." *Economics of Education Review* 13 (March):1–17.

Ehrenberg, Ronald G., and Robert S. Smith. 1991. *Modern Labor Economics: Theory and Public Policy.* 4th ed. Harper Collins.

Ferguson, Ronald F. 1991. "Paying for Public Education: New Evidence on How and Why Money Matters." *Harvard Journal on Legislation* 28 (Summer): 465–98.

Freeman, Richard B., and James L. Medoff. 1984. *What Do Unions Do?* Basic Books.

Grimes, Paul W., and Charles A. Register. 1990. "Teachers' Unions and Student Achievement in High School Economics." *Journal of Economic Education* 21 (Summer):297–306.

———. 1991. "Teacher Unions and Black Students' Scores on College Entrance Exams." *Industrial Relations* 30 (Fall):492–500.

Grogger, Jeff. Forthcoming. "Does School Quality Explain the Recent Black-White Wage Trend?" *Journal of Labor Economics.*

Grogger, Jeff, and Eric Eide. 1995. "Changes in College Skills and the Rise in the College Wage Premium." *Journal of Human Resources* 30 (Spring): 280–310.

Hanushek, Eric A. 1986. "The Economics of Schooling: Production and Efficiency in Public Schools." *Journal of Economic Literature* 24 (September): 1141–77.

———. 1989. "The Impact of Differential Expenditures on School Performance." *Educational Researcher* 4 (May): 45–51, 62.

———. 1991. "When School Finance 'Reform' May Not Be Good Policy." *Harvard Journal on Legislation* 28 (Summer): 423–56.

Hirschman, Albert O. 1970 *Exit, Voice, and Loyalty: Responses to Decline in Firms, Organizations, and States.* Harvard University Press.

Hoxby, Caroline Minter. 1994a. "Does Competition among Public Schools Benefit Students and Taxpayers?" Working Paper 4979. Cambridge, Mass.: National Bureau of Economic Research.

———. 1994b. "Teachers' Unions and the Effectiveness of Policies Designed to Improve School Quality." Harvard University, Department of Economics.

Johnson, George E., and Frank P. Stafford. 1973. "Social Returns to Quantity and Quality of Schooling." *Journal of Human Resources* 8 (Spring):139–55.

Jud, G. Donald, and James L. Walker. 1977. "Discrimination by Race and Class and the Impact of School Quality." *Social Science Quarterly* 57 (March): 731–49.

Kohen, Andrew Ivor. 1971. "Determinants of Early Labor Market Success among Young Men: Ability, Quantity and Quality of Schooling—Preliminary Report." Research report. Ohio State University, Center for Human Resource Research.

Kurth, Michael M. 1987. "Teachers' Unions and Excellence in Education: An Analysis of the Decline in SAT Scores." *Journal of Labor Research* 8 (Fall):351–67.

Lawrance, Emily C. 1991. "Poverty and the Rate of Time Preference: Evidence from Panel Data." *Journal of Political Economy* 99 (February):54–77.

Link, Charles R., and Edward C. Ratledge. 1975a. "The Influence of the Quantity and Quality of Education on Black-White Earnings Differentials: Some New Evidence." *Review of Economics and Statistics* 57 (August):346–50.

———. 1975b. "Social Returns to Quantity and Quality of Education: A Further Statement." *Journal of Human Resources* 10 (Winter): 78–89.

Link, Charles, Edward Ratledge, and Kenneth Lewis. 1976. "Black-White Differences in Returns to Schooling: Some New Evidence." *American Economic Review* 66 (March): 221–23.

———. 1980. "The Quality of Education and Cohort Variation in Black-White Earnings Differentials: Reply." *American Economic Review* 70 (March): 196–203.

Morgan, James, and Ismail Sirageldin. 1968. "A Note on the Quality Dimension in Education." *Journal of Political Economy* 76 (September–October): 1069–77.

Morgenstern, Richard D. 1973. "Direct and Indirect Effects on Earnings of Schooling and Socio-Economic Background." *Review of Economics and Statistics* 55 (May): 225–33.

Murnane, Richard J. 1975. *Impact of School Resources on the Learning of Inner City Children.* Cambridge, Mass.: Ballinger.

———. 1991. "Interpreting the Evidence on 'Does Money Matter?'" *Harvard Journal on Legislation* 28 (Summer): 457–64.

Murnane, Richard J., John B. Willett, and Frank Levy. 1995. "The Growing Importance of Cognitive Skills in Wage Determination." *Review of Economics and Statistics* 77 (May):251–66.

Murnane, Richard J., and others. 1991. *Who Will Teach? Policies That Matter.* Harvard University Press.

Murray, Charles, and R. J. Herrnstein. 1992. "What's Really behind the SAT-Score Decline?" *Public Interest* 106 (Winter): 32–56.

National Commission on Excellence in Education. 1983. *A Nation at Risk: The Imperative for Educational Reform.* Government Printing Office.

Nechyba, Thomas J. 1990. "The Southern Wage Gap, Human Capital, and the Quality of Education." *Southern Economic Journal* 57 (October): 308–22.

Parnes, Herbert S., and Andrew I. Kohen. 1975. "Occupational Information and Labor Market Status: The Case of Young Men." *Journal of Human Resources* 10 (Winter): 44–55.

Ribich, Thomas I., and James L. Murphy. 1975. "The Economic Returns to Increased Educational Spending." *Journal of Human Resources* 10 (Winter): 56–77.

Rizzuto, Ronald, and Paul Wachtel. 1980. "Further Evidence on the Returns to School Quality." *Journal of Human Resources* 15 (Winter): 240–54.

Sander, William. 1993. "Expenditures and Student Achievement in Illinois: New Evidence." *Journal of Public Economics* 52 (October):403–16.

Taubman, Paul. 1989. "Role of Parental Income in Educational Attainment." *American Economic Review* 79 (May):57–61.

Tremblay, Carol Horton. 1986. "The Impact of School and College Expenditures on the Wages of Southern and Non-Southern Workers." *Journal of Labor Research* 7 (Spring): 201–11.

U.S. Bureau of the Census. 1994. *Statistical Abstract of the United States: 1994.* 114th ed. Government Printing Office.

Wachtel, Paul. 1975. "The Effect of School Quality on Achievement, Attainment Levels, and Lifetime Earnings." *Explorations in Economic Research* 2 (Fall): 502–36.

———. 1976. "The Effect on Earnings of School and College Investment Expenditures." *Review of Economics and Statistics* 58 (August): 326–31.

Welch, Finis. 1966. "Measurement of the Quality of Schooling." *American Economic Review* 56 (May, *Papers and Proceedings, 1965*): 379–92.

CHAPTER 7

Does Measured School Quality Really Matter? An Examination of the Earnings-Quality Relationship

James Heckman, Anne Layne-Farrar, and Petra Todd

T HE RELATIONSHIP between educational expenditure and performance in the labor market has been the subject of much debate. Recent empirical studies find conflicting evidence on the extent to which spending on smaller classroom sizes, higher teacher salaries, or longer term lengths influences student educational attainment and labor-market earnings.

Studies showing an impact of schooling quality on earnings identify three distinct channels through which schooling inputs might affect earnings:[1]

—the effect of schooling quality on the intercept of log-earnings equations;

—the effect of schooling quality on the "rate of return" to education (the coefficient on education in a schooling–log earnings relationship); and

—the effect of schooling quality on educational attainment and the consequent increase in earnings that accompanies higher levels of education.

The first effect increases earnings in the same proportion at all education levels. The second effect widens schooling–log earnings differentials. The third effect operates as a consequence of the first two. As the return to schooling increases, students attend school longer.

We are especially grateful to Derek Neal for his helpful comments. Valuable insights were also provided by Casey Mulligan, Bo Honoré, Jose Scheinkman, and Bob Willis. We thank Jonathan Bone for assistance in collecting the schooling quality data. This research was supported, in the main, by the American Bar Association; an earlier version was supported by NSF-SBR-91-11145, NSF-FES-9224079, and the Mellon Foundation. The research for appendix D, Rejoinder to David Card and Alan Krueger, was supported by the Russell Sage Foundation and NSF-91-1145.

1. See, for example, Johnson and Stafford (1973); Card and Krueger (1992a, 1992b).

Despite the accumulated evidence, many economists and most soci-ologists doubt that the earnings-quality relationship is strong. Beginning with the Coleman report and continuing in a literature reviewed by Eric Hanushek, many studies find no systematic relation between quality and achievement test scores.[2] Although the link between achievement test scores and earnings is not well understood, especially when account is taken of family background effects and community effects, the evidence in this literature casts serious doubt on the existence of a strong quality-earnings relationship.

One explanation for the variety of estimates in the literature is differ-ences in the data sets and functional forms used to execute the empirical analyses. Different studies use different quality indexes (for example, pupil-teacher ratios versus current expenditures) or different earnings measures (such as hourly wages versus annual income).[3] Equally prob-lematic are the diverse assumptions made about the specification of the quality-earnings relationship. With different equations estimated, differ-ent results can be expected. Because various studies measure conceptually different earnings-quality relationships, comparisons of estimates across studies are difficult, if not impossible, to make.[4]

The lack of comparability of existing empirical studies is the primary motivation for this chapter. We seek to resolve some of the discrepancies by developing an empirical framework sufficiently broad to encompass all the models used in the main empirical literature. Doing so enables us to make meaningful comparisons among studies and to clarify the as-sumptions required to identify the impact of quality on earnings. There are many channels through which quality can affect earnings. Previous empirical studies typically consider only a single channel through which quality affects earnings, although the channel studied varies across au-

2. Coleman and others (1966); Hanushek (1986, 1989). See also Betts's chapter in this volume and the discussion in Heckman and Neal (forthcoming).

3. Figures 7-1 and 7-2 show the differences between two measures of the pupil-teacher ratio. The first measure is based on pupils enrolled and the second is based on pupils in attendance. The two graphs show the improvements in schooling quality from 1895 to 1985 and the trend towards convergence.

4. Recently researchers have tried to draw conclusions about the effects of schooling quality using meta-analysis, a statistical approach for combining estimated quality effects across different studies. See, for example, Hedges, Laine, and Greenwald (1994) and Card and Krueger (1994). Before combining estimates by this statistical procedure, one should first determine that model estimates are indeed comparable (and justifiable) in a theoretical sense, a procedure that is rarely done because comparability is a subjective condition. Meta-analysis is a mechanical substitute for the more careful empirical reanalysis of data and weighting of the evidence.

Figure 7-1. *Trend in Average Schooling Quality over Time, 1895–1985*

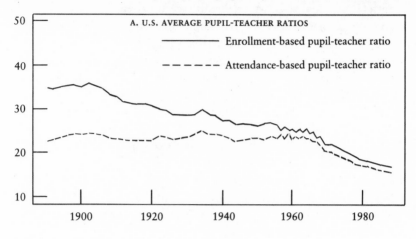

A. U.S. AVERAGE PUPIL-TEACHER RATIOS

Enrollment-based pupil-teacher ratio

Attendance-based pupil-teacher ratio

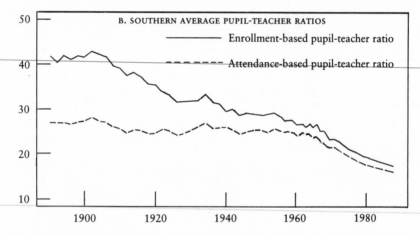

B. SOUTHERN AVERAGE PUPIL-TEACHER RATIOS

Enrollment-based pupil-teacher ratio

Attendance-based pupil-teacher ratio

Source: Authors' computations based on data from the U.S. Department of Education, Biennial Survey of Education.

thors. We consider multiple channels of influence and show that the channel selected critically affects the estimated effect of schooling quality on earnings.

To gain insight into which models are consistent with the data, we conduct statistical tests of the validity of the assumptions used in previous empirical work. We point out a fundamental identifying assumption in the literature: the absence of region of birth–region of residence interactions in the returns to schooling. We find strong evidence of such interactions that is consistent with selective migration and the pursuit of

Figure 7-2. *Convergence in Schooling Quality over Time, 1895–1985*

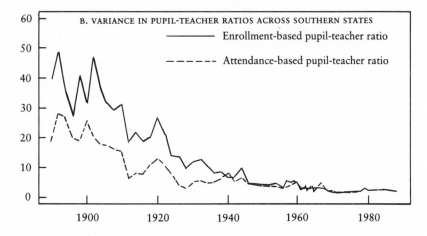

comparative advantage. The evidence calls into question a key identifying assumption of existing models, such as the one presented by David Card and Alan Krueger.[5]

Using that study and features of the 1973 study by George Johnson and Frank Stafford as points of departure, we find that estimated impacts of schooling quality on earnings are fragile with respect to the specification of the earnings function. Log-earnings functions that are linear in years of education are commonly used in the literature. They are re-

5. Card and Krueger (1992b).

jected by the data in favor of a model with "sheepskin" effects.[6] Nonlinear models reveal that the only impact of quality on earnings is on the marginal increment to earnings arising from college attendance and graduation.

This chapter develops in the following way. We first present a general analysis of variance framework for studying the quality-earnings relationship. Within this framework, we compare different estimation strategies taken in the literature for determining the impact of schooling quality on earnings. Of particular interest is our examination of the identification strategy used in aggregate data studies, which relies on observations on migrants in different labor markets to provide crucial identifying information. We show that if individuals educated in particular states of birth have a comparative advantage in the labor markets of particular states of residence, this identification strategy breaks down. Moreover, even under ideal conditions for the application of aggregate methods, aggregate studies cannot solve the problem raised by the Coleman report that family background accounts for virtually all of the measured effects of schooling quality on outcomes. Separating schooling quality from other early environmental factors requires arbitrary assumptions. Different assumptions produce fundamentally different estimates of the effects of quality on earnings.

Second, we discuss the sources of bias that may arise under the aggregate-data and the individual-level-data approaches for estimating the effect of schooling quality on earnings. Third, we question the validity of a key identifying assumption invoked in aggregate-data studies, that there are no patterns of migration on the basis of realized earnings in the destination state. Unfortunately, there is much evidence for selective migration. Fourth, we conduct nonparametric tests of the hypothesis that empirical measures of quality and earnings are monotonically related. The existing literature assumes that quality is an immutable characteristic and that unit increases in quality yield the same return to schooling in all labor markets. In this case, one would expect that in a given labor market, at each education level, wages for workers born in high-quality states should lie above those from low-quality states. Nonparametric rank tests give little evidence of a relation between the measured quality of schooling received by individuals and their wages. Other nonpara-

---

6. Sheepskin effects are discrete increases in the return to education that arise after completing a degree. See Hungerford and Solon (1987) and Jaeger and Page (1996) for recent strong evidence on sheepskin effects.

metric tests reveal an invariance in state-of-birth effects across states of residence, consistent with the evidence from the Coleman report that early environments have a permanent effect on lifetime outcomes.

Finally, we examine the sensitivity of estimated schooling-quality effects to alternative assumptions about functional forms of earnings equations. We highlight differences in the functional forms adopted in the Johnson-Stafford and Card-Krueger schooling-quality studies. We investigate the implications of various maintained assumptions and conduct statistical tests to see whether the data support the assumptions. Besides considering the effect of schooling quality on individual returns to education, our analysis presents new evidence on the effects of aggregate stocks of quality on aggregate pricing relationships.

We test—and reject—the widely used assumption that log earnings are linear in education; instead we find evidence of significant sheepskin effects, especially for completion of college. We note that nonlinearity of the earnings function in terms of years of schooling is consistent with the evidence presented by Daniel Blanchflower and Andrew Oswald that local labor market effects on wages are stronger for less skilled workers.[7] Using a more general model, we reestimate the quality-earnings relationship, allowing for nonlinearities in the return to education. In this empirically more concordant model, the estimated impact of quality on earnings lessens considerably. The only support for the quality hypothesis comes through the marginal return for attending or completing college. Consistent with this evidence, local labor-market effects on wages are found to be sizable for less educated workers and nonexistent for more-educated workers.

We conclude by presenting estimates from an earnings model that allows for systematic differences in returns to schooling for persons born in different regions and living in different regions. Within this model, we relax the assumption that the effect of schooling quality on the rate of return to education is the same in all labor markets. We show that this assumption is rejected for most quality measures. Different valuations of the same quality bundle in different labor markets may be a driving force behind selective migration, as individuals change locations to realize higher returns on their human capital. Relaxing the assumption of uniformity of quality effects on rates of return to schooling generally weakens estimated quality effects.

Our analysis does not prove that higher-quality education is ineffective

---

7. Blanchflower and Oswald (1994).

at enhancing worker productivity and earnings. Rather, it calls into question the strength of the evidence for a strong quality-earnings relationship based on aggregate data. Functional form plays a powerful role in generating this relationship. Estimated quality effects are highly sensitive to the assumption of the linearity of log-earnings function in years of schooling. They also depend on the particular channel of influence used to establish the quality-schooling relationship. Only when arbitrary conventions are adopted can one distinguish effects arising from schooling quality from effects due to early environmental influences. Finally, schooling quality affects the return to education differently across labor markets. If individuals migrate selectively to exploit economic opportunities, the identification strategy used in existing aggregate-data studies breaks down. Appendix D responds to Card and Krueger's summary of our evidence and our previous arguments.

The Empirical Plan and the Framework for Organizing the Evidence

This chapter reexamines existing empirical evidence and presents new evidence on the question whether aggregate secondary schooling quality significantly affects individual earnings. To facilitate comparisons between our analysis and previous aggregate data studies, we use similar data sets. Our observations on individual earnings and demographic characteristics come from the 1970, 1980, and 1990 micro-level census samples. The analysis samples consist of white men born in the United States in the years 1910–59 who worked at least one week and reported positive wage and salary income within a certain range. Our sample restrictions are identical to those used by Card and Krueger, who analyze cohorts of white men from the 1980 census.[8]

We determine the effect of schooling quality on earnings by relating individual-level data on weekly wages to state-level average measures of schooling inputs for the years in which the individual would have attended school. It is assumed that individuals are educated in their state of birth. For example, a person born in Florida in the 1920–29 cohort is imputed an index of that state's schooling inputs averaged over the years in which his birth cohort attended school (1926–47). The empirical

8. Card and Krueger (1992a). See the last section of the text for a detailed description of the data sources and appendixes A and B for additional information.

measures of quality considered in our study are two measures of the pupil-teacher ratio (one based on pupil enrollment and one based on average daily attendance), term length, and relative teacher salary, all of which are derived from published biennial reports from the U.S. Department of Education.

The strategy used in aggregate-data studies to identify an impact of schooling quality on earnings is to compare the earnings of individuals living in the same state but educated in different states. Part of the differential payment to persons from different states of birth is attributed to the quality of schooling and not, for example, to other common early environmental influences or to the operation of selective migration. The method is intrinsically unable to separate out school quality effects from early environmental effects that may be proxied by schooling quality. The analysis using aggregate data is usually conducted within a regression framework in which log earnings are regressed on measures of schooling quality and on additional variables to control for differences in demographic characteristics, labor-market conditions, years of experience, and years of education.[9]

As shown in the next section, empirical strategies in the literature differ in the way the quality variable is introduced into the earnings model. For example, Johnson and Stafford assume that increases in schooling quality act uniformly across education groups: everyone born in a state with relatively high schooling quality receives an identical increase in their log-earnings regardless of their state of residence or their number of years of schooling. An alternative assumption, suggested by Jere Behrman and Nancy Birdsall and used in Card and Krueger's study, is that schooling quality operates by increasing the return to education.[10] This model maintains that individuals with higher levels of education receive more benefit from increases in schooling quality.

Our empirical analyses suggest that many of the earnings functions commonly adopted to model the quality-earnings relationship are too restrictive; key assumptions that identify a quality effect, when tested, are easily rejected by the data. For example, if a unit increase in quality is assumed to have the same effect on the rate of return in all states of residence, an implicit assumption is being made that individuals' residential choices are unrelated to the quality of their education. There is considerable evidence against the assumption that a unit change in quality has a common effect on the rate of return to schooling in all regions. Our empirical evidence also indicates that individuals from certain states of birth have comparative advantages in certain states of residence to which they tend to migrate.

The frequently made assumption that the log-earnings relationship is linear in education is not supported by the data. Moreover, the assumption that schooling quality affects earnings through a single, easily specified channel, such as the rate of return to education, is also of questionable validity. One important restriction implied by a linear specification is that it rules out differential responses to labor-market shocks by different educational classes.

Throughout this chapter and in the entire literature, the quality of schooling available to persons is taken as exogenously given. There is no systematic discussion of the political economy of schooling quality or the migration of families across political jurisdictions, either to pursue a better quality of schooling or to avoid the costs of paying for a higher quality of schooling. This is a serious limitation of the literature because it is likely that family background and labor-market conditions affect the politically determined demand for schooling quality.

To compare the various earnings models adopted in the literature, it is useful to develop a more general framework for thinking about the relation between earnings and schooling quality than has previously been adopted in the literature. Let us express the logarithm of earnings of individual i, born in state b, in birth cohort c, residing in state s, as

$$(7\text{-}1) \quad y_{isbc} = \tilde{\theta}_{sbc} + X_{isbc}\tilde{\beta}_{sbc} + E_{isbc}\tilde{\alpha}_{sbc} + \epsilon_{isbc}$$

$$i = 1, \ldots, I, s = 1, \ldots, S; b = 1, \ldots, B, c = 1, \ldots, C,$$

where $\tilde{\theta}_{sbc}$ is an intercept term, E_{isbc} is education, which may be a vector or a scalar, and $\tilde{\alpha}_{sbc}$ is the associated regression coefficient. It is more familiar to think of E as a scalar determinant of earnings, but the analysis can readily be extended to the vector case, and we do so in some of our empirical work. The term X_{isbc} represents other regressors, such as work experience, which can be parameterized in a symmetric fashion. The term ϵ_{isbc} is a mean zero variable unobserved by the analyst that may or may not be known to person i.

As a model of mean earnings, equation 7-1 is quite general. If E_{isbc} were a vector of dummy variables indicating different levels of educational attainment, equation 7-1 would impose no restrictions on mean earnings at all. Each education–state of residence–state of birth–cohort of birth cell would be fully described by the equation. Linearity of log earnings in years of schooling, E, imposes a strong restriction, which in fact is rejected in our data.

Both the intercept and the slopes can be decomposed into an analysis of variance structure:[11]

(7-2) $\quad \tilde{\theta}_{sbc} = \theta + \theta_s + \theta_b + \theta_c + \theta_{bc} + \theta_{sc} + \theta_{sb} + \theta_{sbc}\theta +,$

(7-3a) $\quad \tilde{\alpha}_{sbc} = \alpha + \alpha_s + \alpha_b + \alpha_c + \alpha_{bc} + \alpha_{sc} + \alpha_{sb} + \alpha_{sbc}\alpha +,$

(7-3b) $\quad \tilde{\beta}_{sbc} = \beta + \beta_s + \beta_b + \beta_c + \beta_{bc} + \beta_{sc} + \beta_{sb} + \beta_{sbc}.$

For simplicity, we restrict β to be identical in all cells, allowing only for cohort effects, β_c. We recognize the peculiar asymmetry that this implies but follow the literature in adopting this convention. In other work, we relax this assumption and find that doing so influences estimates of the effect of quality on the return to education.[12] Conventional regression normalizations of the analysis of variance are adopted to measure effects relative to omitted base-state characteristics.

Aggregate studies of schooling quality generally measure it at an aggregate geographic level, like the state, and assume that a common quality component applies to all persons born in state b in cohort c. The most general analysis of variance form of equations 7-1, 7-2, and 7-3a is fully saturated, so that there are no remaining degrees of freedom to estimate a quality effect on earnings. To make room for such an effect and to estimate the effect of quality on earnings, restrictions have to be imposed on the model. Empirical studies in the literature differ in the way quality is assumed to operate on earnings. For example, if schooling quality is an additive component operating independently of the level of education—as in the Johnson-Stafford model—then it operates solely through $\tilde{\theta}_{sbc}$.

Schooling quality could also operate through slope coefficients. A prototypical restriction is the one used by Card and Krueger:[13]

$$\alpha_{bc} = Q_{bc}\,\varphi,$$

where state-of-birth fixed effects and cohort fixed effects for slope coef-

---

11. Residuals terms could be introduced to both the slope and the intercept equation to put this model in a random coefficient framework.

12. Heckman, Layne-Farrar, and Todd (1996).

13. Card and Krueger (1992b).

ficients are absorbed into α_b and α_c. More general models of quality could be fit as long as the $(B\text{-}1)$ multiplied by $(C\text{-}1)$ degrees of freedom in α_{bc} are not exhausted.

Seeking to avoid bias by using a standard fixed-effects strategy, Card and Krueger do not emphasize estimates of the effect of quality operating through the intercepts in the model (the θ).[14] They include b- and c-specific intercepts in the earnings equation to control for factors such as family income that differ across states of birth and are also likely to affect individual earnings. In several of their specifications, Card and Krueger also entertain the possibility that such factors might operate on slopes. Thus they remove state-of-birth and cohort-specific effects from both the slopes and intercepts of their model, and estimated quality effects are identified through restrictions placed on the interaction terms. Assuming that background effects operate only through intercepts but quality effects operate through interactions is clearly just one possible convention. Equally likely, quality could operate through intercepts while family background operates through interactions.

Quality can determine earnings through other channels as well. The average quality of persons in a labor market could affect earnings through an aggregate supply effect on factor prices. In this case the state of residence–specific components (both the levels, θ_s, θ_{sc}, and slopes, α_s, α_{sc}) would be functions of the total amount of quality employed in the market. Since most studies in the literature focus on only one possible channel through which quality operates, they understate or overstate the contribution of quality to earnings, depending on whether quality increases or decreases the neglected components of the pricing equation. Later, we present some evidence that increasing the total supply of quality in a state labor market depresses the marginal return to education.

Aggregate schooling quality is just one of several aggregate economic variables that are plausible determinants of state-of-residence effects (variables with s-subscripts). In the final section of this chapter, and in our companion study, we present new evidence on the impact of aggregate stocks of human capital, physical capital, industrial structure, and schooling quality on statewide and regional earnings equations.[15] Aggregate economic variables play an important role in determining pricing equations for labor services.

---

14. In the sensitivity analysis section of Card and Krueger (1992b), they do examine a model in which quality affects the intercepts.
15. Heckman, Layne-Farrar, and Todd (1996).

Any empirical study requires that limits be placed on the scope of the work. At issue is how important these limits are in practice. Both Johnson and Stafford, and Card and Krueger, assume that there is no interaction effect between state of birth and state of residence, that is, $\theta_{sb} = 0$, $\theta_{sbc} = 0$, and $\alpha_{sb} = 0$, $\alpha_{sbc} = 0$. These assumptions require that the return to quality (the coefficient of quality in a log-earnings equation) is the same for any state of residence. It also assumes that any common environmental influence, like family background factors emphasized in the Coleman report, has uniform effects in all states or regions of current residence. Moreover, it rules out selective migration by individuals from states of birth to states of residence in response to the level of realized earnings in the destination state. Both studies also assume that the relation between log-earnings and education is linear.[16] In addition, Johnson and Stafford postulate that the slope parameter on education is the same across all states of birth and states of residence ($\alpha_b = 0$, $\alpha_s = 0$, $\alpha_{sb} = 0$, $\alpha_{sc} = 0$, $\alpha_{bc} = 0$, $\alpha_{sbc} = 0$). Any one of these various restrictions, if false, could influence estimated quality effects. Later in this chapter, and in our companion study, we test for the validity of each of these assumptions and find that most are rejected by the data. When these assumptions are relaxed, a different picture of the effect of schooling quality on earnings emerges.

The following two matrixes clarify Card and Krueger's identification strategy and our evidence against it. For simplicity, consider only a single cohort at a given level of education, say twelve years. Let $\bar{y}_{bs}$ be the mean log earnings for people born in b and living in s. Imagine an $S \times B$ matrix of means:

$$
\begin{array}{c}
\text{State of birth} \\
\begin{array}{ccccc}
 & 1 & & \cdots & B
\end{array} \\
\begin{array}{c}
\text{State} \\
\text{of} \\
\text{residence}
\end{array}
\begin{array}{c}
1 \\
\vdots \\
\\
S
\end{array}
\left[
\begin{array}{cccc}
\bar{y}_{11} & \bar{y}_{12} & \cdots & \bar{y}_{1B} \\
\vdots & \bar{y}_{22} & & \vdots \\
 & & \ddots & \\
\bar{y}_{S1} & \bar{y}_{S2} & \cdots & \bar{y}_{SB}
\end{array}
\right]
\end{array}
$$

If all people who are born in b remain in b their entire lifetime, the matrix looks like this:

16. Card and Krueger (1992b) assume that the estimated relationship is linear after the second percentile of the education distribution within each state.

State of birth

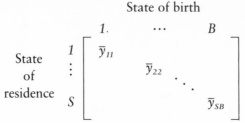

All the information in the matrix is on the diagonal.
Assuming an additive model, mean earnings can be written as

$$\bar{y}_{bs} = \mu + \alpha_b + \beta_s ,$$

where α_b is a state-of-birth effect and β_s is a state-of-residence effect. This model assumes that there is a state-of-birth effect common to persons in different states of residence and a state-of-residence effect common to persons from different states of birth. If no one migrates, then all $b = s$ and one can never separate α_b from β_s; that is, contemporary state-specific economic factors would be confounded with state-specific early environmental quality factors such as parental background and pupil-teacher ratios. The aggregate-data approach to estimating the impact of schooling quality on earnings uses state-of-birth averages as the measure of quality for all persons born in a state.

To identify a state-of-birth endowment effect, α_b, which may or may not be generated by schooling quality, it is necessary to have information on the off-diagonal terms. If there are two or more state-of-birth cohorts residing in a state-of-residence s, one can eliminate the common state-of-residence effect to identify α_b relative to $\alpha_{b'}$ for two states of birth b and b':

$$\bar{y}_{bs} = \mu + \alpha_b + \beta_s,$$

$$\bar{y}_{b's} = \mu + \alpha_{b'} + \beta_s,$$

so

$$\bar{y}_{bs} - \bar{y}_{b's} = \alpha_b - \alpha_{b'} .[17]$$

17. Assuming the normalizations $\sum_b \alpha_b = 0$ and $\sum_s \beta_s = 0$ identifies each component relative to μ. Otherwise, the components are identified relative to an omitted category.

One could identify the change in the value of α_b from one state of birth to another using $\alpha_b - \alpha_{b'}$ so estimated. In a few specifications considered by Card and Krueger, but not in the primary ones, this is what is done, and α_b is parameterized to be a function of quality in the state of birth Q_b. When there is information on more than one cohort, one can estimate α_b for each cohort, $\tilde{\alpha}_{bc}$, where it should be recalled that $\sim$ denotes the cell mean before main effects are eliminated. Taking deviations of $\tilde{\alpha}_{bc}$ around cohort and state-of-birth means gives

$$\tilde{\alpha}_{bc} - \alpha_b - \alpha_c = \alpha_{bc} \, ,$$

where α_{bc} was implicitly defined earlier in equation 7-3a. Card and Krueger assume that this interaction is a linear function of the quality of education for each cohort $c \, (Q_{bc})$, so

(*) $$\alpha_{bc} = \varphi \, Q_{bc}.$$

The term φ is sometimes identified by comparing α_{bc} for two or more states of birth,

(**) $$\alpha_{bc} - \alpha_{b'c} = \varphi(Q_{bc} - Q_{b'c}),$$

where $b \neq b'$; or by comparing any two state-of-birth cohorts, for example,

(***) $$\alpha_{bc} - \alpha_{bc'} = \varphi(Q_{bc} - Q_{bc'}),$$

where $c \neq c'$; or comparing any two distinct groups:

(****) $$\alpha_{bc} - \alpha_{b'c''} = \varphi(Q_{bc} - Q_{b'c''}),$$

where $b \neq b'$ and $c \neq c''$. By dividing the left-hand side by the quality contrast, φ can be identified. If contrasts are taken within states of birth, a b-specific φ, φ_b, can be estimated. If the contrasts are taken only within cohorts, a c-specific φ, φ_c, can be identified. Card and Krueger report results from such a specification. They also report a specification that constrains α_{bc} across c. Each specification embodies an implicit assumption. However, (****) is their fundamental estimation equation, where contrasts are taken across both b and c.

It is important to note that even if these identifying assumptions are satisfied, they do not solve the fundamental identification problem raised by the analysis in the Coleman report.[18] Q_{bc} may proxy family background or other state-specific early environmental influences. This is most easily seen by considering the model in which a separate quality effect is estimated for each cohort. Such a model identifies φ_c from the b-c interactions within cohorts, •

$$\alpha_{bc} - \alpha_{b'c} = \varphi_c(Q_{bc} - Q_{b'c}).$$

One can remove common (across cohorts) state-of-birth effects $\left(\alpha_b = \sum_c \alpha_{bc}\right)$, but any state-specific–cohort-specific effects (for example, the influence of neighbors and communities on promoting schooling in the early part of the century) are assumed to be captured by the quality indexes. Another way to say this is that all b-c interactions are attributable to schooling quality, not family background. One could plausibly argue instead that all schooling quality is attributable to a_b and that family background operates through a_{bc}. Unfortunately, both assumptions are untestable.

Also crucial to the Card-Krueger strategy is the assumption that there are no interactions between state of birth and state of residence, that is, in a model with interaction

$$\bar{y}_{bs} = \mu + \alpha_b + \beta_s + \Delta_{bs},$$

$$\Delta_{bs} = 0.$$

If this is not true, then

$$\bar{y}_{b,s} - \bar{y}_{b',s} = \alpha_b - \alpha_{b'} + \Delta_{bs} - \Delta_{b's}.$$

Estimated relative state-of-birth effects now depend on choices of the states of residence. Although unlikely, it might so happen that a model like (****) could still be true if unit increases in quality had the same effect on the rate of return across all states of residence. That is a testable restriction which we reject in data from 1970, 1980, and 1990. More generally, we test for the absence of interaction ($\Delta_{bs} = 0$) and reject it in all years we consider. The presence of such an interaction is consistent with patterns of comparative advantage for individuals from certain states of birth in certain states of residence, which induce individuals to

18. See the discussion of the evidence in Heckman and Neal (1996).

migrate to exploit favorable economic opportunities.[19] Allowing for a non-zero interaction ($\Delta_{bs} \neq 0$) greatly affects inferences about the size, sign, and statistical significance of estimates of schooling quality on the return to schooling, as we note below.

A Comparison of the Aggregate- and Individual-Level Data Approaches

Previous empirical studies of the quality-earnings relationship can be broadly classified as following either the aggregate-data approach or the individual-level-data approach. Under the individual-level-data approach, individual earnings are related to quality indicators from the school actually attended by the individual. The aggregate approach relates individual earnings to statewide or areawide averages of school quality. In addition, earnings data are sometimes aggregated.

The main criticism directed against the individual-level-data approach is that estimates of the effect of quality on earnings are subject to the problem of sorting bias. The quality of a person's schooling tends to be correlated with family background characteristics. In a regression of earnings on schooling quality, if variables such as family background or child ability affect earnings but are omitted from the analysis, then part of their effect will be wrongly attributed to quality.[20] Researchers attempt to control for sorting bias by including variables in the regression like family income or parental education to proxy for family background, but estimates are nevertheless subject to the uncertainty that the control variables may be inadequate for removing the bias. The bias may be negative or positive, depending on whether quality is negatively or positively associated with omitted ability and background characteristics.

The aggregate-data approach is sometimes promoted as a remedy for the sorting bias problem. By averaging quality variables over large enough areas (such as by school district or by state), there is likely to be less correlation between the quality measure and family background ef-

---

19. See, for example, Heckman and Scheinkman (1987) and Rosen (1983) for discussions of how nonuniform pricing of attributes across sectors in an economy gives rise to the problem of self-selection. Heckman and Scheinkman present empirical evidence against uniform pricing in the U.S. economy.

20. The coefficient on quality will be upwardly biased when the omitted variables positively affect earnings and are positively correlated with quality.

fects, which mitigates the selection problem. However, if quality is positively associated with background or ability, this claim is implausible in light of the empirical evidence. Because the individual-level studies wrongly attribute some of the family background effect to quality, estimates from these studies should provide stronger support for the quality hypothesis than the estimates based on aggregate quality measures. Yet in practice, the opposite occurs: the aggregate studies show a stronger effect of schooling quality on earnings than individual-level studies. However, this evidence is consistent with a negative correlation between quality and background or ability, as would arise if school policies promote egalitarian objectives. Evidence of stronger estimated effects of schooling quality on earnings and test scores as the level of aggregation in the schooling quality measure increases (from schools to states) is also consistent with a story that emphasizes measurement error in schooling quality that is averaged out in state aggregates.[21]

Almost all of the empirical studies, including those by Johnson and Stafford and Card and Krueger, assume that quality is exogenously determined.[22] But this assumption is dubious, given established empirical relationships between family background and education. A more thorough account of the impact of schooling quality on earnings would close the model by including an analysis of how quality is determined. Evidence that aggregate measures of quality produce stronger effects of quality in equations estimated on individual-level data is not consistent with a story of quality determined by schools and parents unless redistribution across school districts is *against* high-achieving students. If school authorities choose to award high-achieving students (or schools) with more resources, and resources raise outcomes, averaging the data should *weaken* and not strengthen estimated input-output relationships. If policies are egalitarian, precisely the opposite result occurs: averaging the data should strengthen estimated quality-earnings relationships.[23] Assumptions about how quality is determined are key to interpreting the results in any analysis of the schooling quality–earnings hypothesis.

21. See Betts's chapter in this volume (chapter 6); Hanushek, Rivkin, and Taylor (1994).

22. Johnson and Stafford (1973); Card and Krueger (1992a).

23. See Heckman, Layne-Farrar, and Todd (1996) for a model of quality determination that reconciles the literature's unusual finding of stronger quality effects for higher levels of aggregation in the data.

Migration: The Source of Identifying Information in Aggregate-Data Models

Sorting bias and measurement error are not the only problems that arise in identifying the effect of schooling quality on earnings. Differences in earnings among individuals with the same educational attainment level can be due to differences in ability, regional differences in cost of living, or regional differences in production technologies. Shifts in demand and supply for different types of human capital can also affect earnings. Finally, individuals can change their earnings simply by moving to different locations. Our ability to isolate the effect of quality on earnings depends on our ability to control for all these other relevant determinants of earnings.

As noted in the discussion surrounding the two matrixes presented earlier, migrants are essential in identifying the impact of schooling quality on earnings when the aggregate approach is used. Recall that if there is no migration across states, one cannot isolate a quality effect from other state-specific effects. If one only observes earnings for people born in a state and living in it, earnings differentials could be due to current state-specific effects like the cost of living, technology, or demand and supply effects that vary across states, as well as family and environmental influences on state earnings that affect initial endowments.

Random migration across states produces exogenous variation in quality, and a background effect on earnings can be identified. This is the most favorable case for the aggregate-data approach if background is interpreted as arising from schooling quality. If migration is nonrandom, however, it is necessary to distinguish state-of-residence effects from background effects. The two are conflated.

To see why, it is fruitful to examine the factors likely to influence a person's decision to migrate. If the prices-of-productivity attributes are uniform across all states, no one has an incentive to migrate. One can earn the same income in all locations.[24] Below, we present evidence against this assumption. If it is not satisfied, migrants will take into account their expectation of their prospective earnings in alternative destination regions. The expected gain from migration depends on the prices paid for quality and quantity of education, which are determined from state aggregates through demand and supply forces. For example, if a

24. After allowing for differences in earnings levels due to differences in amenities across regions.

state experiences an increase in the demand for skilled labor, one would expect to see migration from states producing higher schooling quality to states demanding the skills, if those states are different. There could be a pattern of educational selectivity among migrants, which has often been noted. Horace Hamilton observes that over the period 1940–50 migrants from the South tended to come from the lower and upper ends of the education distribution. Of these migrants, the relatively better educated went to the North and the more poorly educated moved to the West.[25]

Table 7-1, which compares the wages and quality of migrants with those of nonmigrants, reveals a pattern of selective migration for wages and for most measures of schooling quality in most years. The pattern for pupil-teacher ratio is the exception to this rule.[26] For the majority of cohorts and education levels, migrants' wages exceed natives' wages. If migration were random, there should be no systematic difference between the weekly wages of migrants and nonmigrants. Table 7-2, using just the 1980 census data, summarizes the migration patterns of persons born in different regions and provides the strongest evidence against the assumption of random migration. Persons born in a region are much more likely to live in it. This relationship is strongest for persons with less education and for persons born in the Pacific region. Moreover, among persons who move, the pattern of regional migration is not the same for all regions of birth.

Given persuasive evidence in favor of selective migration, and the evidence we present below that quality and education are priced differently in different regions, estimated quality effects produced from models that assume that migration is random are questionable unless one can claim that all relevant factors determining earnings are adequately controlled in estimated earning functions.[27] In the final section we estimate alternative specifications of earnings equations to account for migration. But first we examine the quality-earnings relationship more closely.

25. Hamilton (1959–60).
26. See the last section of the text for a discussion of the data sources and appendixes A and B for detailed information.
27. Theoretically, not accounting for the bias caused by nonrandom migration could result in either over- or underestimating quality effects.

Table 7-1. Proportion of States for Which the Average Educational Quality or Average Weekly Wage of Migrants Exceeds That of Nonmigrants, by Birth Cohort, 1910–59, Census Years 1970, 1980, 1990[a]

Census year and education level	1920–29				1930–39				1940–49				1950–59			
	PT ratio	Term length	Teacher salary	Weekly wage	PT ratio	Term length	Teacher salary	Weekly wage	PT ratio	Term length	Teacher salary	Weekly wage	PT ratio	Term length	Teacher salary	Weekly wage
1970																
<12th grade	.47	.41	.53	.86	.43	.47	.49	.65	.37	.43	.53	.53	…	…	…	…
12th grade	.45	.45	.53	.92	.45	.59	.51	.84	.47	.51	.53	.39	…	…	…	…
1–3 years college	.41	.63	.57	.84	.45	.61	.55	.80	.53	.55	.53	.39	…	…	…	…
4+ years college	.41	.67	.57	.84	.51	.69	.59	.86	.55	.61	.57	.45	…	…	…	…
1980																
<12th grade	.49	.47	.53	.88	.41	.49	.53	.88	.35	.45	.51	.75	…	…	…	…
12th grade	.49	.57	.55	.80	.45	.63	.51	.90	.47	.53	.49	.57	…	…	…	…
1–3 years college	.41	.57	.55	.80	.45	.63	.57	.76	.53	.59	.55	.65	…	…	…	…
4+ years college	.43	.61	.59	.92	.47	.71	.59	.90	.53	.61	.57	.96	…	…	…	…
1990																
<12th grade	…	…	…	…	.39	.43	.47	.65	.29	.41	.45	.67	.43	.41	.51	.69
12th grade	…	…	…	…	.47	.61	.49	.78	.45	.49	.51	.75	.43	.43	.53	.61
1–3 years college	…	…	…	…	.49	.61	.55	.82	.51	.49	.55	.82	.47	.43	.55	.61
4+ years college	…	…	…	…	.47	.69	.59	.92	.53	.57	.57	.96	.55	.45	.53	.98

Source: Author's calculations. The samples used to calculate the numbers in this table are described in appendix A.

a. PT ratio refers to the pupil-teacher ratio based on days enrolled. See appendix B for detailed discussion of the schooling-quality data. The numbers in the "PT ratio" columns are the proportion of states in which the pupil-teacher ratio is *lower* for migrants than for nonmigrants.

Table 7-2. *Distribution of Regional Migration for Birth Cohort 1930–39, with Varying Education Levels, 1980 Census*

Region of birth	Region of residence								
	NE	MA	ENC	WNC	SA	ESC	WSC	Mtn	Pac
	<12 grade								
Northeast	83.97	3.11	1.40	0.39	5.20	0.23	0.91	1.09	3.70
Middle Atlantic	1.47	83.57	3.29	0.38	5.80	0.43	0.89	1.33	2.85
East North Central	0.32	1.01	83.96	2.05	3.64	1.39	1.41	2.02	4.20
West North Central	0.21	0.45	6.73	68.15	1.57	0.54	3.25	6.40	12.69
South Atlantic	0.32	1.92	7.87	0.39	83.81	2.02	1.46	0.69	1.53
East South Central	0.12	0.57	22.73	0.82	7.96	61.70	3.30	0.85	1.96
West South Central	0.14	0.21	3.67	3.52	1.49	1.46	74.52	3.81	11.17
Mountain	0.16	0.60	2.03	2.96	1.87	0.38	3.68	62.90	25.41
Pacific	0.47	0.67	1.14	1.04	2.28	0.47	2.28	5.44	86.21
	12th grade								
Northeast	79.08	3.42	1.72	0.75	6.37	0.73	1.50	1.86	4.55
Middle Atlantic	2.16	77.88	4.07	0.50	8.19	0.52	1.28	1.69	3.73
East North Central	0.46	1.17	80.26	2.54	4.62	1.30	1.88	2.60	5.18
West North Central	0.34	0.62	6.16	65.17	2.50	0.90	3.89	6.83	13.58
South Atlantic	0.49	2.19	6.03	0.76	81.04	2.83	2.43	1.45	2.78
East South Central	0.31	0.61	14.54	1.39	11.22	62.87	4.66	1.30	3.10
West South Central	0.16	0.46	2.43	3.32	2.68	1.85	73.42	4.39	11.30
Mountain	0.38	0.95	2.25	2.85	1.95	0.70	3.88	63.11	23.92
Pacific	0.29	0.53	1.18	1.37	2.51	0.53	1.86	6.21	85.52
	1–3 years college								
Northeast	68.03	5.43	2.17	0.36	9.26	0.87	2.26	2.44	9.17
Middle Atlantic	3.50	63.55	4.75	0.99	11.74	0.84	2.46	2.92	9.24
East North Central	0.88	1.85	66.21	3.03	6.86	1.64	3.38	4.41	11.73
West North Central	0.66	1.25	7.03	48.34	3.96	1.52	6.35	9.05	21.84
South Atlantic	0.62	2.40	4.39	0.74	76.34	3.86	3.81	2.49	5.35
East South Central	0.56	1.39	10.47	1.33	15.32	54.75	7.51	2.37	6.30
West South Central	0.42	0.62	2.27	2.72	3.88	2.83	67.60	5.41	14.25
Mountain	0.58	0.49	2.60	2.73	2.33	0.58	4.03	56.16	30.50
Pacific	0.33	0.76	1.04	1.09	2.37	0.33	2.09	6.65	85.32
	4+ years college								
Northeast	58.27	11.52	4.69	1.25	11.03	0.84	2.25	2.11	8.03
Middle Atlantic	6.27	57.50	6.71	1.41	13.81	1.06	2.41	2.15	8.68
East North Central	2.16	4.96	56.82	4.61	9.46	2.01	3.94	3.87	12.17
West North Central	1.50	3.14	10.60	44.15	6.50	1.27	6.70	8.31	17.84
South Atlantic	1.71	5.43	5.45	1.41	70.01	4.72	3.69	1.92	5.64
East South Central	0.60	2.36	7.77	2.10	20.10	51.49	7.97	2.12	5.49
West South Central	0.82	1.59	3.23	3.88	6.24	3.47	64.79	5.68	10.32
Mountain	1.23	2.21	4.01	4.26	5.43	1.04	5.21	47.49	29.11
Pacific	1.39	2.06	2.66	1.63	4.74	0.89	2.42	5.93	78.30

Source: Author's calculations. The table shows the regional migration patterns for the samples of white males described in appendix A. The table gives percentages of individuals from each region of birth residing in each region of residence.

Testing Monotonicity of the Quality-Earnings Relationship

The central premise of the quality-earnings hypothesis is that higher quality schooling produces higher earnings. In the first matrix on page 203, the column associated with the state with the highest quality should be bigger, element by element, than any other column in the table. This premise alone is almost a tautology, because "quality" per se is something that yields a positive benefit to the recipient—in this case higher earnings. To make the premise empirically interesting, we must further assume that quality levels can be measured in terms of such indexes as pupil-teacher ratios, teacher salaries, and term lengths. We can then devise tests for the hypothesis, since the variables in question are observable.

If we assume that quality has a uniform effect on log earnings at all education levels (as in the Johnson and Stafford model described earlier), then it follows that within every education level the wages of persons with different levels of schooling quality should be ranked according to their quality rankings. This can be seen in figure 7-3A, where we assume that New York's schooling quality is higher than Alabama's.

If we assume that the effect of quality operates only by increasing the rate of return to education (the slope parameter), then it could happen that the ranks by schooling quality and ranks by wages would not coincide at all education levels. Figure 7-3B shows how this might occur.[28] Even if no quality data were available, an implication of the quality through slopes model is that at any education level the ranks by state of birth would be the same in all labor markets.[29] However, this second implication is also consistent with the analysis of the Coleman report. Any early environmental influences that raise earnings could produce a common effect in all markets, or at least a common rank across states of residence.

To illustrate this point, consider figure 7-3B, where the slope is higher in New York but the intercept is lower. Nonetheless, at a given level of education, the relative ranks of persons born in New York and Alabama should remain the same across all labor markets.

This discussion motivates the two rank tests that we perform here: (a) the test that rankings in wage distributions correlate with rankings in

---

28. We thank Gary Burtless for clarifying comments on these points.

29. In the final section of Card and Krueger (1992b), which conducts sensitivity analysis on their model, the authors consider the effect of quality operating through the intercepts. However, their primary model only allows for quality to enter through the slope parameters.

Figure 7-3. Comparison of Wages of Persons with Different School-Quality Levels

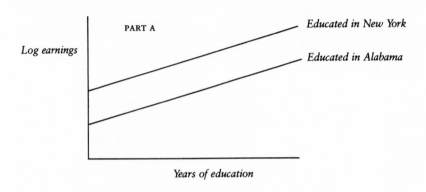

PART A

Log earnings

Educated in New York

Educated in Alabama

Years of education

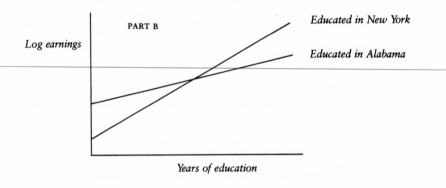

PART B

Log earnings

Educated in New York

Educated in Alabama

Years of education

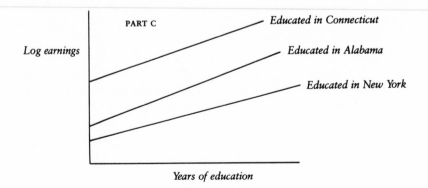

PART C

Log earnings

Educated in Connecticut

Educated in Alabama

Educated in New York

Years of education

quality distributions and (b) the weaker test that relative rankings by states of birth within education levels should be the same in all states of residence. Both are implications of the assumption of no selective migration on the basis of realized earnings.

We now present evidence from the rankings of quality and wages across state and regional labor markets. The evidence generally supports the key idea in figure 7-3A—that the lines do not cross—but does not support the hypothesis that the height of the nonintersecting lines is positively, or negatively, related to schooling quality or that the ranks by state of birth within state earnings distributions are the same for all states at any level of educational attainment. Thus figure 7-3C, which shows no systematic relationship between measured quality and earnings, is a more appropriate summary of our evidence, where Connecticut is assumed to have the highest quality of schooling and Alabama the lowest. Different returns to education for different states of birth may result from common environmental influences (consistent with the Coleman report), or from school quality that is not captured by our indexes.

Tables 7-3 and 7-4 display Kendall-Tau correlations (with *p*-values in parentheses) between the rankings of four different quality measures and mean wages for individuals with twelve and sixteen years of education, respectively.[30] Correlations are calculated separately within regions of residence to allow for cost-of-living differences. The results show no support for a relation between the quality rankings and the mean-wage rankings at either twelve years or sixteen or more years of education. Tests based on median instead of mean earnings yield similar results.

It is useful to ask what explanations are consistent with our finding of no correlation between quality and wage rankings. One possible explanation is that states differ in their production technologies for transforming schooling inputs (the variables that are measured in the literature) into an output of educational quality. This notion is consistent with Hanushek's observation that efficiency in translating educational inputs into outputs, and not just the absolute level of inputs, is important.[31] The level of efficiency can vary across states. It may be affected by factors such as the strength of teacher unions, state laws governing education, and individual teacher proficiency. Educational quality-earnings produc-

---

30. The *p*-value is the smallest level of significance at which the null hypothesis would be rejected. A low *p*-value indicates that the departure of the test statistic from the value specified by the null is an unlikely event under the null and therefore leads to its rejection.

31. Hanushek (1986).

Table 7-3. Kendall-Tau Correlations between Region-of-Birth Quality Rankings and Log-Wage Rankings, by Birth Cohort, 1920–49, with Twelve Years of Education, 1980 Census[a]

Cohort and quality measure[b]	Region of residence[c]								
	NE	MA	ENC	WNC	SA	ESC	WSC	Mtn	Pac
1920–29									
PTR-E	−0.50	−0.17	0.06	0.28	−0.06	−0.33	0.06	−0.50	0.22
	(0.06)	(0.53)	(0.83)	(0.30)	(0.83)	(0.21)	(0.83)	(0.06)	(0.40)
PTR-A	−0.17	0.06	−0.06	0.39	−0.50	−0.11	−0.06	−0.50	0.00
	(0.53)	(0.83)	(0.83)	(0.14)	(0.06)	(0.68)	(0.83)	(0.06)	(1.00)
Teacher salary	0.09	−0.03	0.02	−0.33	0.75	−0.21	0.15	0.09	0.27
	(0.75)	(0.91)	(0.91)	(0.24)	(0.01)	(0.45)	(0.59)	(0.75)	(0.33)
Term length	0.44	−0.11	−0.22	0.22	−0.22	0.28	0.00	0.00	−0.39
	(0.09)	(0.68)	(0.40)	(0.40)	(0.40)	(0.30)	(1.00)	(1.00)	(0.14)
1930–39									
PTR-E	−0.44	0.00	−0.22	0.28	0.17	0.11	0.22	0.06	−0.11
	(0.10)	(1.00)	(0.40)	(0.30)	(0.53)	(0.68)	(0.40)	(0.83)	(0.68)
PTR-A	−0.39	0.17	−0.39	0.33	0.22	−0.06	0.28	−0.11	−0.06
	(0.14)	(0.53)	(0.14)	(0.21)	(0.40)	(0.83)	(0.30)	(0.68)	(0.83)
Teacher salary	−0.47	0.03	−0.55	−0.11	0.18	0.04	−0.04	−0.04	−0.04
	(0.10)	(0.90)	(0.06)	(0.71)	(0.53)	(0.90)	(0.90)	(0.90)	(0.90)
Term length	0.33	−0.22	0.00	−0.28	−0.17	−0.11	−0.11	−0.17	−0.11
	(0.21)	(0.40)	(1.00)	(0.30)	(0.53)	(0.68)	(0.68)	(0.53)	(0.68)
1940–49									
PTR-E	−0.61	0.00	0.06	0.00	0.06	0.39	0.17	−0.17	0.00
	(0.02)	(1.00)	(0.83)	(1.00)	(0.83)	(0.14)	(0.53)	(0.53)	(1.00)
PTR-A	−0.61	−0.11	−0.06	0.11	−0.06	0.28	0.28	−0.17	0.00
	(0.02)	(0.68)	(0.83)	(0.68)	(0.83)	(0.30)	(0.30)	(0.53)	(1.00)
Teacher salary	−0.15	0.45	−0.09	−0.15	−0.03	0.27	−0.21	0.09	−0.27
	(0.59)	(0.11)	(0.75)	(0.59)	(0.91)	(0.33)	(0.45)	(0.75)	(0.33)
Term length	0.67	0.39	0.00	−0.17	0.00	0.00	−0.33	−0.22	−0.28
	(0.01)	(0.14)	(1.00)	(0.53)	(1.00)	(1.00)	(0.21)	(0.40)	(0.30)

Source: Authors' calculations. Correlations were done separately within the nine regions of residence. The table was constructed by (1) calculating mean log wages within region-of-residence–region-of-birth cells; (2) calculating average quality measures for regions of birth (these are weighted averages of the state quality data); (3) for each region of residence, calculating the correlation of the ranks of log wages by region of birth with the corresponding ranks in quality. In addition to doing the rankings by region of birth, we did them by state of birth. The results were similar.

a. The numbers in parentheses are p-values. The p-value is the smallest level of significance at which the null hypothesis would be rejected. In this table, a low p-value indicates that the observed departure of the statistic from 0 is unlikely to be a result of chance.

b. PTR-E = enrollment-based pupil-teacher ratio; PTR-A = attendance-based pupil-teacher ratio.

c. NE: New England; WNC: West North Central; WSC: West South Central; MA: Middle Atlantic; SA: South Atlantic; Mtn: Mountain; ENC: East North Central; ESC: East South Central; Pac: Pacific.

Table 7-4. *Kendall-Tau Correlations between Region-of-Birth Quality Rankings and Log-Wage Rankings, by Birth Cohort, 1920–49, with Four or More Years of College, 1980 Census*[a]

Cohort and quality measure[b]	Region of residence[c]								
	NE	MA	ENC	WNC	SA	ESC	WSC	Mtn	Pac
1920–29									
PTR-E	0.56	−0.22	−0.11	0.00	−0.39	−0.11	−0.11	0.39	0.00
	(0.04)	(0.40)	(0.68)	(1.00)	(0.14)	(0.68)	(0.68)	(0.14)	(1.00)
PTR-A	0.44	−0.22	−0.44	0.22	−0.50	0.11	−0.11	0.50	0.11
	(0.10)	(0.40)	(0.10)	(0.40)	(0.06)	(0.68)	(0.68)	(0.06)	(0.68)
Teacher salary	−0.15	0.62	0.45	−0.21	0.57	−0.27	0.03	−0.21	−0.15
	(0.59)	(0.02)	(0.10)	(0.45)	(0.04)	(0.33)	(0.91)	(0.45)	(0.59)
Term length	−0.50	−0.17	−0.06	0.50	0.00	0.28	0.50	0.22	0.17
	(0.06)	(0.53)	(0.83)	(0.06)	(1.00)	(0.30)	(0.06)	(0.40)	(0.53)
1930–39									
PTR-E	0.17	0.17	−0.33	0.17	−0.22	−0.28	0.06	−0.28	−0.28
	(0.53)	(0.53)	(0.21)	(0.53)	(0.40)	(0.30)	(0.83)	(0.30)	(0.30)
PTR-A	0.00	0.11	−0.39	0.33	−0.28	−0.33	0.22	−0.33	−0.11
	(1.00)	(0.68)	(0.14)	(0.21)	(0.30)	(0.21)	(0.40)	(0.21)	(0.68)
Teacher salary	−0.47	−0.47	0.04	0.11	0.04	0.11	0.40	−0.25	−0.11
	(0.10)	(0.10)	(0.90)	(0.71)	(0.90)	(0.71)	(0.17)	(0.38)	(0.71)
Term length	−0.50	−0.50	0.44	−0.06	0.00	0.28	0.28	−0.06	0.06
	(0.06)	(0.06)	(0.09)	(0.83)	(1.00)	(0.30)	(0.30)	(0.83)	(0.83)
1940–49									
PTR-E	0.22	0.06	−0.17	0.06	−0.50	−0.44	−0.11	0.22	−0.11
	(0.40)	(0.83)	(0.53)	(0.83)	(0.06)	(0.10)	(0.68)	(0.40)	(0.68)
PTR-A	0.11	0.06	−0.28	−0.06	−0.50	−0.56	−0.22	0.11	−0.22
	(0.68)	(0.83)	(0.30)	(0.83)	(0.06)	(0.04)	(0.40)	(0.68)	(0.40)
Teacher salary	−0.15	0.39	0.33	−0.03	−0.03	0.15	−0.14	0.27	0.21
	(0.59)	(0.16)	(0.24)	(0.91)	(0.91)	(0.60)	(0.60)	(0.33)	(0.45)
Term length	−0.17	−0.33	0.00	0.22	0.00	0.39	0.39	−0.28	0.17
	(0.53)	(0.21)	(1.00)	(0.40)	(1.00)	(0.14)	(0.14)	(0.29)	(0.53)

Source: See table 7-3.
a. See note a, table 7-3.
b. See note b, table 7-3.
c. See note c, table 7-3.

tion functions at the state level may not be monotonic in quality; that is, as schooling quality changes, earnings may not change uniformly.

Selective migration based on prospective gains and individual-specific costs is another possible explanation for the observed patterns. Suppose that persons born in different regions receive different quality endowments, face different costs of migrating, and expect different payoffs in different destination regions. Even if higher schooling quality raises productivity in all regions, the pattern of migration choices need not imply strict dominance of the wages of persons from high-quality origins in all destination regions. Persons migrating long distances will tend to have higher earnings in all destination regions than those persons making short moves or no moves at all. The results we presented earlier in tables 7-1 and 7-2 are consistent with this hypothesis. Although we find that migrants' wages consistently lie above nonmigrants', no strong link with schooling quality is evident.

Nonmonotonic schooling quality–earnings relationships, the operation of selective migration, or measurement error in the quality indexes could account for the lack of correlation between wage and quality rankings. This evidence casts doubt both on the empirical validity of simple quality-of-schooling models and on the existence of invariant schooling-quality measures that successfully predict relative success in different economic environments.

Even if schooling quality determines ranks in wages but cannot be measured by our indexes, or if the reversal depicted in figure 7-3B occurs, it is still possible to test a weaker form of the quality-earnings hypothesis nonparametrically. If the hypothesis is true, and there is no selective migration, persons at a given education level from a particular state of birth will tend to have the same relative rank in the wage distributions across all regions of residence.[32] The quality hypothesis would predict invariance in the state-of-birth wage rankings across all regions of residence for each education level under either of the wage-education relationships depicted in figures 7-3A and 7-3B. Table 7-5 presents Kendall coefficient-of-concordance statistics (and p-values) for stability in the region-of-birth–wage rankings across regions of residence and provides some support for this implication of the hypothesis. The 1990 census data show the strongest support for stability in the rankings, with several significant p-values. Thus, while rankings of the widely used empirical measures of schooling quality and earnings appear to be uncorrelated, rankings of earnings by region of birth show some evidence of stability. The stability of the ranks is consistent with unobserved quality producing a stable earnings relationship and in this sense is consistent with the

---

32. When making wage comparisons across different labor markets, rank comparisons are much more robust than level comparisons, since they are not sensitive to regional differences in the cost of living.

Table 7-5. Nonparametric Tests for Agreement in Region-of-Birth Average Wage Rankings across Regions of Residence, by Birth Cohort, 1910–59, with Varying Education Levels, Census Years 1970, 1980, 1990[a]

P = values in parentheses

Census year and cohort	12th grade	1–3 years college	4 + years college
1970			
1910–19	0.18 (0.13)	0.06 (0.81)	0.09 (0.61)
1920–29	0.20 (0.08)	0.21 (0.05)	0.22 (0.04)
1930–39	0.18 (0.11)	0.06 (0.81)	0.25 (0.027)
1940–49	0.14 (0.28)	0.06 (0.81)	0.18 (0.12)
1980			
1920–29	0.10 (0.50)	0.13 (0.31)	0.10 (0.50)
1930–39	0.20 (0.07)	0.24 (0.03)	0.09 (0.60)
1940–49	0.19 (0.09)	0.26 (0.02)	0.33 (0.002)
1990			
1930–39	0.32 (0.004)	0.14 (0.25)	0.22 (0.04)
1940–49	0.26 (0.02)	0.32 (0.004)	0.35 (0.002)
1950–59	0.17 (0.13)	0.52 (0.0001)	0.48 (0.0003)

Source: Author's calculations. The Kendall coefficient of concordance for measuring the relative agreement between m rankings of n objects is given by $W = \dfrac{12S}{m^2(n^3 - n)}$, where $S = \sum_{i=1}^{n} \left[R_i - \dfrac{m(n + 1)}{2} \right]^2$ and R_i is the sum of the ranks for object i. For $n > 7$, $\chi_r^2 = m(n - 1)W$ is approximately χ^2 with $n - 1$ degrees of freedom. When all rankings agree, $W = 1$. As W gets closer to 0, there is less agreement in the rankings.

a. Regions of birth and regions of residence refer to the nine census regions: New England, Middle Atlantic, East North Central, West North Central, South Atlantic, East South Central, West South Central, Mountain, and Pacific. The p-value is the smallest level of significance at which the null hypothesis would be rejected. In this table, a low p-value indicates that the observed departure of the statistic from 0 is unlikely to be a result of chance.

schooling-quality model. The evidence is, of course, also consistent with a model motivated by the evidence from the Coleman report that unobserved family background or income effects determine earnings. Any early environmental variable that differs across states of birth is a candidate for explaining this relationship.

It is striking that the measures used in the literature to establish a schooling quality–earnings relationship do not survive a nonparametric test. This rejection of the measured schooling quality hypothesis suggests that the earnings–schooling-quality relationships reported in the literature may be artifacts of arbitrary functional form assumptions or other empirical procedures. Keeping this evidence in mind, we next examine the models used in two representative studies of schooling quality that find significant effects of measured schooling quality variables on earnings. We focus on the question of choosing an appropriate functional form for the earnings-quality relationship.

An Empirical Exploration of Two Representative Models

Empirical studies using different functional forms find different effects of schooling quality on earnings. To gain an understanding of how sensitive estimated effects are to changes in model specification, we examine two representative models. The first is that of Card and Krueger and the second is a version of their model adapted to accommodate certain features of the Johnson-Stafford model.[33] Both studies estimate quality effects on earnings using aggregated data.

Description of the Data

As mentioned, our data come from the 1970, 1980, and 1990 census samples. To maintain close comparability between our results and those of Card and Krueger, we replicate as closely as possible their 1980 census samples and construct samples from the 1970 and 1990 censuses in the same way. Our study focuses on white males from five birth cohorts: 1910–19, 1920–29, 1930–39, 1940–49, and 1950–59. Appendix A summarizes the sample exclusion restrictions and gives exact sample sizes for the different extractions. The sample sizes for the individual-level data regressions are large, ranging from about 100,000 to nearly 600,000.

Our study draws on state-level data quantifying three broad aspects of schooling quality for full-time public primary and secondary day schools (grades *K-12*): average term length, average annual instructional staff salary, and pupil-teacher ratios. For the most part, our quality data come from the *Biennial Survey of Education*. The data sources, as well as descriptions of the quality variables, are given in detail in appendix

33. Card and Krueger (1992a); Johnson and Stafford (1973).

B.[34] We consider two measures of the pupil-teacher ratio, one based on pupil enrollment and one based on average daily attendance. For the earlier cohorts, which were not subject to mandatory schooling laws, and for more rural areas with family farming demands, the attendance-based measure is probably a better proxy for true quality.[35]

A fundamental problem in establishing an empirical quality-earnings relationship is how to obtain consistent measures of schooling quality. The commonly used indexes are sometimes inversely related to one another. If budget constraints are binding, as teacher salaries rise there should be a concurrent increase in classroom size. That is, one measure would indicate an improvement in quality while another would indicate a decline. In table 7-6 we present evidence demonstrating conflicts among alternative measures of quality. Alternative measures are not always positively correlated, and even when they are, the correlation is far from perfect.

Specific Functional Forms: The Card and Krueger Model

Card and Krueger postulate a linear equation for log weekly earnings, y. In their specification, y depends on a person's state of birth (b), state of residence (s), years of education (E), and several demographic variables (X). Their definition of education is somewhat unusual: E is the years of education above the level attained by the bottom two percent of people in the education distribution. The demographic variables included in X are a marital status indicator, potential work experience, potential work experience squared, and an indicator for whether an individual resides in a metropolitan area. The earnings function for individual i is written as

$$(7\text{-}4) \qquad y_{isbc} = \delta_{bc} + \mu_{sc} + X_{ic} \cdot \beta_c + E_{ibc}\,(\gamma_{bc} + \rho_{rc}) + \epsilon_{ibsc}$$

$$E_{ibc} = Max(e_{ibc} - T_{bc}, 0).$$

—r refers to the region of residence (the nine regions defined by the

---

34. We use a different regional deflator from that used by Card and Krueger to construct our relative teacher salary measure. Also, we use a term-length measure that refers only to whites for the states that report a race-specific measure. These differences are discussed in detail in appendix B.

35. Most state mandatory school attendance laws were not passed until the early 1920s. Sometimes state or district educational funding depended on enrollment, in which case there was an incentive for schools to inflate enrollment numbers.

Table 7-6. Kendall-Tau Correlations between Different Quality Measures, by Birth Cohort, 1920–49[a]

Birth cohort and quality measure[b]	Measure of schooling quality[b]		
	PTR-E	PTR-A	Teacher salary
1920–29			
PTR-A	0.79	...	...
	(0.00)		
Teacher salary	0.05	0.21	...
	(0.61)	(0.03)	
Term length	−0.15	0.00	0.27
	(0.13)	(0.98)	(0.01)
1930–39			
PTR-A	0.83	...	...
	(0.00)		
Teacher salary	0.10	0.09	...
	(0.07)	(0.35)	
Term length	−0.13	−0.10	0.10
	(0.02)	(0.033)	(0.30)
1940–49			
PTR-A	0.80	...	...
	(0.00)		
Teacher salary	0.10	0.08	...
	(0.07)	(0.41)	
Term length	−0.13	−0.11	0.43
	(0.02)	(0.27)	(0.00)

Source: Authors' calculations. The quality indexes are described in detail in appendix B. The pairwise rank correlations are calculated by ranking the states according to two quality measures and calculating the correlation among the ranks.

a. The numbers in parentheses are *p*-values. The *p*-value is the smallest level of significance at which the null hypothesis would be rejected. In this table, a low *p*-value indicates that the observed departure of the statistic from 0 is unlikely to be a result of chance.

b. PTR-E = enrollment-based pupil-teacher ratio; PTR-A = attendance-based pupil-teacher ratio.

census are geographically contiguous groups of states); c indicates the birth cohort.

—e_{ibsc} is the actual number of years of schooling completed; T_{bc} is the bottom second percentile of the education distribution for men born in state b of cohort c.

—γ_{bc} is the "return" to education for an individual in cohort c, born in state b.

—δ_{bc} is a cohort-specific fixed effect for state of birth b.

—μ_{sc} is a cohort-specific fixed effect for state-of-residence s.

—ρ_{rc} is a region of residence effect that is meant to capture regional labor market shocks to the return to education; the region of residence coefficients are normalized to give deviations around a national mean.[36] —ϵ_{ibsc} is a stochastic error term assumed to be identically and independently distributed across individuals.

Using a model of the impact of quality on earnings suggested by Behrman and Birdsall's 1983 study, Card and Krueger introduce schooling quality into the earnings function by assuming that quality increases the rate of return to education, γ_{bc}. They posit a linear relation between the rate of return for individuals born in state b in cohort c and educational quality (Q_{bc}), as measured by the pupil-teacher ratio, term length, and teacher salary:

$$(7\text{-}5) \qquad \gamma_{bc} = \alpha_b + \alpha_c + Q_{bc}\varphi.$$

The return to education is allowed to depend on the state of birth (through fixed effects α_b) and on the cohort (through α_c), but the marginal effect of quality is assumed to be the same for all birth cohorts and for all states of birth. The key parameter in the quality-earnings relationship is φ. Estimates of φ are obtained from a two-stage procedure regressing estimates of γ_{bc} on Q_{bc}.[37] This method uses variation in quality both within and across cohorts to identify φ.

Several features of this specification are noteworthy. First, observe that the parameterization of work experience (included in X_{ic}) is not symmetric with respect to the parameterization of education. The effect of experience is permitted to vary by birth cohorts but not across states of birth, as is permitted for the effect of education. Since work experience is a form of human capital that is complementary to formal schooling, and since participation in formal schooling increases the rate of accu-

---

36. Card and Krueger set $\sum_r f_{rc} \cdot \rho_{rc} = 0$, where f_{rc} is the fraction of cohort c living in one of the nine census regions. Therefore, the γ_{bc} parameter includes the national cohort mean education return.

37. Finis Welch, in discussion, made the observation regarding two-stage estimation that, in general, it is incorrect to deviate the second-stage dependent variable around regional means, but not to deviate the regressor variables. However, the Card-Krueger specification assumes that the state-of-birth component of the return to education depends only on personal characteristics, Q_{bc}, that are invariant across regions. Therefore in their model the regressors do not need to be deviated around regional means. We relax this assumption by allowing the state-of-birth return to depend not only on birth-specific characteristics, but also on factors that may influence where individuals choose to work, such as migration costs. See Heckman, Layne-Farrar, and Todd (1996) for a more detailed discussion.

mulation of job training,[38] it is not obvious that experience should be treated asymmetrically. When we parameterize experience more generally, we find that estimated schooling quality effects operating through the return to education weaken, but there is little evidence of a quality effect operating through estimated returns-to-work experience.[39]

Second, this model assumes that the log-earnings–quality relationship is linear above a 2 percent threshold and that there is no return to education until the 2 percent level.[40] Later we test and reject the assumption that earnings are linear in education for all three census years. In the data there is evidence of sheepskin effects, or discrete jumps in the return to education on completion of a degree. When the linearity assumption is relaxed to account for these effects, the only support of an effect of school quality on earnings comes through the marginal return to college attendance.

Third, the specification in equation 7-4 rules out state-of-birth–region-of-residence interactions both in slopes and intercepts. We test this hypothesis and reject it. There are differential returns to skills, including quality, across different regions of residence that depend on region of birth. Differential pricing of individual productivity attributes, such as quality, could induce selective migration, in which case the residual, ϵ_{isbc}, is unlikely to be exogenous with respect to state- and region-of-residence indicators. When we estimate a model that includes interactions between region of birth and region of residence to account for nonrandom migration decisions, estimated effects of schooling quality often reverse sign or become imprecisely determined. These estimates indicate the sensitivity of the Card-Krueger findings to this identifying assumption. But introducing such interactions does not solve the selection problem in general; a more involved analysis is required.

Fourth, the specification in equation 7-4 assumes that returns to education are region specific. The addition of an education-specific regional component to the education return is a valuable contribution of the Card-Krueger model. We test and do not reject the hypothesis that returns are region specific. However, when we allow for nonlinearity in the earnings equation, we reject this specification for higher (more than twelve years)

---

38. Mincer (1974).

39. See Heckman, Layne-Farrar, and Todd (1996) for this evidence.

40. The second percentile of most states for the later cohorts is about eight to nine years of education. In our sensitivity analysis we find that assuming linearity above a 2 percent threshold versus assuming linearity in actual years of education makes little difference to the estimated effects of quality. Card and Krueger (1992b) report similar results.

levels of education. For persons with college degrees there is a national labor market; regional labor-market effects are unimportant. This finding suggests a new argument for nonlinearity in the earnings function that goes beyond the traditional model of sheepskin effects.[41] Models that force labor-market shocks to have the same effects on the return to education at all skill levels are at odds with our data and with the evidence assembled by Blanchflower and Oswald.[42] In our companion study we examine the theoretical implications of the evidence of statistically significant education-specific regional interaction effects for conventional efficiency-units models of labor quality.[43] We reject the efficiency-units specification of labor input and other common specifications of labor services that are widely used in macroeconomic labor-market analyses.

Finally, as noted earlier, the specification given in equations 7-4 and 7-5 defines the effect of schooling quality on earnings solely as the effect of Q on the slope coefficient, γ_{bc} ($\gamma_{bc} = \alpha_b + \alpha_{bc}$ in the notation of the analysis of variance model presented earlier). This disregards the possible contribution of quality through the intercepts in the model, δ_{bc} and μ_{sc} (the θ components in our earlier analysis of variance—ANOVA—decomposition). Focusing only on the effect of quality operating through γ_{bc} may understate or overstate the contribution of quality to the level of wages.

The specifications considered by Card and Krueger ignore the effects of quality and other economic aggregates on the location-of-residence component to the return to education, ρ_{rc} (α_{sc} in our previous notation). We introduce such aggregates into the analysis and produce a richer economic model of the earnings function in the tradition of Jan Tinbergen and Michael Sattinger.[44] Of importance to the immediate discussion is our finding that quality aggregates often act like a supply shock and *depress* returns to skill. Measuring the effect of quality solely through γ_{bc} (α_b or $\alpha_b + \alpha_{bc}$) usually *overstates* the contribution of quality to the total educational return.

Because there are components in the model that could plausibly be affected by schooling quality that are not considered in equation 7-5, evidence that $\varphi = 0$ is not necessarily evidence that schooling quality does not affect earnings. Conversely, evidence that $\varphi \neq 0$ is not evidence

41. See, for example, Hungerford and Solon (1987) and Jaeger and Page (1996).
42. Blanchflower and Oswald (1994).
43. Heckman, Layne-Farrar, and Todd (1996).
44. Tinbergen (1975); Sattinger (1980).

that schooling quality raises earnings, because an offsetting reverse effect could operate through δ_{bc} or ρ_{rc}. In the next two subsections, we shed light on this question by presenting empirical evidence of how quality affects earnings through the various channels just discussed.

Replicating and Extending the Card-Krueger Model

We have replicated Card and Krueger's study using both their schooling-quality data (presented in table 1 of their paper) and ours. The results of the two replications are similar, so we present only the results using our quality data. We use the ANOVA notation to focus attention on the different components of the return to education that might be affected by schooling quality. Our current notation differs slightly, because some components of the model are stated in terms of region of residence and region of birth, denoted by $r(s)$ and $r(b)$, instead of state of residence and state of birth. For now, we consider the effect of quality operating through the slope parameters, $\tilde{\alpha}_{r(s)bc}$. In our second-stage regressions, we employ the total return to education as the dependent variable so that we can examine the effect of quality both on the state-of-birth and on the region-of-residence components of the return. Later we also examine the effects of quality on intercepts (θ terms in equation 7-1). In the ANOVA framework, the second-stage regression model decomposing the total rate of return to education into cohort, state-of-birth, and region-of-residence components is given by

$$(7\text{-}6) \quad total\ rate\ of\ return \equiv \tilde{\alpha}_{r(s)bc}$$

$$= \alpha + \alpha_b + \alpha_c + \alpha_{r(s)} + \alpha_{bc} + \alpha_{r(s)c} + \alpha_{r(s)r(b)} + \alpha_{r(s)b(s)c}.$$

The term α_c allows for a cohort-specific mean, α_b and α_{bc} are the state-of-birth components, $\alpha_{r(s)}$ and $\alpha_{r(s)c}$ are the region-of-residence components, and $\alpha_{r(s)r(b)}$ and $\alpha_{r(s)r(b)c}$ are interactions between the state of birth, region of residence, and cohort. As noted earlier, the Card-Krueger model assumes the effect of quality operates through the state-of-birth components α_b and α_{bc} and suppresses region-of-birth–region-of-residence interaction terms ($\alpha_{r(s)r(b)} = 0$, $\alpha_{r(s)r(b)c} = 0$). We initially maintain the assumption of no interaction effects but later relax it.

Table 7-7 presents results from our analysis of the 1980 census. The specifications similar to the Card and Krueger model write α_{bc} and α_b as a function of quality and include unrestricted region-of-residence and cohort intercepts (α_c, α_r, and α_{rc}—see columns 1, 2, and 3 in the table).

Table 7-7. *Effect of Schooling Quality on the Rate of Return to Education, Linear Model, 1980 Census*[a]

				Second-stage model restrictions					
				(4) $\alpha_{bc} = \varphi_c Q_{bc}$					
Measure[b]	(1) $\alpha_{bc} = \varphi Q_{bc}$	(2) $\alpha_{bc} = \varphi Q_{bc}$	(3) $\alpha_b + \alpha_{bc} = \varphi Q_{bc}$	1920–29	1930–39	1940–49	(5) $\alpha_{bc} = \varphi Q_{bc}$ $\alpha_{r(s)} + \alpha_{r(s)c} = \pi_1 Q_{r(s)}$	(6) $\alpha_{bc} = \varphi Q_{bc}$ $\alpha_{r(s)} + \alpha_{r(s)c} = \pi_1 Q_{r(s)}$	(7) $\alpha_{bc} = \varphi Q_{bc}$ $\alpha_{r(s)} + \alpha_{r(s)c} = \pi_1 Q_{r(s)} + \pi_2 D_{r(s)}$
Pupil-teacher ratio	−5.66 (1.48)	−6.27 (1.49)	1.36 (0.55)	−0.09 (1.03)	2.58 (0.75)	2.02 (0.97)	−6.27 (2.69)	−6.27 (2.55)	−6.27 (1.86)
Term length	...	1.07 (0.49)	3.06 (0.24)	2.23 (0.33)	3.59 (0.44)	4.39 (0.66)	1.07 (0.98)	1.07 (1.01)	1.07 (0.67)
Relative teacher salary	...	2.08 (0.24)	0.98 (0.08)	1.27 (0.11)	0.83 (0.12)	0.54 (0.19)	2.08 (0.43)	2.08 (0.44)	2.08 (0.31)
Demand and supply aggregates									
Regional average pupil-teacher ratio	...	...	...	...	...	...	21.52 (1.20)	20.27 (1.13)	−38.88 (2.41)
Regional average term length	...	...	...	...	...	...	...	1.91 (0.36)	11.36 (0.74)
Percent 12 years of school	...	...	...	...	...	...	...	...	−0.33 (0.01)
Percent 1–3 years college	...	...	...	...	...	...	...	...	−0.16 (0.01)
Percent 4+ years college	...	...	...	...	...	...	...	...	−0.19 (0.02)
Percent manufacturing	...	...	...	...	...	...	...	...	−0.0002 (0.005)

Source: Author's calculations. The number of observations = 1,323 (49 states of birth × 9 regions × 3 cohorts). The percent of the work force in the manufacturing industry was computed from the 1980 census (sample A), using all workers (male and female) aged eighteen to sixty-five. The mean quality within a region of residence was calculated using the 1920–29, 1930–39, and 1940–49 birth cohorts.

a. Second-stage model: rate of return = $\alpha + \alpha_b + \alpha_{r(s)} + \alpha_c + \alpha_{bc} + \alpha_{r(s)c}$. The numbers in parentheses are Eicker-White standard errors.

b. The omitted education category is < 12 years. The pupil-teacher ratio and term length were divided by 100 in the regression. The attendance-based pupil-teacher ratio was used.

Column 1 reports estimates of the effect of Q, as measured by the pupil-teacher ratio, on α_{bc}. We use the more interpretable pupil-teacher ratio based on days attended rather than the measure based on days enrolled. The only difference between columns 1 and 2 is the addition of two other quality measures: teacher salary and term length. The third specification is similar to the second, except that α_b is suppressed, resulting in a single intercept term rather than a set of state-of-birth-specific intercepts.[45]

The coefficients in columns 1 through 3 are not identical to Card and Krueger's because we impose linearity instead of 2 percent linearity in education, use an attendance-based instead of an enrollment-based pupil-teacher ratio, use a different definition of teacher wages, and report different standard errors.[46] Despite these differences, our empirical results are very similar to theirs.[47] Using days attended instead of days enrolled weakens but does not eliminate the estimated impact of the pupil-teacher ratio on earnings.

In the first two columns of table 7-7, which include state-of-birth intercepts, the effect of quality is identified by using variation in the rates of return for state of birth and cohort of birth, removing cohort and state-of-birth means. Column 3 reports results from a model that suppresses the state-of-birth intercepts. This specification adds back the state-of-birth means and so identifies the effect of quality by using variation in the rates of return for state of birth and cohort of birth, removing only cohort-of-birth means. The estimated effect is not robust to the exclusion of the state-of-birth intercepts: the third column shows the weakest quality effects and frequently the sign on the pupil-teacher ratio reverses. However, if one wished to remove state-of-birth fixed effects from the estimated rate of return, the estimates reported in the third column would be of no interest.

The results for 1970 and 1990 data are found in tables 7C-1 and 7C-2 in appendix C.[48] For the first three columns, which extend Card

45. The numbers in column 3 show the total effect of quality operating through both α_b and α_{bc}. Columns 1 and 2 show the effect of quality operating through α_{bc} alone.

46. We use Eicker-White robust standard errors in the second stage instead of estimating by generalized least squares (GLS). This usually reduces the magnitude of the quality coefficients slightly, but the differences are not substantial. An appendix showing comparable results using GLS estimation as well as results using the enrollment-based pupil-teacher ratio is available from the authors on request.

47. When we used Card and Krueger's exact model and quality data, we were able to replicate their estimated coefficients almost exactly.

48. We focus on the 1980 census data to facilitate comparison with Card and Krueger's results. Note that the 1970 sample contains one more cohort than do the 1980 and 1990

Table 7-8. *Effect of Hypothetical Improvements in Quality on Earnings for High School Graduates (HSG) and College Graduates (CG), Extension of Linear Model, Census Years 1970, 1980, 1990*[a]

Percent

	1970		1980		1990	
Change in quality	HSG	CG	HSG	CG	HSG	CG
Decrease pupil-teacher ratio (attendance-based) by five	↑ 5.33	↑ 7.12	↑ 3.76	↑ 5.01	↑ 6.40	↑ 8.53
Increase relative teacher wage by 30 percent	↑ 4.32	↑ 5.76	↑ 7.49	↑ 9.98	↑ 9.32	↑ 12.4
Increase term length by ten days	↑ 0.89	↑ 1.18	↑ 1.28	↑ 1.71	↑ 7.74	↑ 10.3

Source: Authors' calculations. Because returns are assumed to be linear in quality, the effects of other magnitudes of quality changes are easily found by rescaling the numbers in the table.

a. The coefficients are given in column 2 of table 7-7 and in appendix C, tables 7C-1, 7C-2.

and Krueger's analysis to different data sets, the pattern found in the 1980 data of significant quality coefficients is upheld in the 1970 and 1990 data. The insignificance of the coefficient on the term-length variable in 1970 is one exception. The quality effects estimated for 1990 are stronger (in absolute value terms) and are statistically more significant.

As an aid in interpreting the estimated quality (Q_{bc}) coefficients, table 7-8 shows the effects of hypothetical improvements in schooling quality on earnings for two education levels. No single quality variable emerges as the most important for affecting a change in earnings. The potential increases in earnings from changes in the relative teacher wage and term length are larger in 1990. This pattern of amplification of estimated quality effects in 1990 is consistent with other evidence that the returns to schooling and ability increased between 1980 and 1990. Contrary to claims in the literature, the effect of schooling inputs on earnings increased over the period 1980–90 as the returns to education increased.[49]

The remaining columns in table 7-7 extend the model beyond the original Card and Krueger specification. The model reported in specification 4 differs from those in the previous columns by allowing each element of quality to have a cohort-specific effect. The estimates in that specification thus indicate how measures of schooling quality affect returns to education for different cohorts. As tables 7-7, 7C-1, and 7C-2

---

samples. We include the 1940–49 cohort in the 1970 sample so that one cohort may be followed across all three census years.

49. Recall, though, that aggregate quality measures were virtually identical across the states by 1940 (see figures 7-1 and 7-2). It is therefore important to distinguish between changes in the quality measures observed in the data and potential changes.

show, estimated effects of the pupil-teacher ratio weaken or become perverse for more recent cohorts. This evidence supports the argument of diminishing variability in schooling quality in recent cohorts. Contrary to this argument, however, variability in term length also declined considerably, but its estimated effect is strongest for more recent cohorts.[50]

The specifications reported in columns 5 and 6 investigate how regional aggregates of schooling quality affect the regional component of the return to education ($\alpha_{r(s)}$ and $\alpha_{r(s)c}$). Earnings functions are not solely determined by individual attributes but also depend on how the attributes are valued in the labor market. Therefore, we examine how the return to education is affected by variables that describe the local labor market, including the aggregate stocks of human capital. We allow the regional component of the educational return ($\alpha_{r(s)}$ and $\alpha_{r(s)c}$ in equation 7-6) to depend on regional demand and supply aggregates Z:

$$\alpha_{r(s)c} = Z_{r(s)c} \, \pi,$$

$$\alpha_{r(s)} = Z_{r(s)} \, \tilde{\pi}.$$

It is through these channels that the first-order effects of economic aggregates should flow. The regional aggregates (Z) considered are average schooling quality, education levels, and industrial composition.

The estimates reported in columns 5 and 6 of tables 7-7, 7C-1, and 7C-2 are consistent with a supply-shift hypothesis. When regional averages of the quality measures are added to the model, higher aggregate quality levels produce lower rates of return.[51] In column 7 we consider additional regional aggregates: the regional stocks of different levels of education and the percent of the work force in manufacturing, interpreted as a demand shifter. In this specification the coefficients on the quality variables are not consistent with the hypothesis that aggregates act like supply shifters. Instead, higher levels of quality in the region of residence increase the returns to an individual's education. The variables capturing the educational distribution of the work force are highly statistically significant. Increases in the proportion of the labor force with schooling above high school depress returns at the mean, while increases in dropouts raise the return at the mean. This is consistent with comple-

50. The coefficients in column 4 appear to be most strongly affected by the estimation method. Generalized least squares yields more significant quality coefficients than ordinary least squares (OLS) with Eicker-White standard errors.
51. Recall that a positive coefficient on the pupil-teacher ratio means that as quality worsens, the rate of return rises.

mentarity in production for inputs across different skill groups. An increase in the proportion of workers near the educational mean depresses mean earnings. Except for 1980, increases in the percentage of the work force in manufacturing reduce the returns to schooling (tables 7C-1 and 7C-2). Specifications 5 through 7 also reveal that the estimated quality effects operating through α_{bc} are robust to the inclusion of regional aggregates in the model. The coefficients on individual state-of-birth quality measures are not in variant to the addition of the regional aggregates (compare with column 2).

Overall, these results show that two additional census years replicate Card and Krueger's general findings of statistically and numerically significant quality effects. Quality effects are especially strong in 1990.

The Effect of Quality Operating through the Intercepts of the Card-Krueger Model

The earlier work of Johnson and Stafford models the effect of schooling quality operating through intercepts of the earnings equation rather than through slope parameters.[52] Quality has a uniform effect on log earnings regardless of the level of education, as is shown in figure 7-3A. However, the nonparametric rank tests discussed in conjunction with the figure decisively reject a simple monotonic relationship between quality and earnings. Therefore, we do not replicate Johnson and Stafford's model here.

Nevertheless, their findings motivate us to consider the effect of quality on the intercept parameters in Card and Krueger's model. This is an interesting exercise because it informs us how quality may operate through yet another channel, one largely ignored by Card and Krueger in an attempt to control for fixed-effects bias arising from omitted state-of-birth-specific and state-of-residence-specific intercepts. In the ANOVA notation, the equation decomposing the model intercepts into the cohort, state-of-birth, and state-of-residence components is

$$(7\text{-}7) \qquad \tilde{\theta}_{sbc} = \theta + \theta_s + \theta_b + \theta_c + \theta_{bc} + \theta_{sc} + \theta_{sb} + \theta_{sbc}.$$

We maintain the assumption of their model that $\theta_{sbc} = \theta_{sb} = 0$ and now

---

52. Johnson and Stafford (1973) test for both a slope and an intercept effect and find only the intercept effect to be significant, so they use an intercept model as their preferred specification.

estimate the effect of the empirical measures of schooling quality on θ_b, θ_{bc}, θ_s, and θ_{sc}.

In columns 1 through 3 of table 7-9, the state-of-birth intercept terms are parameterized as functions of quality. This table contains results for the 1980 census, and analogous tables for 1970 and 1990, tables 7C-3 and 7C-4, are found in appendix C. The specifications given by each of the columns are analogous to those discussed in relation to the slope parameters. In our treatment of the intercept terms, we use state of residence instead of region of residence to index the current location variables. Most of the estimated coefficients on the quality variables are statistically significant. In table 7C-3, for 1970, the pupil-teacher ratio operating through the intercepts supports the quality hypothesis and reinforces the slope effect seen earlier in table 7C-1. In 1980 and 1990, however, the effect of the pupil-teacher ratio operating through the intercept sometimes reinforces and sometimes counters the slope effect, depending on the model specification. For the term-length and teacher-salary variables, we find evidence that the effect of quality on earnings operates through the intercept parameters in a direction opposite to its effect through the slope coefficients for all three years. Hence focusing only on an estimated quality effect operating through slope coefficients leads to an *overstatement* of the effect of the quality variables on earnings. Specification 4, which allows the quality coefficients to differ across cohorts, generally supports these conclusions.

In columns 5 through 7, the state-of-residence intercepts are parameterized to be functions of regional aggregates. The signs of the coefficients on regional average quality measures, $Q_{r(s)}$, are affected by whether other regional aggregates are included in the model. The coefficients are not always consistent across census years. The coefficients of the state-of-birth quality variables, Q_{bc}, are robust to the inclusion of these aggregates.

Questioning Linearity

Another critical assumption, and one that is standard throughout the literature, is the specification that log-earnings equations are linear in years of education.[53] This assumption implies that the percent earnings gain from a one-year increase in schooling attainment is the same from

---

53. An exception is a study by Wachtel (1976), in which the quality relationship is estimated separately by educational attainment level.

Table 7-9. *Effect of Schooling Quality on Fixed Effects, Linear Model, 1980 Census*[a]

				Model specification					
	(1)	(2)	(3)	(4) $\theta_{bc} = \varphi_c Q_{bc}$			(5) $\theta_{bc} = \varphi Q_{bc}$ $\theta_s + \theta_{sc} = \pi_1 Q_{r(s)}$	(6) $\theta_{bc} = \varphi Q_{bc}$ $\theta_s + \theta_{r(s)c} = \pi_1 Q_{r(s)}$	(7) $\theta_{bc} = \varphi Q_{bc}$ $\theta_s + \theta_{r(s)c} = \pi_1 Q_{r(s)} + \pi_2 D_{r(s)}$
Measure[b]	$\theta_{bc} = \theta Q_{bc}$	$\theta_{bc} = \varphi Q_{bc}$	$\theta_b + \theta_{bc} = \varphi Q_{bc}$	1920–29	1930–39	1940–49			
Pupil-teacher ratio	0.93 (0.14)	1.02 (0.14)	−0.38 (0.05)	−0.19 (0.08)	−0.59 (0.07)	−0.40 (0.09)	1.02 (0.23)	1.02 (0.23)	1.02 (0.17)
Term length	...	−0.18 (0.05)	−0.52 (0.02)	−0.41 (0.03)	−0.60 (0.04)	−0.69 (0.07)	−0.18 (0.09)	−0.18 (0.09)	−0.18 (0.06)
Relative teacher salary	...	−0.27 (0.02)	−0.10 (0.01)	−0.13 (0.01)	−0.08 (0.01)	−0.07 (0.02)	−0.27 (0.04)	−0.27 (0.04)	−0.27 (0.03)
Demand and supply aggregates									
Regional average pupil-teacher ratio	...	...	...	...	...	...	−0.03 (0.001)	−0.02 (0.001)	0.11 (0.002)
Regional average term length	...	...	...	...	...	...	...	−0.01 (0.0003)	−0.02 (0.001)
Percent 12 years of school	...	...	...	...	...	...	...	...	0.06 (0.001)
Percent 1–3 years college	...	...	...	...	...	...	...	...	0.04 (0.001)
Percent 4+ years college	...	...	...	...	...	...	...	...	0.03 (0.002)
Percent manufacturing	...	...	...	...	...	...	...	...	0.002 (0.001)

Source: Authors' calculations. The number of observations = 7,497 (49 states of birth × 51 states of residence × 3 cohorts). The percent of the work force in the manufacturing industry was computed from the 1980 census (sample A), using male and female workers aged eighteen to sixty-five. The mean quality within a region of residence was calculated using the 1920–29, 1930–39, and 1940–49 birth cohorts.

a. Second-stage model: $\theta_{bsc} = \theta + \theta_b + \theta_s + \theta_c + \theta_{bc} + \theta_{sc} + \theta_{r(s)c}$. The numbers in parentheses are Eicker-White standard errors.

b. The pupil-teacher ratio and term length were divided by 100 in the regression. The attendance-based pupil-teacher ratio was used.

the ninth to tenth grade as it is from three to four years of college. The linear model does not allow for possible sheepskin effects, which might be expected to occur on completion of a high school or college degree. It constrains national and regional labor-market shocks to have the same effect on the rate of return to schooling at all schooling levels. Furthermore, the linearity assumption imposes a severe limitation on the way quality is allowed to affect earnings. In the model given by equations 7-4 and 7-5, quality enters only interactively with education, imposing the restriction that a change in quality has a progressively larger effect at higher levels of educational attainment.

We test the linearity assumption by adding sheepskin effects (dummy variables for grade completion) at grades 8, 12, and 16 to equation 7-4. We then perform simple F-tests on the significance of the sheepskin effects, presented in table 7-10.[54] The data strongly reject linearity for most cohorts in the three census samples and support the notion of sheepskin effects, especially for postsecondary schooling. To illustrate the magnitude of the sheepskin coefficients, they are plotted for the 1980 census, 1930–39 cohort, in figure 7-4. Because the census sample sizes are rather large, there is a tendency to reject the null hypothesis of no sheepskin effects using conventional statistical levels. We therefore show the significance of the coefficients at the 0.1 percent significance level (+ indicates significant at this level). There is clear evidence of discrete jumps in the return to education, especially for completion of a college degree. There is no support for the linearity hypothesis, a finding consistent with previously reported results in Thomas Hungerford and Gary Solon's study.[55]

A Nonlinear Model

The data indicate that the return to additional years of education varies with the level of education, so we revise the earnings model to allow for nonlinearities in the log-earnings equation. Given the evidence of strong and statistically significant sheepskin effects at the college level, we estimate a model that allows for discrete jumps in the return to education at one to three years of college and at four or more years of

---

54. The F-tests are joint across all states of birth for each cohort at each level of schooling (grades 8 and 12 and four years of college).
55. Hungerford and Solon (1987). See also Jaeger and Page (1996).

Table 7-10. **F-Tests for Linear Functional Form by Birth Cohort, 1910–59, and by Education Level, Census Years 1970, 1980, 1990**

Birth cohort	1970			1980			1990		
	8 years	12 years	16 years	8 years	12 years	16 years	8 years	12 years	16 years
1910–19									
F-statistic	1.62	0.90	8.38	...	...	...	...	...	...
P-value	0.00	0.66	0.00						
1920–29									
F-statistic	1.35	1.15	14.45	1.31	2.48	25.5	...	...	...
P-value	0.05	0.22	0.00	0.00	0.00	0.00			
1930–39									
F-statistic	1.96	1.04	9.27	3.30	6.91	35.1	3.67	2.00	14.07
P-value	0.00	0.40	0.00	0.00	0.00	0.00	0.00	0.00	0.00
1940–49									
F-statistic	3.56	3.91	9.15	4.21	12.6	22.1	6.21	2.99	16.37
P-value	0.00	0.00	0.00	0.00	0.00	0.00	0.00	0.00	0.00
1950–59									
F-statistic	...	...	...	...	...	...	14.35	16.22	49.53
P-value							0.00	0.00	0.00

Source: Authors' calculations.

Figure 7-4. *Evidence of Sheepskin Effects in the Return to Education, 1930–39 Cohort, 1980 Census*

Number of states

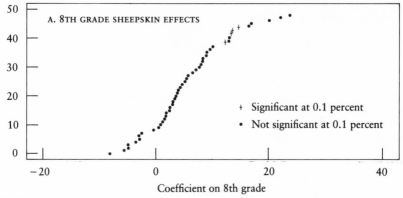

Coefficient on 8th grade

Number of states

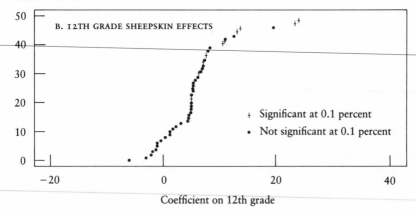

Coefficient on 12th grade

Number of states

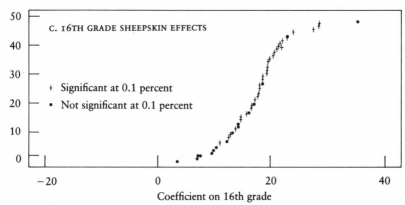

Coefficient on 16th grade

college.[56] Thus the model is more flexible than the standard linear model.[57]

Since the samples we use are very large, it might be argued that the statistical rejections reported above are of little economic consequence. Linearity may not be grossly at odds with the data. If this is so, relaxing the linearity assumption would then have only a slight impact on estimates of the effect of quality on schooling. We test and reject this hypothesis below.

The nonlinear model can be written as

$$(7\text{-}8) \quad y_{ibsc} = \tilde{\theta}_{sbc} + \tilde{\alpha}^0_{r(s)bc} \cdot e_{isbc} + \tilde{\alpha}^1_{r(s)bc} \cdot \tau^1_{isbc}$$

$$+ \tilde{\alpha}^2_{r(s)bc} \cdot \tau^2_{isbc} + X_{isbc} \cdot \beta_c + \epsilon_{isbc},$$

where

$$\tilde{\alpha}^j_{r(s)bc} = \tilde{\alpha}^j_c + \tilde{\alpha}^j_b + \tilde{\alpha}^j_{r(s)} + \alpha^j_{bc} + \tilde{\alpha}^j_{r(s)c}, j = 0,1,2,$$

$$\tilde{\theta}_{sbc} = \tilde{\theta}_c + \tilde{\theta}_b + \tilde{\theta}_{bc} + \tilde{\theta}_s + \tilde{\theta}_{sc},$$

$$\tau^1_{isbc} = \begin{cases} 1 & \text{if individual } i \text{ completed some college but} \\ & \text{less than four years,} \\ 0 & \text{else,} \end{cases}$$

$$\tau^2_{isbc} = \begin{cases} 1 & \text{if individual } i \text{ completed four or} \\ & \text{more years of college,} \\ 0 & \text{else,} \end{cases}$$

and where e_{isbc} is actual years of education. The term X_{isbc} represents the same demographic variables as used in the linear model (defined under equation 7-4).

Since $\tilde{\alpha}^0_{r(s)bc}$ represents the per year return to school, it is multiplied by the total number of years of education to obtain the total return to

56. Since each additional education category adds from 76 to 120 parameters to the model (depending on the specification), we did not introduce more than two marginal returns. Even though the nonlinear model is highly parameterized, our sample sizes are large (see appendix A) and the coefficients are still precisely determined.

57. Our model also improves over a model that assumes 2 percent linearity, which constrains persons below the 2 percent threshold in the cohort-of-birth educational distribution to have the earnings of a person with no education (zero years of school up to the 2 percent cutoff are grouped together). Such a constraint is extreme for the later cohorts, for whom the 2 percent threshold is as high as nine years of school.

schooling for someone with a high school degree or less. For example, for someone with thirteen years of school, the total return to education would be the linear effect plus the marginal effect, $\tilde{\alpha}^0_{r(s)bc}$ *13 + $\tilde{\alpha}^1_{r(s)bc}$. If an individual has a master's degree (assumed to be eighteen years of school), his or her return is given by $\tilde{\alpha}^0_{r(s)bc}$ *18 + $\tilde{\alpha}^2_{r(s)bc}$. To illustrate the magnitude of the estimated education returns for the model given in equation 7-8, figure 7-5 plots them for a few representative states.

To determine the effect of schooling quality on the rate of return to education, we parameterize the different components of the return as functions of the quality variables. Note that the second-stage equation is estimated separately for the linear base return, $\tilde{\alpha}^0_{r(s)bc}$, and for each of the marginal returns, $\tilde{\alpha}^1_{r(s)bc}$ and $\tilde{\alpha}^2_{r(s)bc}$. As with the linear model, we consider the effect of quality in the state of birth operating through the state-of-birth components, $\tilde{\alpha}^j_b$ and $\tilde{\alpha}^j_{bc}$, as well as the effect of aggregate quality on regional labor-market conditions, operating through region-of-residence components, $\tilde{\alpha}^j_{r(s)}$ and $\tilde{\alpha}^j_{r(s)c}$.

Tables 7-11 through 7-13 present the 1980 census results obtained from estimating $\tilde{\alpha}^j_{r(s)bc}$ in equation 7-8 and using those estimates as the dependent variables in second-stage regressions. The procedure we follow is analogous to that described for the linear model, and the estimated coefficients can be compared to those in table 7-7. In specifications 3 through 4 of table 7-11, which parameterize $\tilde{\alpha}^j_b$ and $\tilde{\alpha}^j_{bc}$ as functions of quality, the signs of the quality coefficients are often reversed or else become statistically insignificant. Interestingly, support for an effect of secondary school quality on earnings comes through the marginal return for some college or for a college degree (see tables 7-12 and 7-13). This finding is consistent with evidence reported by Paul Wachtel.[58] As with the linear model, estimated quality effects in the nonlinear model differ in magnitude depending on whether fixed effects for state of birth are included. The final three specifications examine the effect of quality operating through the regional return, $\tilde{\alpha}^j_{r(s)}$ and $\tilde{\alpha}^j_{r(s)c}$. The last column upholds our earlier finding that higher average levels of quality among workers in the region of residence lead to increased returns. However, the level of educational attainment in the region has mixed effects, and the coefficient estimates reverse signs across census years.

The second-stage regression results for 1970 and 1990 census data are given in tables 7C-5 through 7C-7 and 7C-8 through 7C-10, respectively. For 1970 there is some evidence of an effect of term length on the base

58. Wachtel (1976).

Figure 7-5. *Plots of Estimated Education Returns for Four States, 1930–39 Cohort, 1980 Census*

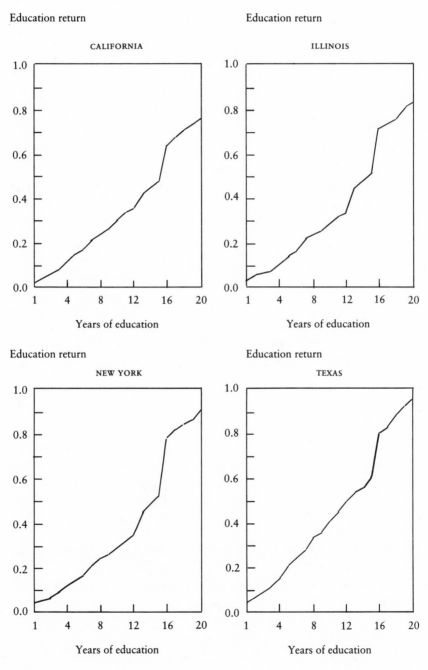

Table 7-11. *Effect of Schooling Quality on the Linear Base Return to Education, Nonlinear Model, 1980 Census*[a]

				Model specification					
	(1) $\alpha_{bc} = \varphi Q_{bc}$	(2) $\alpha_{bc} = \varphi Q_{bc}$	(3) $\alpha_b + \alpha_{bc} = \varphi Q_{bc}$	(4) $\alpha_{bc} = \varphi_c Q_{bc}$			(5) $\alpha_{bc} = \varphi Q_{bc}$ $\alpha_{r(s)} + \alpha_{r(s)c} = \pi_1 Q_{r(s)}$	(6) $\alpha_{bc} = \varphi Q_{bc}$ $\alpha_{r(s)} + \alpha_{r(s)c} = \pi_1 Q_{r(s)}$	(7) $\alpha_{bc} = \varphi Q_{bc}$ $\alpha_{r(s)} + \alpha_{r(s)c} = \pi_1 Q_{r(s)} + \pi_2 D_{r(s)}$
Measure[b]				1920–29	1930–39	1940–49			
Pupil-teacher ratio	−3.27 (1.83)	−2.95 (1.86)	3.53 (0.71)	3.97 (0.92)	6.21 (1.31)	−1.14 (1.51)	−2.95 (2.79)	−2.95 (2.79)	−2.94 (2.46)
Term length	...	−1.89 (0.67)	0.49 (0.33)	−0.037 (0.40)	1.20 (0.66)	0.08 (1.07)	−1.89 (1.08)	−1.89 (1.08)	−1.89 (1.08)
Relative teacher salary	...	1.03 (0.36)	0.06 (0.12)	0.48 (0.11)	−1.13 (0.26)	0.88 (0.28)	1.03 (0.50)	1.03 (0.50)	1.03 (0.49)
Demand and supply aggregates									
Regional average pupil-teacher ratio	...	...	...	...	...	...	0.28 (0.02)	0.28 (0.02)	−0.11 (0.04)
Regional average term length	...	...	...	...	...	...	...	−0.002 (0.004)	−0.08 (0.01)
Percent 12 years of school	...	...	...	...	...	...	...	...	−0.18 (0.01)
Percent 1–3 years college	...	...	...	...	...	...	...	...	−0.09 (0.02)
Percent 4+ years college	...	...	...	...	...	...	...	...	−0.25 (0.02)
Percent manufacturing	...	...	...	...	...	...	...	...	−0.03 (0.01)

Source: Author's calculations. The number of observations = 1,323 (49 states of birth × 9 regions × 3 cohorts). The percent of the work force in the manufacturing industry was computed from the 1980 census (sample A) using male and female workers aged eighteen to sixty-five. The mean quality within a region of residence was calculated using the 1920–29, 1930–39, and 1940–49 birth cohorts.

a. Second-stage model: rate of return = $\alpha + \alpha_b + \alpha_{r(s)} + \alpha_c + \alpha_{bc} + \alpha_{r(s)c}$. The numbers in parentheses are Eicker-White standard errors.

b. The pupil-teacher ratio and term length were divided by 100 in the regression. The attendance-based pupil-teacher ratio was used.

Table 7-12. *Effect of Schooling Quality on the Marginal Rate of Return to One to Three Years of College, Nonlinear Model, 1980 Census*[a]

Measure[b]	(1) $\alpha_{bc} = \varphi Q_{bc}$	(2) $\alpha_{bc} = \varphi Q_{bc}$	(3) $\alpha_b + \alpha_{bc} = \varphi Q_{bc}$	(4) $\alpha_{bc} = \varphi_c Q_{bc}$ 1920–29	(4) 1930–39	(4) 1940–49	(5) $\alpha_{bc} = \varphi Q_{bc}$; $\alpha_{r(s)} + \alpha_{r(s)c} = \pi_1 Q_{r(s)}$	(6) $\alpha_{bc} = \varphi Q_{bc}$; $\alpha_{r(s)} + \alpha_{r(s)c} = \pi_1 Q_{r(s)}$	(7) $\alpha_{bc} = \varphi Q_{bc}$; $\alpha_{r(s)} + \alpha_{r(s)c} = \pi_1 Q_{r(s)} + \pi_2 D_{r(s)}$
Pupil-teacher ratio	−23.51 (13.03)	−29.01 (12.59)	12.25 (3.79)	−5.95 (7.06)	18.99 (5.58)	32.24 (5.66)	−29.00 (14.63)	−29.01 (14.10)	−29.01 (13.22)
Term length	…	17.36 (3.30)	15.04 (1.68)	16.28 (2.48)	10.12 (3.00)	17.85 (4.85)	17.36 (4.45)	17.36 (4.13)	17.36 (3.70)
Relative teacher salary	…	6.56 (2.21)	2.97 (0.74)	2.62 (1.15)	8.44 (1.02)	−5.18 (1.08)	6.56 (2.52)	6.56 (2.44)	6.56 (2.32)
Demand and supply aggregates									
Regional average pupil-teacher ratio	…	…	…	…	…	…	−0.18 (0.08)	−0.39 (0.07)	−2.16 (0.19)
Regional average term length	…	…	…	…	…	…	…	0.32 (0.02)	0.43 (0.06)
Percent 12 years of school	…	…	…	…	…	…	…	…	−0.89 (0.09)
Percent 1–3 years college	…	…	…	…	…	…	…	…	−0.37 (0.09)
Percent 4+ years college	…	…	…	…	…	…	…	…	−0.31 (0.13)
Percent manufacturing	…	…	…	…	…	…	…	…	0.24 (0.04)

Source: Author's calculations. The number of observations = 1,323 (49 states of birth × 9 regions × 3 cohorts). The percent of the work force in the manufacturing industry was computed from the 1980 census (a sample) using male and female workers aged eighteen to sixty-five. The mean quality within a region of residence was calculated using the 1920–29, 1930–39, and 1940–49 birth cohorts.

a. Second-stage model: rate of return = $\alpha + \alpha_b + \alpha_{r(s)} + \alpha_c + \alpha_{bc} + \alpha_{r(s)c}$. The numbers in parentheses are Eicker-White standard errors.

b. The pupil-teacher ratio and term length were divided by 100 in the regression. The attendance-based pupil-teacher ratio was used.

Table 7-13. *Effect of Schooling Quality on the Marginal Rate of Return to Four or More Years of College, Nonlinear Model, 1980 Census*[a]

				Model specification					
	(1) $\alpha_{bc} = \varphi Q_{bc}$	(2) $\alpha_{bc} = \varphi Q_{bc}$	(3) $\alpha_b + \alpha_{bc} = \varphi Q_{bc}$	(4) $\alpha_{bc} = \varphi_c Q_{bc}$			(5) $\alpha_{bc} = \varphi Q_{bc}$; $\alpha_{r(s)} + \alpha_{r(s)c} = \pi_1 Q_{r(s)}$	(6) $\alpha_{bc} = \varphi Q_{bc}$; $\alpha_{r(s)} + \alpha_{r(s)c} = \pi_1 Q_{r(s)}$	(7) $\alpha_{bc} = \varphi Q_{bc}$; $\alpha_{r(s)} + \alpha_{r(s)c} = \pi_1 Q_{r(s)} + \pi_2 D_{r(s)}$
Measure[b]				1920–29	1930–39	1940–49			
Pupil-teacher ratio	−22.35 (16.53)	−28.14 (16.35)	−4.54 (6.00)	−22.36 (11.13)	−10.10 (8.46)	34.23 (9.56)	−28.14 (20.64)	−28.14 (20.25)	−28.14 (18.56)
Term length	...	17.95 (5.01)	9.19 (2.59)	7.28 (3.53)	2.77 (4.80)	30.46 (6.86)	17.95 (7.10)	17.95 (6.88)	17.95 (6.10)
Relative teacher salary	...	7.41 (2.42)	4.99 (0.82)	4.39 (0.97)	12.46 (1.64)	−5.03 (1.65)	7.41 (3.19)	7.41 (3.12)	7.41 (2.83)
Demand and supply aggregates									
Regional average pupil-teacher ratio	...	...	...	...	...	...	−0.60 (0.12)	−0.77 (0.13)	−2.32 (0.29)
Regional average term length	...	...	...	...	...	...	...	0.27 (0.03)	0.35 (0.09)
Percent 12 years of school	...	...	...	...	...	...	...	...	−1.14 (0.13)
Percent 1–3 years college	...	...	...	...	...	...	...	...	−0.53 (0.13)
Percent 4+ years college	...	...	...	...	...	...	...	...	0.50 (0.19)
Percent manufacturing	...	...	...	...	...	...	...	...	0.27 (0.06)

Source: Author's calculations. The number of observations = 1,323 (49 states of birth × 9 regions × 3 cohorts). The percent of the work force in the manufacturing industry was computed from the 1980 census (sample A) using male and female workers aged eighteen to sixty-five. The mean quality within a region of residence was calculated using the 1920–29, 1930–39, and 1940–49 birth cohorts.

a. Second-stage model: rate of return = $\alpha + \alpha_b + \alpha_{r(s)} + \alpha_c + \alpha_{bc} + \alpha_{r(s)c}$. The numbers in parentheses are Eicker-White standard errors.

b. The pupil-teacher ratio and term length were divided by 100 in the regression. The attendance-based pupil-teacher ratio was used.

Table 7-14. *Effect of Hypothetical Improvements in Quality on Earnings for High School Graduates (HSG) and College Graduates (CG), Nonlinear Model including Region-Education Interactions, Census Years 1970, 1980, 1990*[a]

Percent

	1970		1980		1990	
Change in quality	*HSG*	*CG*	*HSG*	*CG*	*HSG*	*CG*
Decrease pupil-teacher ratio (attendance-based) by five	↓ 1.39	↑ 0.89	↑ 1.77	↑ 3.77	↓ 5.08	↓ 2.21
Increase relative teacher wage by 30 percent	↑ 0.79	↑ 1.81	↑ 3.71	↑ 7.17	↑ 6.16	↑ 6.95
Increase term length by ten days	↑ 3.24	↑ 2.00	↓ 2.27	↓ 1.23	↑ 5.06	↑ 7.14

Source: Authors' calculations.
a. The coefficients are given in column 2 of tables 7-11 through 7-13 and appendix C, tables 7C-5 through 7C-10.

return in specification 2, but the signs of the other estimated quality coefficients are generally inconsistent with the quality hypothesis. Support for an effect of quality on earnings again comes mainly through the marginal return to attending some college or to completing college. For the 1990 census data, the pupil-teacher ratio is consistently of the expected sign only when the dependent variable is the marginal return to completing four or more years of college.

Relaxing the false assumption of linearity yields models that provide little support for an effect of quality on earnings.[59] The weak surviving support for the hypothesis is the estimated effect of quality on the marginal returns to college. It is likely that students from higher-quality schools attend better colleges, in which case part of the estimated effect of secondary schooling quality is more properly attributable to college quality, a variable omitted from our regression. However, in results available from the authors, we find that when college quality is entered as a direct argument in the rate of return equations, our estimates of the effect of precollege quality on the return to schooling are not affected.

To illustrate the effects of schooling quality on earnings implied by the estimated coefficients, we again tabulate the effects of counterfactual changes in quality in table 7-14. The results are unstable across measures and years and do not provide strong support for the quality hypothesis.

---

59. The one exception appears to be quality operating through regional aggregates, which has a fairly consistent effect on returns in both the linear and nonlinear models for each census year.

Table 7-15. *F-Tests for Significance of Region of Birth–Region of Residence Interactions, Both in Intercepts and in Slopes for the Linear Model, by Birth Cohort 1910–59, Census Years 1970, 1980, 1990*[a]

Birth cohort	1970		1980		1990	
	θ_{rb}	α_{rb}	θ_{rb}	α_{rb}	θ_{rb}	α_{rb}
1910–19						
F-statistic	1.47	2.20	. . .	. . .	. . .	. . .
P-value	0.01	0.00				
1920–29						
F-statistic	1.96	2.44	1.81	2.25	. . .	. . .
P-value	0.00	0.00	0.00	0.00		
1930–39						
F-statistic	1.67	1.67	2.40	2.59	2.02	2.51
P-value	0.00	0.00	0.00	0.00	0.00	0.00
1940–49						
F-statistic	2.33	1.64	3.06	3.03	3.62	4.65
P-value	0.00	0.00	0.00	0.00	0.00	0.00
1950–59						
F-statistic	. . .	. . .	. . .	. . .	6.77	7.15
P-value					0.00	0.00

Source: Authors' calculations.
a. θ_{rb} is an intercept term and α_{rb} is a slope term for education. Each of the tests is joint over sixty-four coefficients.

Accounting for Comparative Advantage by Region of Birth in Regions of Residence

Earlier in the chapter we discussed the importance of random migration by individuals across states to securing identification of state-of-birth effects from region-of-residence effects in aggregate-data models. We provided evidence that individuals from particular states of birth tend to migrate to particular states of residence, presumably because of lower migration costs or higher expected gains. If their expected gains are correlated with realized values of the disturbance term in the earnings equation, ϵ_{ibsc}, the disturbances are no longer exogenous with respect to the regressors, and identification strategies like the one pursued by Card and Krueger break down.

To allow for the possibility that individuals born in a certain state may have a comparative advantage in particular geographic regions, we relax the assumption that $\alpha_{r(s)r(b)} = 0$ and $\alpha_{r(s)r(b)c} = 0$ within the context of the linear model. *F*-tests of the assumption of no interactions, reported in table 7-15 for each cohort in each census year, decisively reject it. Therefore, we augment the model in equation 7-4 to include region-of-birth–region-of-residence interactions both in intercepts and in slopes. In the notation from the earlier section, the model is written as

$$y_{isbc} = \tilde{\theta}_{sbc} + X_{isbc} \cdot \tilde{\beta}_c + E_{isbc} \cdot \tilde{\alpha}_{r(s)bc} + \epsilon_{isbc}$$

$$\tilde{\theta}_{sbc} = \theta + \theta_s + \theta_b + \theta_c + \theta_{bc} + \theta_{sc} + \theta_{r(s)r(b)} + \theta_{r(s)r(b)c}$$

$$\tilde{\alpha}_{r(s)bc} = \alpha + \alpha_{r(s)} + \alpha_b + \alpha_c + \alpha_{bc}$$

(7-9)
$$+ \alpha_{r(s)c} + \alpha_{r(s)r(b)} + \alpha_{r(s)r(b)c}$$

$$i = 1, \ldots, I, s = 1, \ldots, S; b = 1, \ldots, B,$$

$$c = 1, \ldots, C, r = 1, \ldots, R,$$

where $\tilde{\beta}_c$ is constrained to be the same across states but is permitted to vary across cohorts. Interactions are introduced in terms of regions of birth, $r(b)$, and regions of residence, $r(s)$, instead of states of birth and states of residence.

The effect of quality on the return to education is estimated in two stages. First, estimates of the total return to education, $\tilde{\alpha}_{r(s)}r_b$, are obtained for each (b,s,c) cell from equation 7-9. In the second stage, components of the return to education are parameterized as functions of quality as before. In the most general treatment of the interaction terms, $\alpha_{r(s)r(b)}$ and $\alpha_{r(s)r(b)c}$, the quality effect operating through α_b and α_{bc} could be estimated without imposing restrictions on the interactions. This general model is difficult to interpret. However, when the hypothesis of no interactions is tested with the general model, most interaction coefficients are statistically significant and the estimated quality effects become statistically insignificant or perverse for both linear- and nonlinear-in-education models.[60]

In this study, we parameterize the interaction terms in a simple and interpretable way. We relax the assumption maintained in all the models considered thus far that the effect of a unit increase in schooling quality on the rate of return to education is the same across regions. We also allow the rate of return to education for individuals born in region b and living in region r to depend on the physical distance between regions.

---

60. Heckman, Layne-Farrar, and Todd (1996) discuss the problem—common to all models with interactions—of interpreting non-zero interactions. Estimated quality effects may be nonrobust to the choice of the reference state for measuring interactions. In that paper we explore these issues and show that for data used in this paper, the choice of a base state does not affect the qualitative conclusions of our analysis. We estimate a fully interacted model, using the conventional base state—the mean across all effects.

Since longer distances traveled are usually associated with higher costs of migration (both economic and psychological costs), we would expect the rate of return to increase with the distance of the move. Formally, we write,

$$(7\text{-}10) \quad \tilde{\alpha}_{br(s)c} = \alpha + \alpha_b + \alpha_c + \alpha_{r(s)} + \alpha_{r(s)c}$$
$$+ \varphi_{r(s)} Q_{bc} + \eta_1 d_{r(s)r(b)} + \eta_2 d^2_{r(s)r(b)} ,$$

where φ_{rs} varies across regions, and d is the distance between regions of birth and regions of residence.[61] Card and Krueger assume that $\varphi_{rs} = \varphi$ for all regions and ignore any effects of distance on returns to schooling. There is some evidence that the model in equation 7-10 is too simple.[62] A more general model of self-selection in migration is required to account for the patterns we find here. Estimated effects cannot be interpreted causally. The estimates obtained from (7-10) dramatically alter the evidence of how quality affects earnings. More general, statistically significant, though less interpretable interactions produce a pattern of estimated quality effects on earnings that strongly rejects the schooling-quality hypothesis.

Table 7-16 contains the estimated coefficients from the second-stage model. These estimates are for a model that imposes linearity in schooling on the earnings equation. Results for a nonlinear schooling model are qualitatively similar.[63] The specifications reported in the first three columns are for three different quality measures, taken one at a time, in a model that includes fixed effects for the state of birth. The effect of the pupil-teacher ratio on the rate of return varies by region of residence. In most regions a lower pupil-teacher ratio is associated with a higher rate of return, but this is not true in New England, which has historically been a region of high schooling quality. The coefficient on distance and its square is highly significant and in the expected direction in all specifications. Longer distance implies higher wages. As seen by columns 2 and 3, relative teacher salary has a similar effect on the rate of return across regions, but estimated effects of term length are always statistically insignificant or perversely signed. Columns 4 and 5 consider all three quality measures in specifications with and without fixed effects for state

61. See Heckman, Layne-Farrar, and Todd (1996), for details on how physical distance between regions was measured.
62. See Heckman, Layne-Farrar, and Todd (1996).
63. See Heckman, Layne-Farrar, and Todd (1996).

Table 7-16. *Effect of Schooling Quality on the Return to Education, Linear Model with Region of Birth–Region of Residence Interactions, 1980 Census*[a]

Coefficent estimates[b]	(1)	(2)	(3)	(4)	(5)
	$\alpha_{bc} + \alpha_{r(b)r(s)} + \alpha_{r(b)r(s)c} = \varphi_{r(s)}Q_{bc} + \eta d$				$\alpha_b + \alpha_{bc} + \alpha_{r(b)r(s)} + \alpha_{r(b)r(s)c} = \varphi_{r(s)}Q_{bc} + \eta d$
Pupil-teacher ratio					
New England	8.85	...	...	7.58	15.34
	(4.52)			(4.44)	(3.97)
Middle Atlantic	−7.07	...	...	−7.23	0.39
	(3.35)			(3.40)	(2.55)
East North Central	−8.22	...	...	−6.84	1.28
	(3.03)			(3.04)	(2.09)
West North Central	−5.46	...	...	−5.18	3.89
	(3.47)			(3.51)	(2.74)
South Atlantic	−9.29	...	...	−9.30	−1.77
	(3.18)			(3.17)	(2.17)
East South Central	−6.65	...	...	−6.18	1.85
	(3.75)			(3.72)	(3.32)
West South Central	−3.37	...	...	−2.75	5.60
	(2.94)			(2.88)	(2.07)
Mountain	−3.88	...	...	−2.47	6.40
	(3.09)			(3.08)	(2.32)
Pacific	−6.77	...	...	−5.40	3.14
	(2.93)			(2.93)	(1.77)
Teacher salary					
New England	...	2.58	...	3.49	1.21
		(0.69)		(0.63)	(0.59)
Middle Atlantic	...	2.59	...	3.42	1.13
		(0.46)		(0.49)	(0.37)
East North Central	...	2.59	...	3.06	0.74
		(0.42)		(0.43)	(0.28)
West North Central	...	2.55	...	3.37	1.01
		(0.53)		(0.58)	(0.52)
South Atlantic	...	2.58	...	3.38	1.06
		(0.42)		(0.45)	(0.31)
East South Central	...	2.60	...	3.27	0.92
		(0.51)		(0.53)	(0.46)
West South Central	...	2.58	...	3.19	0.82
		(0.39)		(0.42)	(0.34)
Mountain	...	2.56	...	3.03	0.67
		(0.46)		(0.48)	(0.45)
Pacific	...	2.57	...	3.06	0.72
		(0.44)		(0.45)	(0.23)

Model restrictions spans columns (1)–(5).

Table 7-16. (Continued)

Coefficent estimates[b]	Model restrictions				
	(1)	(2)	(3)	(4)	(5)
	$\alpha_{bc} + \alpha_{r(b)r(s)} + \alpha_{r(b)r(s)c}$ $= \varphi_{r(s)}Q_{bc} + \eta d$				$\alpha_b + \alpha_{bc} + \alpha_{r(b)r(s)} + \alpha_{r(b)r(s)c}$ $= \varphi_{r(s)}Q_{bc} + \eta d$
Term length					
New England	...	...	−7.51	−9.92	−5.50
			(2.09)	(2.03)	(2.02)
Middle Atlantic	...	...	−1.58	−5.18	−0.69
			(1.47)	(1.49)	(1.21)
East North Central	...	...	2.78	−0.38	4.44
			(1.32)	(1.32)	(0.97)
West North Central	...	...	−2.29	−5.58	−0.48
			(1.56)	(1.68)	(1.48)
South Atlantic	...	...	−0.64	−4.28	0.66
			(1.11)	(1.13)	(0.92)
East South Central	...	...	−0.01	−3.26	1.90
			(1.51)	(1.58)	(1.40)
West South Central	...	...	−0.45	−3.32	2.01
			(1.13)	(1.11)	(1.05)
Mountain	...	...	1.40	−1.36	3.83
			(1.46)	(1.48)	(1.46)
Pacific	...	...	2.19	−0.89	4.12
			(1.17)	(1.19)	(1.00)
Distance[c]	1.19	1.24	1.16	1.11	0.94
	(0.15)	(0.14)	(0.15)	(0.15)	(0.17)
Distance squared[c]	−0.22	−0.24	−0.23	−0.21	−0.18
	(0.05)	(0.05)	(0.05)	(0.05)	(0.06)

Source: Authors' calculations. The number of observations = 1,343 (49 states of birth × 9 regions × 3 cohorts). The percent of the work force in the manufacturing industry was computed from the 1980 census using male and female workers aged eighteen to sixty-five. The mean quality within a region of residence was calculated using the 1920–29, 1930–39, and 1940–49 cohorts.

a. Second-stage model: rate of return = $\alpha + \alpha_b + \alpha_{r(s)} + \alpha_c + \alpha_{bc} + \alpha_{r(s)c} + \alpha_{r(s)r(b)} + \alpha_{r(s)r(b)c}$. The numbers in parentheses are Eicker-White standard errors.

b. The omitted education category is < 12 years. The pupil-teacher ratio and term length were divided by 100 in the regression. The attendance-based pupil-teacher ratio was used.

c. Distance is measured in thousands of miles.

of birth, respectively. Permitting differential effects of quality on the returns to education across regions of residence is what produces the results reported here.

As was found in the previous models, estimated coefficients are not robust to the exclusion of state-of-birth fixed effects. In column 5 the coefficient on pupil-teacher ratio is consistently of the wrong sign, and the coefficient on teacher salary is diminished in magnitude and significance. The significant coefficients on term length are generally positive, but again the effect in New England runs counter to that in other regions, and counter to the schooling-quality hypothesis.

Tables 7C-11 and 7C-12 contain analogous results for the 1970 and

Table 7-17. *F-Tests for the Restriction That Quality Effects Are Equal across Regions of Residence in the Linear Second-Stage Model with Interactions, Census Years 1970, 1980, 1990*

	Census year		
Quality variable	1970	1980	1990
Pupil-teacher ratio			
F-statistic	4.72	4.34	3.86
P-value	0.0001	0.0001	0.0002
Term length			
F-statistic	2.77	4.07	3.03
P-value	0.0048	0.0001	0.0021
Teacher salary			
F-statistic	0.48	0.20	0.14
P-value	0.8737	0.9913	0.9975

Source: Author's calculations. These tests are conducted on the second-stage equation relating the total return to education to the quality measures. For the 1970 census regression, n = 1,764 and for the 1980 and 1990 census regressions, n = 1,323. The tests are conducted on the form of the model that contains an intercept, cohort dummies, region-of-residence and state-of-birth indicators, region-of-residence interacted with cohort indicators, distance between region of residence and region of birth, and indicators for region of residence interacted with each of the quality variables. Each test considers eight restrictions on the model.

1990 census years. In models with state-of-birth intercepts, the pupil-teacher ratio and teacher salary again show statistically significant effects, while the effect of term length is usually insignificant or in the wrong direction. The strongest effects for the first two quality variables are seen in the 1990 data. Excluding state-of-birth effects normally leads to a reduction in the magnitude of the estimated pupil-teacher ratio and teacher salary effects, with some sign reversals for the pupil-teacher ratio in regions in 1970. The exclusion leads to an increase in the estimated effect of term length, which becomes strongly significant for most regions in 1990.

Table 7-17 tests the restriction that the coefficients associated with the quality variables are identical across regions, $\varphi = \varphi_{rs}$, for all census years. This assumption, maintained in all the models considered earlier and maintained in the previous literature, is rejected for the coefficients on the pupil-teacher ratio and term length but is not rejected for the coefficients on teacher salary.[64] Therefore, unit increases in quality usually have different effects on the rate of return to schooling in different regions. This disparity could arise because of differential regional demand factors, or for other reasons previously discussed regarding comparative

64. Note that our measure for average teacher salary eliminates a great deal of variation. We calculate teacher salary in a state relative to the regional mean so that the measure is between zero and one.

advantage and selective migration. Our evidence speaks against the crucial identifying assumptions used in previous studies. When those assumptions are relaxed, the empirical findings challenge the claim that measured schooling quality raises earnings.

The Effect of Schooling Quality on Educational Attainment Levels

In the introduction we identified three ways that schooling quality can affect earnings. Thus far we have considered only the first two: the effect of schooling quality on the intercepts and the effect of quality on the slopes of the earnings-schooling relationship, holding constant the level of educational attainment. We now consider a third: the role of schooling quality in increasing the incentive for students to further their education. Students attending higher-quality secondary schools may be more likely to graduate from high school or more likely to go to college. This relationship has been found in several previous studies.[65]

To examine the impact of schooling quality on years of education completed, we estimate the relation between the proportions of college graduates, high school graduates without postsecondary degrees, and high school dropouts in each state and our quality indicators:

$$(7\text{-}11) \qquad \ln[N_{ed.level(b,c)}/Population_{bc}] = \alpha_c + \ln(Q_{bc})\beta_c \,.$$

As before, c designates the cohort and b the state of birth. The variable $N_{ed.\ level\ (b,c)}$ is the total number of individuals born in state b in cohort c with a specific level of education. Dividing by the total number of individuals born in state b in cohort c gives the proportion of the population with that education level. The three education levels considered are college graduation, high school graduation (without college degree), and high school dropout.

The proportions of different education levels show considerable variation across states and over time. The region with the lowest percentage of college graduates is East South Central, comprising Alabama, Kentucky, and Tennessee. In 1970 data only 8 percent of the 1910–19 cohort born in that region had received a college degree or higher. Fully 59 percent of them were high school dropouts. These figures improve somewhat over time, but educational attainment is the lowest here among the

---

65. See Card and Krueger (1992a) and Johnson and Stafford (1973).

nine regions: in the 1990 data 22 percent of the 1950–59 cohort had graduated from college and only 14 percent were high school dropouts. The Pacific region, with California, Oregon, and Washington, and the Mid-Atlantic region, with New York, New Jersey, and Pennsylvania, produce the highest percentages of college graduates. About 15 percent of the 1910–19 cohort born in these regions have college degrees according to 1970 census data. This number increases to 28 percent for the Pacific region and 35 percent for the Mid-Atlantic region for the 1950–59 cohort in 1990 census data.

We estimate equation 7-11 by regressing the proportion of college graduates in each state, by cohort, on the four quality measures. Table 7C-13 in appendix C displays the coefficient estimates for the 1980 census. Tables 7C-14 and 7C-15 show the results from the 1970 and 1990 data. The proportion of college graduates, shown in the top panel, is consistently positively related to all the schooling-quality indexes for all cohorts. Because the relationship is expressed as a log-log model, we can interpret the quality coefficients as the percent change in the proportion of college graduates resulting from a 1 percent change in quality. For example, if average classroom size decreased by 1 percent for the 1920–29 cohort, we would expect a 0.42 percent increase in the proportion of college graduates. The model for the proportion of high school graduates, presented in the middle panel, shows a weaker relationship. Although the estimated coefficients have the expected signs, they are often statistically insignificant. The bottom panel, however, which regresses the proportion of high school dropouts on quality, shows strong results. Increasing schooling quality decreases the proportion of dropouts. The results for 1970 and 1990 are analogous.

This evidence provides some support for the hypothesis, previously found in the literature, that schooling quality has a positive effect on schooling attainment. It is interesting to note that the same pattern found in the quality-earnings regressions is found here as well: the weakest link between secondary school quality and outcomes is for high school graduates. The connection is much stronger for college graduates and high school dropouts.

Although the relationship is robust across census years, it may be spurious. Estimated quality effects are confounded with family background and state-of-residence effects on the schooling decision. Differences across states in educational attainment levels could be due, in part, to differences in family backgrounds or to different local labor-market conditions at the time schooling decisions are made. In principle, one could regress deviations in schooling attainment over cohorts and within states on deviations in average quality across cohorts and within states to eliminate "permanent" state effects on educational attainment and schooling quality. However, such a fixed effect procedure reduces the variation in the data and does not eliminate state- and cohort-specific shocks to enrollment and quality that could produce a spurious empirical relationship.

Conclusion

In this chapter we have examined the empirical and conceptual foundations of recent studies designed to estimate the impact of schooling quality on earnings. We have set forth a general analysis of variance framework within which we nest all previously estimated models. We have made explicit the identifying assumptions and definitions of the quality effect of interest that were implicit in previous studies. And we have estimated more general models and tested restrictions imposed in previous studies. Having done so, we reach the following six main conclusions about the existing evidence on whether measured quality affects earnings.

—Aggregate estimation approaches secure identification of quality effects by comparing the earnings of people living in the same labor market but born (and presumably educated) in different states. This strategy separates state-of-current-residence effects from state-of-birth effects, but does not separate out schooling-quality effects from other early environmental effects. Quality effects on earnings are estimated by attributing some state-of-birth effects isolated by this procedure to schooling quality. Which state-of-birth effects are used to estimate the impact of schooling quality crucially affects the estimates. If measures of schooling quality are less erroneous than family background measures, a standard errors in variables argument suggests that schooling quality may proxy the family background effects demonstrated by the Coleman report to have a strong effect on outcome measures. The strategy of using migrants to separate state-of-birth effects from state-of-residence effects breaks down altogether when individuals migrate selectively on the basis of expected earnings in the destination region and there is some relation between their expectations and the unobservables in destination-earnings equations. Evidence on nonrandom sorting by region of residence and region of birth, and evidence on the higher wages of the migrant population, point to the empirical importance of selective migration.

—The leading models in the literature predict that quality and earnings are monotonically related. This can be tested nonparametrically. Nonparametric rank tests comparing state-of-birth rankings by quality with rankings by wages suggest no relation between the empirical measures of schooling quality and wages. Earnings ranks by state of birth show some stability across regions of residence, but the sources of stability are unrelated to the aggregate measures of quality. Our evidence on the stability of ranks of state of birth in wage distributions across regions of residence is consistent with many other stories besides ones that emphasize schooling quality. For example, a story based on the Coleman report that emphasizes the importance of family background on raising earnings can also account for this evidence.

—Empirical studies in the literature differ in the parameters they estimate and in the functional forms assumed for the earnings equation. Imposing the identifying assumptions of Card and Krueger's model, we find that their analysis can be replicated in 1970 and 1990. Within their framework there is evidence for a quality effect, and it is the strongest in 1990. We also find statistically significant effects of aggregate measures of quality and aggregate supply and demand variables on the regional return to education.

—Extending the analysis of Card and Krueger to estimate the effect of quality operating through intercepts, we find evidence that quality operates not only through slope parameters but also through model intercepts. Quality lowers intercepts, so empirical studies that focus solely on slopes overstate the total effect of quality on earnings.

—The assumption that log earnings and education are linearly related is decisively rejected by the data. Local labor-market shocks affect low skill workers much more than high skill workers, implying that linearity is a poor assumption. There are nonlinearities in the return to education associated with significant sheepskin effects, particularly at the college level. In an earnings model that relaxes linearity, support for the quality hypothesis weakens considerably. The only evidence for a positive relation between schooling quality and earnings is among those who attend college.

—Estimated quality effects are sensitive to changes in model specification to allow for selective migration and region-of-birth–region-of-residence interactions in earnings equations. We stress, however, that introducing interactions in the fashion of this paper only enables us to test the hypothesis of no selective migration into regions of residence from regions of birth. We reject the hypothesis of no interactions, but our estimation procedure does not, in general, correct for the selection bias. Thus, in the general case, estimated schooling quality effects cannot be interpreted causally.

Allowing for differential effects of quality across regions, we find that the effect of the pupil-teacher ratio on the rate of return to education differs across labor markets and that term length has little or no effect on the return to schooling. However, there is some support in this model for a positive effect of relative teacher salary that is uniform across labor markets. This support vanishes, however, when statistically significant region-of-birth–region-of-residence interactions for an unrestricted model are introduced.[66]

The evidence in this chapter, like the evidence in the literature that precedes it, is not decisive on the question whether schooling inputs can increase earnings. All we have done is to raise considerable doubts about the reliability of the evidence on schooling quality based on aggregated quality data.

The available measures of schooling quality are crude. Estimating equations used in the literature do not capture explicit choice mechanisms for parents and school authorities or the detailed schooling production processes required to justify specific policy interventions. As Hanushek notes, the absence of a strong empirical relation between measured outcomes and measured inputs may reflect the quality of the measures and the inefficiency of most schooling organizations in transforming inputs to outputs.[67]

This study, like the studies that precede it, takes as exogenously given the quality of schooling in a person's state of birth. Until the mechanism of quality determination and its statistical consequences are understood, and until the full effects of selective migration and family background are accounted for, any evidence about quality-earnings effects is at best tentative.

Appendix A: Description of the Analysis Samples

Our samples are taken from the 1970, 1980, and 1990 censuses. The 1970 sample is taken from two 1 percent public-use A samples: the 1

66. Heckman, Layne-Farrar, and Todd (1996).
67. Hanushek (1991).

Table 7A-1. *Summary of Sample Restrictions, Census Years 1970, 1980, 1990*

Sex	Male
Race	White
Place of birth	48 mainland states and District of Columbia
Place of residence	Living in any one of the 50 states or District of Columbia as of the census year.
Wage/salary[a]	1970 census: Annual 1969 wage or salary income of at least $51 and weekly wage or salary falling in the range $18–$1,264.
	1980 census: Annual 1979 wage or salary income of at least $101 and weekly average wage or salary of $26–$2,500.
	1990 census: Annual 1989 wage or salary income of at least $173 and average weekly wage or salary of $60–$4,270
Other	Individuals with imputed information on age, race, sex, education, weeks worked, or income are excluded. Also, individuals who have not worked at least one week are excluded.

a. Salary ranges for the 1970 and 1990 censuses are equal to the 1980 range adjusted by the CPI for the appropriate year.

percent state sample (5 percent form) and the 1 percent state sample (15 percent form). It is a self-weighting sample of 2 percent of the population. The 1980 Census and the 1990 census samples are both 5 percent public-use A samples. The 1980 census sample is self-weighted, but the 1990 sample is not. Therefore, for 1990, our regressions take into account the weight of each individual in the sample.

To maintain comparability of our empirical results with those of Card and Krueger, we impose identical restrictions on our 1980 sample. To the extent possible, we construct the 1970 and 1990 extractions in the same way. The 1970 census reports the number of weeks worked in intervals, whereas the 1980 and 1990 censuses report integer amounts. To get a point estimate for the number of weeks worked in 1970, we calculate the mean number of weeks worked in 1980 within the 1970 intervals and impute these interval means for individuals in the 1970 sample. Point estimates of annual earnings are computed by assigning to individuals the midpoint of their earnings interval. Table 7A-1 summarizes the full set of restrictions for each of the three census samples.

Each census sample is divided into ten-year birth cohorts. The year of birth for each individual is determined from information on age and

Table 7-A2. *Sample Sizes for Birth Cohorts, Census Years 1970, 1980, 1990*

Birth cohort	1970 census	1980 census	1990 census
1910–19	119,894	. . .	. . .
1920–29	152,245	277,601	. . .
1930–39	148,281	302,941	239,373
1940–49	193,808	447,691	418,335
1950–59	. . .	. . .	571,808

quarter of birth. The sample sizes for each of the birth cohorts is given in table 7A-2.

Regression Variables

The *log weekly wage* variable used in the regressions is constructed by dividing the annual wage and salary income by the number of weeks worked. Number of weeks worked is reported directly in the 1980 and 1990 censuses, but not in the 1970 census. In 1970 number of weeks worked is reported by category: 0–13 weeks, 14–26, 27–39, 40–47, 48–49, and 50–52 weeks. To arrive at a single number for weeks worked, we calculate the distribution of weeks worked in each of these categories by age, race, and education level using the 1980 census data. We then impute the mean number of weeks worked for each category in 1980 to the 1970 data.

The *experience* variable refers to "potential" experience, calculated as age minus years of schooling minus 6. Information on *SMSA* (standard metropolitan statistical area) and *marital status* variables are available in each census year's documentation.

Years of education is reported differently in the three census samples we use. In 1970 and 1980, the census reports the highest grade completed. In 1990, the census reports categories of education for first through fourth grade and fifth through eighth grade, and then reports the highest grade completed for ninth through twelfth grades (twelve years of school with no degree is reported separately from high school graduation). For high school and beyond, the census reports only the degree obtained. To make it comparable to the other two census samples, we impute the number of years of education associated with each level and degree. For twelve years of school with and without a high school degree, we assign twelve years. For both some college but no degree and an associate (academic or occupational) degree we assign fourteen years of school. If a bachelor's degree is reported, we assign sixteen years of

For the eighteen historically segregated public education school systems,[71] data sources allowed compilation of white-specific measures covering much of the 1916–68 time period. Unfortunately, we were able to find teacher salaries on an aggregate level only.

Virtually complete white-specific PTR-E and PTR-A series were extracted from the *Biennial Surveys*, various federal Office of Education studies appearing under such rubrics as *Statistics of the Education of Negroes: A Decade of Progress* (1943), and state education reports for the years 1916–54. In the wake of the *Brown v. Board of Education* decision that year, the federal government and many of the historically segregated states ceased publishing racially disaggregated educational statistics. However, the pace and timing of post-*Brown* school desegregation varies widely.

Where post-*Brown* legal desegregation[72] was relatively immediate, as in the District of Columbia and a number of border states, white-specific pupil-teacher ratios and white term lengths were immediately replaced by the nondifferentiated, aggregate ratios used to characterize historically nonsegregated systems. Where legal desegregation lagged, particularly in the deep South, white-specific pupil-teacher ratios were extracted to the extent that available data (mainly from SERS publications and state reports) allowed. Since racially differentiated data in these instances typically were unavailable well before full desegregation had taken effect, a smoothing procedure was employed to merge white-specific pupil-teacher ratios and the somewhat larger aggregate ratios.

Based on data appearing in the SERS gazette *Southern School News*, the increasing percentages of legally desegregated schools within individual states were calculated post-*Brown* through 1968 (when full legal desegregation was assumed). Partially segregated states were assigned an average of the last reported white-specific pupil-teacher ratio and the current aggregate ratio, weighted according to the current level of desegregation.[73] Aggregate measures were only assigned once the legal desegregation in a given states schools reached a 95 percent threshold.

71. These were the states of Alabama, Arkansas, Delaware, Florida, Georgia, Kentucky, Louisiana, Maryland, Mississippi, Missouri, North Carolina, Oklahoma, South Carolina, Tennessee, Texas, Virginia, and West Virginia, and the District of Columbia.

72. That is, certified compliance with the then-prevailing interpretations of federal law: nominal integration as far as the legal right to enroll, as distinguished from the de facto integration later sought by such court-mandated measures as busing plans.

73. That is, a state whose schools were 40 percent desegregated in a given year was assigned the pupil-teacher ratios equivalent to 60 percent of the last reported white-specific ratios and 40 percent of the relevant aggregate ratios.

We took an average of the quality measures over each birth cohort for the years those born in that cohort would have attended school. We assumed all individuals complete twelve years of elementary and secondary schooling.[74] Specifically, we took twelve-year averages of each quality measure for each year of birth.[75] For example, a high school graduate born in 1910 would have begun school in 1916 and remained in school through 1927. Therefore, for individuals born in 1910 the state-level quality indexes were averaged over 1916–27. We then averaged the twelve-year measures to obtain birth cohort averages. For the 1910–19 cohort, the averages were taken for birth years 1910 through 1919. This procedure is identical to the calculations in Card and Krueger's study.

Appendix C: Additional Tables

All tables included with the text are for 1980. In this appendix we also present evidence for 1970 and 1990.

74. We also tried attendance specific averages. That is, if an individual only completed eight years of school, then he or she would receive an eight-year average beginning six years after his or her birth year. This correction did not change any of the results and is therefore not presented here.

75. For 1990 birth cohorts, we restricted the quality data to every other year. Because the data were available every other year for some periods, and every year for other periods, taking a straight average would place disproportionate weight on the periods with more frequently reported data. Restricting the data to every other year results in giving equal weight to each data point. The 1970 and 1980 cohorts were not restricted in this fashion, due to oversight. The quality averages and the regression coefficients are affected only minimally by this procedure. None of the conclusions are affected.

Table 7C-1. *Effect of Schooling Quality on the Rate of Return to Education, Linear Model, 1970 Census*[a]

				Second-stage model restrictions						
	(1)	(2)	(3)	(4) $\alpha_{bc} = \varphi_c Q_{bc}$				(5)	(6)	(7)
Measure[b]	$\alpha_{bc} = \varphi Q_{bc}$	$\alpha_{bc} = \varphi Q_{bc}$	$\alpha_b + \alpha_{bc} = \varphi Q_{bc}$	1910–19	1920–29	1930–39	1940–49	$\alpha_{bc} = \varphi_c Q_{bc}$ $\alpha_{r(s)} + \alpha_{r(s)c} = \pi_1 Q_{r(s)}$	$\alpha_{bc} = \varphi_c Q_{bc}$ $\alpha_{r(s)} + \alpha_{r(s)c} = \pi_1 Q_{r(s)}$	$\alpha_{bc} = \varphi_c Q_{bc}$ $\alpha_{r(s)} + \alpha_{r(s)c} = \pi_1 Q_{r(s)} + \pi_2 D_{r(s)}$
Pupil-teacher ratio	−8.10 (1.48)	−8.89 (1.50)	−2.14 (0.70)	−8.38 (1.28)	−1.79 (1.21)	4.66 (0.89)	0.36 (1.77)	−8.89 (2.16)	−8.89 (2.13)	−8.89 (1.82)
Term length	…	0.74 (0.39)	1.85 (0.27)	−0.16 (0.32)	4.59 (0.37)	3.45 (0.55)	7.08 (1.35)	0.74 (0.63)	0.74 (0.62)	0.74 (0.51)
Relative teacher salary	…	1.20 (0.31)	0.33 (0.09)	0.97 (0.19)	0.07 (0.12)	0.39 (0.15)	−0.46 (0.30)	1.20 (0.45)	1.20 (0.44)	1.20 (0.38)
Demand and supply aggregates										
Regional average pupil-teacher ratio	…	…	…	…	…	…	…	25.65 (1.50)	21.02 (1.55)	−31.76 (3.36)
Regional average term length	…	…	…	…	…	…	…	…	−4.46 (0.45)	−5.17 (1.64)
Percent 12 years school	…	…	…	…	…	…	…	…	…	−0.20 (0.02)
Percent 1–3 years college	…	…	…	…	…	…	…	…	…	−0.20 (0.03)
Percent 4+ years college	…	…	…	…	…	…	…	…	…	0.17 (0.05)
Percent manufacturing	…	…	…	…	…	…	…	…	…	0.03 (0.007)

Source: Author's calculations. The number of observations = 1,764 (49 states of birth × 9 regions × 4 cohorts). The percent of the work force in the manufacturing industry was computed from the 1970 census using male and female workers aged eighteen to sixty-five. The mean quality within a region of residence was calculated using the 1910–19, 1920–29, 1930–39, and 1940–49 birth cohorts.

a. Second-stage model: rate of return = $\alpha + \alpha_b + \alpha_{r(s)} + \alpha_c + \alpha_{bc} + \alpha_{r(s)c}$. The numbers in parentheses are Eicker-White standard errors.

b. The omitted education category is < 12 years. The pupil-teacher ratio and term length were divided by 100 in the regression. The attendance-based pupil-teacher ratio was used.

Table 7C-2. *Effect of Schooling Quality on the Rate of Return to Education, Linear Model, 1990 Census*[a]

Measure[b]	(1) $\alpha_{bc} = \varphi Q_{bc}$	(2) $\alpha_{bc} = \varphi Q_{bc}$	(3) $\alpha_b + \alpha_{bc} = \varphi Q_{bc}$	(4) $\alpha_{bc} = \varphi_c Q_{bc}$			(5) $\alpha_{bc} = \varphi Q_{bc}$ $\alpha_{r(s)} + \alpha_{r(s)c} = \pi_1 Q_{r(s)}$	(6) $\alpha_{bc} = \varphi Q_{bc}$ $\alpha_{r(s)} + \alpha_{r(s)c} = \pi_1 Q_{r(s)}$	(7) $\alpha_{bc} = \varphi Q_{bc}$ $\alpha_{r(s)} + \alpha_{r(s)c} = \pi_1 Q_{r(s)} + \pi_2 D_{r(s)}$
				1930–39	1940–49	1950–59			
Pupil-teacher ratio	−9.22 (1.52)	−10.66 (1.47)	1.55 (0.74)	0.71 (0.85)	3.06 (1.39)	1.58 (2.34)	−10.66 (2.57)	−10.65 (1.72)	−10.66 (1.76)
Term length	...	6.45 (0.62)	8.29 (0.46)	8.92 (0.51)	7.81 (0.96)	5.87 (1.93)	6.45 (1.29)	6.45 (0.79)	6.45 (0.79)
Relative teacher salary	...	2.59 (0.32)	2.06 (0.12)	1.88 (0.18)	1.78 (0.22)	2.98 (0.30)	2.59 (0.59)	2.59 (0.39)	2.59 (0.39)
Demand and supply aggregates									
Regional average pupil-teacher ratio	...	...	...	...	...	...	15.54 (1.48)	17.06 (1.47)	−27.61 (3.42)
Regional average term length	...	...	...	...	...	...	...	−4.25 (0.42)	8.31 (1.26)
Percent 12 years school	...	...	...	...	...	...	...	...	−0.35 (0.03)
Percent 1–3 years college	...	...	...	...	...	...	...	...	−0.34 (0.01)
Percent 4+ years college	...	...	...	...	...	...	...	...	−0.35 (0.02)
Percent manufacturing	...	...	...	...	...	...	...	...	−0.10 (0.007)

Source: Authors' calculations. The number of observations = 1,323 (49 states of birth × 9 regions × 3 cohorts). The percent of the work force in the manufacturing industry was computed from the 1990 census (sample A), using male and female workers aged eighteen to sixty-five. The mean quality within a region of residence was calculated using the 1930–39, 1940–49, and 1950–59 birth cohorts.

a. Second-stage model: rate of return = $\alpha + \alpha_b + \alpha_{r(s)} + \alpha_c + \alpha_{bc} + \alpha_{r(s)c}$. The numbers in parentheses are Eicker-White standard errors.

b. The omitted education category is < 12 years. The pupil-teacher ratio and term length were divided by 100 in the regression. The attendance-based pupil-teacher ratio was used.

Table 7C-3. Effect of Schooling Quality on Fixed Effects, Linear Model, 1970 Census[a]

Measure[b]	(1) $\theta_{bc} = \varphi Q_{bc}$	(2) $\theta_{bc} = \varphi Q_{bc}$	(3) $\theta_b + \theta_{bc} = \varphi Q_{bc}$	(4) $\theta_{bc} = \varphi_c Q_{bc}$ 1910–19	1920–29	1930–39	1940–49	(5) $\theta_{bc} = \varphi Q_{bc}$ $\theta_s + \theta_{r(s)c} = \pi_1 Q_{r(s)}$	(6) $\theta_{bc} = \varphi Q_{bc}$ $\theta_s + \theta_{r(s)c} = \pi_1 Q_{r(s)}$	(7) $\theta_{bc} = \varphi Q_{bc}$ $\theta_s + \theta_{sc} = \pi_1 Q_{r(s)} + \pi_2 D_{r(s)}$
				Second-stage model restrictions						
Pupil-teacher ratio	0.77 (0.11)	0.86 (0.12)	0.03 (0.05)	0.86 (0.10)	−0.06 (0.08)	−0.94 (0.07)	−0.08 (0.11)	0.86 (0.17)	0.86 (0.17)	0.86 (0.14)
Term length	...	−0.06 (0.03)	−0.19 (0.02)	0.06 (0.03)	−0.50 (0.04)	−0.39 (0.04)	−0.80 (0.10)	−0.06 (0.05)	−0.06 (0.05)	−0.06 (0.04)
Relative teacher salary	...	−0.19 (0.02)	−0.01 (0.01)	−0.12 (0.02)	0.01 (0.01)	0.004 (0.01)	0.09 (0.02)	−0.19 (0.04)	−0.19 (0.03)	−0.19 (0.03)
Demand and supply aggregates										
Regional average pupil-teacher ratio	...	...	...	...	...	...	...	−0.02 (0.001)	−0.02 (0.001)	0.09 (0.002)
Regional average term length	...	...	...	...	...	...	...	...	0.01 (0.0004)	−0.003 (0.002)
Percent 12 years school	...	...	...	...	...	...	...	...	...	0.05 (0.002)
Percent 1–3 years college	...	...	...	...	...	...	...	...	...	−0.01 (0.003)
Percent 4+ years college	...	...	...	...	...	...	...	...	...	0.03 (0.004)
Percent manufacturing	...	...	...	...	...	...	...	...	...	−0.0006 (0.006)

Source: Author's calculations. The number of observations = 9,996 (49 states of birth × 51 states of residence × 4 cohorts). The percent of the work force in the manufacturing industry was computed from the 1970 census using male and female workers aged eighteen to sixty-five. The mean quality within a region of residence was calculated using the 1910–19, 1920–29, 1930–39, and 1940–49 birth cohorts.

a. Second-stage model: $\theta_{bsc} = \theta + \theta_b + \theta_s + \theta_c + \theta_{bc} + \theta_{r(s)c}$. The numbers in parentheses are Eicker-White standard errors.

b. The omitted education category is < 12 years of school. The pupil-teacher ratio and term length were divided by 100 in the regression. The attendance-based pupil-teacher ratio was used.

Table 7C-4. *Effect of Schooling Quality on Fixed Effects, Linear Model, 1990 Census*[a]

	(1) $\theta_{bc} = \varphi Q_{bc}$	(2) $\theta_{bc} = \varphi Q_{bc}$	(3) $\theta_b + \theta_{bc} = \varphi Q_{bc}$	(4) $\theta_{bc} = \varphi_c Q_{bc}$			(5) $\theta_{bc} = \varphi Q_{bc}$; $\theta_s + \theta_{r(s)c} = \pi_1 Q_{r(s)}$	(6) $\theta_{bc} = \varphi Q_{bc}$; $\theta_s + \theta_{r(s)c} = \pi_1 Q_{r(s)}$	(7) $\theta_{bc} = \varphi Q_{bc}$; $\theta_s + \theta_{r(s)c} = \pi_1 Q_{r(s)} + \pi_2 D_{r(s)}$
							Second-stage model restrictions		
Measure[b]				1930–39	1940–49	1950–59			
Pupil-teacher ratio	1.14 (0.14))	1.37 (0.14)	−0.64 (0.06)	−0.55 (0.07)	−0.81 (0.10)	−0.60 (0.17)	1.37 (0.21)	1.37 (0.21)	1.37 (0.15)
Term length	...	−1.15 (0.07)	−1.03 (0.04)	−1.17 (0.04)	−0.91 (0.08)	−0.31 (0.16)	−1.15 (0.11)	−1.15 (0.11)	−1.15 (0.08)
Relative teacher salary	...	−0.41 (0.03)	−0.24 (0.01)	−0.22 (0.01)	−0.19 (0.02)	−0.36 (0.02)	−0.41 (0.05)	−0.41 (0.50)	−0.41 (0.36)
Demand and supply aggregates									
Regional average pupil-teacher ratio	...	...	...	...	...	...	0.01 (0.001)	−0.002 (0.002)	0.09 (0.003)
Regional average term length	...	...	...	...	...	...	...	0.01 (0.0004)	−0.02 (0.001)
Percent 12 years school	...	...	...	...	...	...	...	...	0.06 (0.003)
Percent 1–3 years college	...	...	...	...	...	...	...	...	0.05 (0.001)
Percent 4+ years college	...	...	...	...	...	...	...	...	0.08 (0.002)
Percent manufacturing	...	...	...	...	...	...	...	...	0.02 (0.01)

Source: Authors' calculations. The number of observations = 7,497 (49 states of birth × 51 states of residence × 3 cohorts). The percent of the work force in the manufacturing industry was computed from the 1990 census (sample A) using male and female workers aged eighteen to sixty-five. The mean quality within a region of residence was calculated using the 1930–39, 1940–49, and 1950–59 birth cohorts.

a. Second-stage model: = $\theta_{bsc} = \theta + \theta_b + \theta_s + \theta_c + \theta_{bc} + \theta_{sc}$. The numbers in parentheses are Eicker-White standard errors.

b. The omitted education category is < 12 years of schooling. The pupil-teacher ratio and term length were divided by 100 in the regression. The attendance-based pupil-teacher ratio was used.

Table 7C-5. *Effect of Schooling Quality on the Linear Base Return to Education, Nonlinear Model, 1970 Census*[a]

				Second-stage model restrictions						
	(1)	(2)	(3)	(4)				(5)	(6)	(7)
	$\alpha_{bc} = \varphi Q_{bc}$	$\alpha_{bc} = \varphi Q_{bc}$	$\alpha_b + \alpha_{bc} = \varphi Q_{bc}$	$\alpha_{bc} = \varphi_c Q_{bc}$				$\alpha_{bc} = \varphi Q_{bc}$, $\alpha_{r(s)c} = \pi_1 Q_{r(s)}$	$\alpha_{bc} = \varphi Q_{bc}$, $\alpha_{r(s)} + \alpha_{r(s)c} = \pi_1 Q_{r(s)}$	$\alpha_{bc} = \varphi Q_{bc}$, $\alpha_{r(s)} + \alpha_{r(s)c} = \pi_1 Q_{r(s)} + \pi_2 D_{r(s)}$
Measure[b]				1910–19	1920–29	1930–39	1940–49			
Pupil-teacher ratio	3.67 (2.49)	2.31 (2.52)	0.37 (1.18)	−12.93 (2.17)	6.19 (1.42)	6.99 (1.92)	6.72 (3.07)	2.31 (3.06)	2.31 (2.97)	2.31 (2.65)
Term length	…	2.70 (0.48)	0.96 (0.31)	−0.98 (0.38)	3.93 (0.64)	0.82 (0.60)	10.00 (1.70)	2.70 (0.72)	2.70 (0.69)	2.70 (0.54)
Relative teacher salary	…	−0.22 (0.53)	0.91 (0.14)	1.84 (0.23)	−0.09 (0.19)	0.98 (0.31)	1.83 (0.51)	−0.22 (0.65)	−0.22 (0.63)	−0.22 (0.57)
Demand and supply aggregates										
Regional average pupil-teacher ratio	…	…	…	…	…	…	…	0.26 (0.02)	0.18 (0.02)	−0.28 (0.05)
Regional average term length	…	…	…	…	…	…	…	…	−0.08 (0.01)	−0.20 (0.03)
Percent 12 years school	…	…	…	…	…	…	…	…	…	0.03 (0.03)
Percent 1–3 years college	…	…	…	…	…	…	…	…	…	−0.44 (0.04)
Percent 4 + years college	…	…	…	…	…	…	…	…	…	0.40 (0.08)
Percent manufacturing	…	…	…	…	…	…	…	…	…	0.02 (0.01)

Source: Authors' calculations. The number of observations = 1,764 (49 states of birth × 9 regions × 4 cohorts). The percent of the work force in the manufacturing industry was computed from the 1970 census, using male and female workers aged eighteen to sixty-five. The mean quality within a region of residence was calculated using the 1910–19, 1920–29, 1930–39, and 1940–49 birth cohorts.

a. Second-stage model: rate of return = $\alpha + \alpha_b + \alpha_{r(s)} + \alpha_c + \alpha_{bc} + \alpha_{r(s)c}$. The numbers in parentheses are Eicker-White standard errors.

b. The omitted education category is < 12 years of schooling. The pupil-teacher ratio and term length were divided by 100 in the regression. The attendance-based pupil-teacher ratio was used.

Table 7C-6. Effect of Schooling Quality on the Marginal Rate of Return to One to Three Years of College, Nonlinear Model, 1970 Census[a]

Measure[b]	(1) $\alpha_{bc} = \varphi Q_{bc}$	(2) $\alpha_{bc} = \varphi Q_{bc}$	Second-stage model restrictions							
			(3) $\alpha_b + \alpha_{bc} = \varphi Q_{bc}$	(4) $\alpha_{bc} = \varphi_c Q_{bc}$				(5) $\alpha_{bc} = \varphi Q_{bc}$; $\alpha_{r(s)} + \alpha_{r(s)c} = \pi_1 Q_{r(s)}$	(6) $\alpha_{bc} = \varphi Q_{bc}$; $\alpha_{r(s)} + \alpha_{(s)c} = \pi_1 Q_{r(s)}$	(7) $\alpha_{bc} = \varphi Q_{bc}$; $\alpha_{r(s)} + \alpha_{r(s)c} = \pi_1 Q_{r(s)} + \pi_2 D_{r(s)}$
				1910–19	1920–29	1930–39	1940–49			
Pupil-teacher ratio	−19.72 (13.69)	−16.56 (13.24)	−1.92 (5.73)	7.81 (7.80)	−40.72 (14.29)	43.56 (7.82)	−23.02 (12.24)	−16.56 (13.69)	−16.56 (13.40)	−16.56 (13.29)
Term length	...	−19.33 (3.58)	−1.62 (1.86)	−2.65 (2.52)	−6.75 (3.83)	3.07 (3.64)	−8.25 (9.18)	−19.32 (3.75)	−19.32 (3.61)	−19.33 (3.59)
Relative teacher salary	...	21.20 (2.52)	−0.89 (0.90)	−0.79 (1.48)	5.64 (2.05)	−4.47 (1.21)	−13.38 (2.80)	21.20 (2.60)	21.20 (2.59)	21.20 (2.54)
Demand and supply aggregates										
Regional average pupil-teacher ratio	...	...	...	...	...	...	...	0.04 (0.09)	0.29 (0.10)	−0.48 (0.24)
Regional average term length	...	...	...	...	...	...	...	...	0.24 (0.03)	0.95 (0.13)
Percent 12 years school	...	...	...	...	...	...	...	...	...	−1.16 (0.16)
Percent 1–3 years college	...	...	...	...	...	...	...	...	...	1.23 (0.22)
Percent 4+ years college	...	...	...	...	...	...	...	...	...	−2.29 (0.42)
Percent manufacturing	...	...	...	...	...	...	...	...	...	0.07 (0.05)

Source: Authors' calculations. The number of observations = 1,764 (49 states of birth × 9 regions × 4 cohorts). The percent of the work force in the manufacturing industry was computed from the 1970 census, using male and female workers aged eighteen to sixty-five. The mean quality within a region of residence was calculated using the 1910–19, 1920–29, 1930–39, and 1940–49 birth cohorts.

a. Second-stage model: rate of return = $\alpha + \alpha_b + \alpha_{r(s)} + \alpha_c + \alpha_{bc} + \alpha_{r(s)c}$. The numbers in parentheses are Eicker-White standard errors.

b. The omitted education category is < 12 years of schooling. The pupil-teacher ratio and term length were divided by 100 in the regression. The attendance-based pupil-teacher ratio was used.

Table 7C-7. *Effect of Schooling Quality on the Marginal Rate of Return to Four or More Years of College, Nonlinear Model, 1970 Census*[a]

	(1) $\alpha_{bc} = \varphi Q_{bc}$	(2) $\alpha_{bc} = \varphi Q_{bc}$	(3) $\alpha_b + \alpha_{bc} = \varphi Q_{bc}$	(4) $\alpha_{bc} = \varphi_c Q_{bc}$				(5) $\alpha_{bc} = \varphi Q_{bc}$ $\alpha_{r(s)} + \alpha_{r(s)c} = \pi_1 Q_{r(s)}$	(6) $\alpha_{bc} = \varphi Q_{bc}$ $\alpha_{r(s)} + \alpha_{r(s)c} = \pi_1 Q_{r(s)}$	(7) $\alpha_{bc} = \varphi Q_{bc}$ $\alpha_{r(s)} + \alpha_{r(s)c} = \pi_1 Q_{r(s)} + \pi_2 D_{r(s)}$
Measure[b]				1910–19	1920–29	1930–39	1940–49			
Pupil-teacher ratio	−66.13 (19.30)	−54.69 (19.14)	8.33 (8.09)	72.84 (14.99)	−40.35 (12.58)	2.53 (15.28)	−17.65 (20.15)	−54.69 (21.01)	−54.69 (21.01)	−54.69 (19.36)
Term length	...	−23.16 (4.67)	−8.54 (2.64)	−7.31 (3.61)	−17.97 (5.44)	6.22 (4.91)	−25.85 (13.06)	−23.16 (5.37)	−23.16 (4.96)	−23.16 (4.96)
Relative teacher salary	...	2.52 (3.67)	−7.23 (1.28)	−9.89 (2.83)	−0.95 (2.15)	−9.24 (1.94)	−16.68 (4.01)	2.52 (4.19)	2.52 (4.07)	2.52 (3.78)
Demand and supply aggregates										
Regional average pupil-teacher ratio	...	...	...	...	...	...	...	−0.49 (0.15)	0.06 (0.14)	−0.32 (0.36)
Regional average term length	...	...	...	...	...	...	...	...	0.52 (0.04)	1.49 (0.20)
Percent 12 years school	...	...	...	...	...	...	...	...	...	−1.78 (0.25)
Percent 1–3 years college	...	...	...	...	...	...	...	...	...	2.00 (0.33)
Percent 4+ years college	...	...	...	...	...	...	...	...	...	−1.98 (0.65)
Percent manufacturing	...	...	...	...	...	...	...	...	...	0.04 (0.08)

Source: Authors' calculations. The number of observations = 1,764 (49 states of birth × 9 regions × 4 cohorts). The percent of the work force in the manufacturing industry was computed from the 1970 census, using male and female workers aged eighteen to sixty-five. The mean quality within a region of residence was calculated using the 1910–19, 1920–29, 1930–39, and 1940–49 birth cohorts.

a. Second-stage model: rate of return = $\alpha + \alpha_b + \alpha_{r(s)} + \alpha_c + \alpha_{bc} + \alpha_{r(s)c}$. The numbers in parentheses are Eicker-White standard errors.

b. The omitted education category is < 12 years of schooling. The pupil-teacher ratio and term length were divided by 100 in the regression. The attendance-based pupil-teacher ratio was used.

Table 7C-8. *Effect of Schooling Quality on the Linear Base Return to Education, Nonlinear Model, 1990 Census*[a]

Measure[b]	(1) $\alpha_{bc} = \varphi Q_{bc}$	(2) $\alpha_{bc} = \varphi Q_{bc}$	(3) $\alpha_b + \alpha_{bc} = \varphi Q_{bc}$	(4) $\alpha_{bc} = \varphi_c Q_{bc}$ 1930–39	(4) 1940–49	(4) 1950–59	(5) $\alpha_{bc} = \varphi Q_{bc}$; $\alpha_{r(s)} + \alpha_{r(s)c} = \pi_1 Q_{r(s)}$	(6) $\alpha_{bc} = \varphi Q_{bc}$; $\alpha_{r(s)} + \alpha_{r(s)c} = \pi_1 Q_{r(s)}$	(7) $\alpha_{bc} = \varphi Q_{bc}$; $\alpha_{r(s)} + \alpha_{r(s)c} = \pi_1 Q_{r(s)} + \pi_2 D_{r(s)}$
				Second-stage model restrictions					
Pupil-teacher ratio	9.42 (4.65)	8.47 (4.64)	0.28 (1.78)	6.26 (2.82)	3.66 (2.03)	−25.91 (5.60)	8.47 (5.49)	8.47 (5.53)	8.47 (5.20)
Term length	...	4.22 (1.57)	8.12 (0.89)	7.05 (0.87)	11.43 (1.85)	7.92 (5.51)	4.22 (2.25)	4.22 (2.26)	4.22 (2.26)
Relative teacher salary	...	1.71 (0.87)	1.72 (0.29)	1.81 (0.48)	1.30 (0.33)	1.60 (0.64)	1.71 (1.13)	1.71 (1.13)	1.71 (1.13)
Demand and supply aggregates									
Regional average pupil-teacher ratio	...	...	...	...	...	...	0.14 (0.03)	0.19 (0.03)	−0.15 (0.08)
Regional average term length	...	...	...	...	...	...	...	−0.05 (0.01)	0.04 (0.03)
Percent 12 years school	...	...	...	...	...	...	...	...	−0.18 (0.07)
Percent 1–3 years college	...	...	...	...	...	...	...	...	−0.19 (0.03)
Percent 4+ years college	...	...	...	...	...	...	...	...	−0.31 (0.06)
Percent manufacturing	...	...	...	...	...	...	...	...	−0.09 (0.02)

Source: Authors' calculations. The number of observations = 1,323 (49 states of birth × 9 regions × 3 cohorts). The percent of the work force in the manufacturing industry was computed from the 1990 census (sample A) using male and female workers aged eighteen to sixty-five. The mean quality within a region of residence was calculated using the 1930–39, 1940–49, and 1950–59 birth cohorts.

a. Second-stage model: rate of return = $\alpha + \alpha_b + \alpha_{r(s)} + \alpha_c + \alpha_{bc} + \alpha_{r(s)c}$. The numbers in parentheses are Eicker-White standard errors.
b. The omitted education category is < 12 years of schooling. The pupil-teacher ratio and term length were divided by 100 in the regression. The attendance-based pupil-teacher ratio was used.

Table 7C-9. *Effect of Schooling Quality on the Marginal Rate of Return to One to Three Years of College, Nonlinear Model, 1990 Census*[a]

				(4) $\alpha_{bc} = \varphi_c Q_{bc}$			Second-stage model restrictions		
Measure[b]	(1) $\alpha_{bc} = \varphi Q_{bc}$	(2) $\alpha_{bc} = \varphi Q_{bc}$	(3) $\alpha_b + \alpha_{bc} = \varphi Q_{bc}$	1930–39	1940–49	1950–59	(5) $\alpha_{bc} = \varphi Q_{bc}$ $\alpha_{r(s)} + \alpha_{r(s)c} = \pi_1 Q_{r(s)}$	(6) $\alpha_{bc} = \varphi Q_{bc}$ $\alpha_{r(s)} + \alpha_{r(s)c} = \pi_1 Q_{r(s)}$	(7) $\alpha_{bc} = \varphi Q_{bc}$ $\alpha_{r(s)} + \alpha_{r(s)c} = \pi_1 Q_{r(s)} + \pi_2 D_{r(s)}$
Pupil-teacher ratio	1.76 (15.39)	−1.60 (15.46)	52.23 (5.40)	24.95 (7.92)	57.06 (5.55)	125.94 (15.62)	−1.60 (17.22)	−1.60 (16.77)	−1.60 (16.66)
Term length	...	0.92 (5.72)	−12.31 (3.86)	−7.60 (4.22)	−14.18 (6.59)	−53.85 (19.68)	0.92 (7.15)	0.92 (6.71)	0.92 (6.63)
Relative teacher salary	...	6.78 (2.85)	1.60 (0.99)	0.95 (1.60)	4.39 (1.34)	0.58 (2.17)	6.78 (3.44)	6.78 (3.24)	6.78 (3.21)
Demand and supply aggregates									
Regional average pupil-teacher ratio	...	...	...	...	...	...	0.37 (0.10)	0.10 (0.09)	−1.03 (0.28)
Regional average term length	...	...	...	...	...	...	...	0.32 (0.03)	0.35 (0.10)
Percent 12 years school	...	...	...	...	...	...	...	...	−0.75 (0.21)
Percent 1–3 years college	...	...	...	...	...	...	...	...	−0.94 (0.10)
Percent 4+ years college	...	...	...	...	...	...	...	...	−0.40 (0.18)
Percent manufacturing	...	...	...	...	...	...	...	...	0.05 (0.06)

Source: Authors' calculations. The number of observations = 1,323 (49 states of birth × 9 regions × 3 cohorts). The percent of the work force in the manufacturing industry was computed from the 1990 census (sample A) using male and female workers aged eighteen to sixty-five. The mean quality within a region of residence was calculated using the 1930–39, 1940–49, and 1950–59 birth cohorts.

a. Second-stage model: rate of return = $\alpha + \alpha_b + \alpha_{r(s)} + \alpha_c + \alpha_{bc} + \alpha_{r(s)c}$. The numbers in parentheses are Eicker-White standard errors.

b. The omitted education category is < 12 years of schooling. The pupil-teacher ratio and term length were divided by 100 in the regression. The attendance-based pupil-teacher ratio was used.

Table 7C-10. *Effect of Schooling Quality on the Marginal Rate of Return to Four or More Years of College, Nonlinear Model, 1990 Census*[a]

			Second-stage model restrictions						
				(4) $\alpha_{bc} = \varphi_c Q_{bc}$					
Measure[b]	(1) $\alpha_{bc} = \varphi Q_{bc}$	(2) $\alpha_{bc} = \varphi Q_{bc}$	(3) $\alpha_b + \alpha_{bc} = \varphi Q_{bc}$	1930–39	1940–49	1950–59	(5) $\alpha_{bc} = \varphi Q_{bc}$ $\alpha_{r(s)} + \alpha_{r(s)c} = \pi_1 Q_{r(s)}$	(6) $\alpha_{bc} = \varphi Q_{bc}$ $\alpha_{r(s)} + \alpha_{r(s)c} = \pi_1 Q_{r(s)}$	(7) $\alpha_{bc} = \varphi Q_{bc}$ $\alpha_{r(s)c} = \alpha_{r(s)c} = \pi_1 Q_{r(s)} + \pi_2 D_{r(s)}$
Pupil-teacher ratio	−93.37 (23.55)	−91.40 (23.77)	33.57 (10.31)	−9.48 (16.03)	31.05 (11.30)	182.51 (33.63)	−91.40 (27.91)	−91.40 (28.07)	−91.40 (27.94)
Term length	...	3.89 (8.74)	−13.38 (5.87)	−6.50 (5.88)	−26.32 (12.14)	−29.81 (32.38)	3.89 (11.87)	3.89 (11.83)	3.89 (11.76)
Relative teacher salary	...	−4.19 (5.95)	−4.18 (2.13)	−7.01 (3.70)	−2.63 (2.53)	4.02 (3.92)	−4.19 (6.94)	−4.19 (6.91)	−4.19 (6.89)
Demand and supply aggregates									
Regional average pupil-teacher ratio	...	...	...	...	...	...	−0.08 (0.17)	−0.32 (0.17)	−0.46 (0.49)
Regional average term length	...	...	...	...	...	...	...	0.28 (0.04)	0.18 (0.18)
Percent 12 years school	...	...	...	...	...	...	...	...	−0.42 (0.39)
Percent 1–3 years college	...	...	...	...	...	...	...	...	−0.73 (0.18)
Percent 4+ years college	...	...	...	...	...	...	...	...	0.14 (0.32)
Percent manufacturing	...	...	...	...	...	...	...	...	−0.14 (0.11)

Source: Authors' calculations. The number of observations = 1,323 (49 states of birth × 9 regions × 3 cohorts). The percent of the work force in the manufacturing industry was computed from the 1990 census (sample A) using male and female workers aged eighteen to sixty-five. The mean quality within a region of residence was calculated using the 1930–39, 1940–49, and 1950–59 birth cohorts.

a. Second-stage model: rate of return = $\alpha + \alpha_b + \alpha_{r(g)} + \alpha_c + \alpha_{bc} + \alpha_{r(s)c}$. The numbers in parentheses are Eicker-White standard errors. The pupil-teacher ratio and term length were divided by 100 in the regression. The attendance-based pupil-teacher ratio was used.

b. The omitted education category is < 12 years of schooling.

Table 7C-11. *The Effect of Schooling Quality on the Return to Education, Linear Model, with Region of Birth–Region of Residence Interactions, 1970 Census*[a]

Coefficent estimates	Second-stage model restrictions				
	(1)	(2)	(3)	(4)	(5)
	$\alpha_{bc} + \alpha_{r(b)r(s)} + \alpha_{r(b)r(s)c}$ $= \phi_{r(s)}Q_{bc} + \eta d$				$\alpha_b + \alpha_{bc} + \alpha_{r(b)r(s)} + \alpha_{r(b)r(s)c}$ $= \phi_{r(s)}Q_{bc} + \eta d$
Pupil-teacher ratio					
New England	2.67	...	...	2.68	12.24
	(5.05)			(5.11)	(4.76)
Middle Atlantic	− 8.55	...	...	− 9.71	− 0.36
	(3.72)			(3.74)	(2.76)
East North Central	− 12.15	...	...	− 12.33	2.52
	(3.48)			(3.55)	(2.56)
West North Central	− 3.27	...	...	− 5.81	5.01
	(4.00)			(4.00)	(2.93)
South Atlantic	− 16.57	...	...	− 17.32	− 7.97
	(3.61)			(3.64)	(2.37)
East South Central	2.77	...	...	2.83	12.59
	(4.90)			(4.97)	(4.12)
West South Central	− 11.58	...	...	− 13.47	− 3.39
	(3.89)			(3.87)	(2.72)
Mountain	− 7.14	...	...	− 7.69	2.86
	(3.99)			(4.06)	(2.90)
Pacific	− 11.26	...	...	− 11.89	− 1.96
	(3.52)			(3.66)	(2.45)
Teacher salary					
New England	...	1.03	...	0.40	− 0.44
		(0.78)		(0.85)	(0.64)
Middle Atlantic	...	1.07	...	1.12	0.28
		(0.56)		(0.64)	(0.40)
East North Central	...	1.07	...	0.72	− 0.17
		(0.55)		(0.60)	(0.38)
West North Central	...	1.10	...	1.43	0.50
		(0.74)		(0.76)	(0.57)
South Atlantic	...	1.03	...	1.06	0.17
		(0.60)		(0.66)	(0.37)
East South Central	...	1.08	...	0.42	− 0.49
		(0.75)		(0.80)	(0.64)
West South Central	...	1.05	...	1.38	0.45
		(0.72)		(0.80)	(0.52)
Mountain	...	1.06	...	0.70	− 0.21
		(0.69)	...	(0.75)	(0.58)
Pacific	...	1.04	...	0.90	0.02
		(0.58)		(0.63)	(0.36)

Table 7C-11. (Continued)

Coefficent estimates	(1)	(2)	(3)	(4)	(5)
	Second-stage model restrictions				
	$\alpha_{bc} + \alpha_{r(b)r(s)} + \alpha_{r(b)r(s)c} = \phi_{r(s)}Q_{bc} + \eta d$				$\alpha_b + \alpha_{bc} + \alpha_{r(b)r(s)} + \alpha_{r(b)r(s)c} = \phi_{r(s)}Q_{bc} + \eta d$
Term length					
New England	...	...	2.36	3.04	4.22
			(2.16)	(2.45)	(2.44)
Middle Atlantic	...	...	0.09	−0.36	0.88
			(1.17)	(1.34)	(1.34)
East North Central	...	...	3.61	3.47	4.96
			(1.18)	(1.31)	(1.23)
West North Central	...	...	−2.97	−3.47	−1.82
			(1.79)	(1.84)	(1.72)
South Atlantic	...	...	1.79	1.18	2.82
			(1.12)	(1.22)	(0.98)
East South Central	...	...	2.44	3.21	4.97
			(1.82)	(2.00)	(1.85)
West South Central	...	...	−1.32	−2.05	−0.18
			(1.26)	(1.48)	(1.28)
Mountain	...	...	2.59	2.63	4.25
			(1.32)	(1.51)	(1.44)
Pacific	...	...	1.96	1.61	3.03
			(1.01)	(1.11)	(0.99)
Distance[b]	1.17	1.28	1.35	1.28	1.04
	(0.24)	(0.23)	(0.23)	(0.25)	(0.25)
Distance squared[b]	−0.22	−0.26	−0.28	−0.25	−0.19
	(0.09)	(0.09)	(0.09)	(0.09)	(0.10)

Source: Authors' calculations. The number of observations = 1,764 (49 states of birth × 9 regions × 3 cohorts). The percent of the work force in the manufacturing industry was computed from the 1970 census using male and female workers aged eighteen to sixty-five. The mean quality within a region of residence was calculated using the 1910–19, 1920–29, 1930–39, and 1940–49 cohorts. The omitted education category is < 12 years. The pupil-teacher ratio and term length were divided by 100 in the regression. The attendance-based pupil-teacher ratio was used.

a. Second-stage model: rate of return = $\alpha + \alpha_b + \alpha_{r(s)} + \alpha_c + \alpha_{bc} + \alpha_{r(s)c} + \alpha_{r(s)r(b)} + \alpha_{r(s)r(b)c}$. The numbers in parentheses are Eicker-White standard errors.

b. Distance is measured in thousands of miles.

Table 7C-12. *The Effect of Schooling Quality on the Return to Education, Linear Model, with Region of Birth–Region of Residence Interactions, 1990 Census*[a]

	Second-stage model restrictions				
	(1)	(2)	(3)	(4)	(5)
Coefficent estimates					
	$\alpha_{bc} + \alpha_{r(b)r(s)} + \alpha_{r(b)r(s)c}$ $= \phi_{r(s)}Q_{bc} + \eta d$				$\alpha_b + \alpha_{bc} + \alpha_{r(b)r(s)} + \alpha_{r(b)r(s)c}$ $= \phi_{r(s)}Q_{bc} + \eta d$
Pupil-teacher ratio					
New England	−26.44	...	...	−27.57	−13.52
	(6.90)			(6.83)	(6.47)
Middle Atlantic	−29.07	...	...	−31.22	−17.47
	(8.39)			(8.41)	(7.79)
East North Central	−30.47	...	...	−32.10	−18.22
	(6.11)			(6.01)	(5.62)
West North Central	−24.09	...	...	−26.84	−11.55
	(7.20)			(7.12)	(6.62)
South Atlantic	−46.50	...	...	−48.90	−34.72
	(5.77)			(5.78)	(6.04)
East South Central	−28.10	...	...	−32.07	−18.09
	(6.38)			(6.18)	(5.15)
West South Central	−22.50	...	...	−25.95	−11.35
	(5.75)			(5.61)	(4.56)
Mountain	−14.85	...	...	−14.01	−0.24
	(8.22)			(8.07)	(7.99)
Pacific	−17.53	...	...	−18.57	−6.90
	(5.23)			(5.18)	(5.36)
Teacher salary					
New England	...	2.97	...	4.08	1.65
		(1.50)		(1.54)	(1.05)
Middle Atlantic	...	3.19	...	4.50	2.10
		(1.52)		(1.53)	(1.28)
East North Central	...	2.97	...	4.21	1.79
		(1.32)		(2.32)	(1.14)
West North Central	...	3.12	...	4.35	1.90
		(1.65)		(1.66)	(1.26)
South Atlantic	...	3.00	...	4.63	2.19
		(1.31)		(1.31)	(1.25)
East South Central	...	3.07	...	4.65	2.21
		(1.48)		(1.43)	(0.93)
West South Central	...	3.11	...	4.51	2.07
		(1.49)		(1.45)	(0.88)
Mountain	...	2.99	...	3.61	1.24
		(1.53)		(1.53)	(1.39)
Pacific	...	3.23	...	4.21	1.92
		(1.14)		(1.16)	(0.81)

Table 7C-12. *(Continued)*

| Coeffcent estimates | \multicolumn{5}{c}{Second-stage model restrictions} |
| | (1) | (2) | (3) | (4) | (5) |
	\multicolumn{4}{c}{$\alpha_{bc} + \alpha_{r(b)r(s)} + \alpha_{r(b)r(s)c}$ $= \phi_{r(s)}Q_{bc} + \eta d$}	$\alpha_b + \alpha_{bc} + \alpha_{r(b)r(s)} + \alpha_{r(b)r(s)c}$ $= \phi_{r(s)}Q_{bc} + \eta d$
Term length					
New England	...	...	−1.58	−3.19	16.09
			(3.38)	(3.53)	(3.89)
Middle Atlantic	...	...	−5.49	−7.73	10.80
			(4.27)	(4.40)	(5.10)
East North Central	...	...	−3.26	−5.12	13.60
			(2.86)	(2.85)	(4.28)
West North Central	...	...	−6.43	−7.50	11.50
			(4.35)	(4.49)	(4.91)
South Atlantic	...	...	−5.81	−9.67	9.46
			(3.67)	(3.51)	(4.92)
East South Central	...	...	−14.47	−16.21	2.80
			(3.57)	(3.64)	(3.91)
West South Central	...	...	−12.30	−13.10	5.68
			(3.38)	(3.49)	(3.61)
Mountain	...	...	5.63	6.38	23.34
			(4.17)	(4.14)	(5.11)
Pacific	...	...	−2.79	−3.14	11.95
			(2.38)	(2.36)	(3.81)
Distance[b]	2.09	2.27	2.44	2.26	1.65
	(0.26)	(0.25)	(0.25)	(0.25)	(0.32)
Distance squared[b]	−0.52	−0.57	−0.63	−0.58	−0.20
	(0.08)	(0.08)	(0.08)	(0.08)	(0.10)

Source: Authors' calculations. The number of observations = 1,343 (49 states of birth × 9 regions × 3 cohorts). The percent of the work force in the manufacturing industry was computed from the 1990 census using male and female workers aged eighteen to sixty-five. The mean quality within a region of residence was calculated using the 1930–39, 1940–49, and 1950–59 cohorts. The omitted education category is < 12 years. The pupil-teacher ratio and term length were divided by 100 in the regression. The attendance-based pupil-teacher ratio was used.

a. Second-stage model: rate of return = $\alpha + \alpha_b + \alpha_{r(s)} + \alpha_c + \alpha_{bc} + \alpha_{r(s)c} + \alpha_{r(s)r(b)} + \alpha_{r(s)r(b)c}$. The numbers in parentheses are Eicker-White standard errors.

b. Distance is measured in thousands of miles.

Table 7C-13. *Effect of Quality on Educational Attainment, by Birth Cohort, 1920–49, and Education Level, 1980 Census*[a]

Birth cohort and model	Pupil-teacher ratio[b]	Teacher salary	Term length
	College graduates		
1920–29			
(1)	−0.42	...	...
	(0.20)		
(2)	−0.44	1.08	0.36
	(0.18)	(0.74)	(0.13)
1930–39			
(1)	−0.59	...	...
	(0.22)		
(2)	−0.59	2.83	0.52
	(0.18)	(0.98)	(0.15)
1940–49			
(1)	−0.73	...	...
	(0.22)		
(2)	−0.75	2.38	0.73
	(0.18)	(1.19)	(0.16)
	High school graduates without college degrees[c]		
1920–29			
(1)	−0.34	...	...
	(0.14)		
(2)	−0.34	0.96	0.16
	(0.13)	(0.53)	(0.09)
1930–39			
(1)	−0.11	...	...
	(0.07)		
(2)	−0.10	0.61	−0.01
	(0.07)	(0.36)	(0.05)
1940–49			
(1)	−0.02	...	...
	(0.07)		
(2)	−0.01	−0.30	−0.14
	(0.07)	(0.46)	(0.06)

Table 7C-13. *(Continued)*

Birth cohort and model	Pupil-teacher ratio[b]	Teacher salary	Term length
	High school dropouts		
1920–29			
(1)	0.67	. . .	. . .
	(0.28)		
(2)	0.70	−1.60	−0.44
	(0.26)	(1.04)	(0.18)
1930–39			
(1)	0.78	. . .	. . .
	(0.32)		
(2)	0.77	−3.77	−0.61
	(0.28)	(1.51)	(0.23)
1940–49			
(1)	1.50	. . .	. . .
	(0.46)		
(2)	1.53	−3.43	−1.09
	(0.43)	(2.82)	(0.37)

Source: Authors' calculations. The dependent variable is the log of the proportion of people in each education category. The estimated coefficients give the percent change in the proportion of the state's population with a given education level for a 1 percent change in the quality measure.

a. [ln $(N_{Ed.\ level}$/Population) $= a + \ln(Q_{bc})\beta_c$]. The numbers in parentheses are standard errors.

b. Attendance based.

c. Includes men with some college.

Table 7C-14. *Effect of Quality on Educational Attainment, by Birth Cohort, 1910–49, and Education Level, 1970 Census*[a]

Birth cohort and model	Pupil-teacher ratio[b]	Teacher salary	Term length
	College graduates		
1910–19			
(1)	−0.56	...	...
	(0.23)		
(2)	−0.61	1.36	0.39
	(0.20)	(0.50)	(0.16)
1920–29			
(1)	−0.54	...	...
	(0.24)		
(2)	−0.53	1.97	0.32
	(0.21)	(0.86)	(0.15)
1930–39			
(1)	−0.79	...	...
	(0.25)		
(2)	−0.79	3.01	0.58
	(0.21)	(1.11)	(0.17)
1940–49			
(1)	−0.92	...	...
	(0.25)		
(2)	−0.92	3.03	0.67
	(0.21)	(1.41)	(0.18)
	High school graduates without college degrees[c]		
1910–19			
(1)	−0.51	...	...
	(0.20)		
(2)	−0.54	1.36	0.30
	(0.17)	(0.43)	(0.14)
1920–29			
(1)	−0.38	...	...
	(0.16)		
(2)	−0.39	0.93	0.22
	(0.15)	(0.61)	(0.10)
1930–39			
(1)	−0.20	...	...
	(0.09)		
(2)	−0.18	0.88	−0.05
	(0.09)	(0.48)	(0.07)
1940–49			
(1)	−0.21	...	...
	(0.08)		
(2)	−0.21	0.35	−0.10
	(0.09)	(0.57)	(0.07)

Table 7C-14. *(Continued)*

Birth cohort and model	Pupil-teacher ratio[b]	Teacher salary	Term length
	High school dropouts		
1910–19			
(1)	0.51	. . .	. . .
	(0.22)		
(2)	0.57	−1.11	−0.40
	(0.19)	(0.47)	(0.15)
1920–29			
(1)	0.57	. . .	. . .
	(0.26)		
(2)	0.59	−1.47	−0.39
	(0.24)	(0.97)	(0.17)
1930–39			
(1)	0.83	. . .	. . .
	(0.29)		
(2)	0.82	−3.17	−0.52
	(0.26)	(1.41)	(0.21)
1940–49			
(1)	1.35	. . .	. . .
	(0.38)		
(2)	1.35	−3.40	−0.87
	(0.36)	(2.35)	(0.31)

Source: Authors' calculations. The dependent variable is the log of the proportion of people in each education category. The estimated coefficients give the percent change in the proportion of the state's population with a given education level for a 1 percent change in the quality measure.

a. $[\ln (N_{Ed.\ level}/\text{Population}) = a + \ln(Q_{bc})\beta_c]$. The numbers in parentheses are standard errors.

b. Attendance based.

c. Includes men with some college.

Table 7C-15. *Effect of Quality on Educational Attainment, by Birth Cohort, 1930–59, and Education Level, 1990 Census*[a]

Birth cohort and model	Pupil-teacher ratio[b]	Teacher salary	Term length
	College graduates		
1930–39			
(1)	−0.62	. . .	. . .
	(0.22)		
(2)	−0.64	2.59	0.62
	(0.17)	(0.92)	(0.14)
1940–49			
(1)	−0.80	. . .	. . .
	(0.23)		
(2)	−0.83	2.34	0.78
	(0.18)	(1.20)	(0.16)
1950–51			
(1)	−0.94	. . .	. . .
	(0.30)		
(2)	−0.79	7.20	0.78
	(0.23)	(1.96)	(0.17)
	High school graduates without college degrees[c]		
1930–39			
(1)	−0.07	. . .	. . .
	(0.06)		
(2)	−0.06	0.63	0.02
	(0.06)	(0.34)	(0.05)
1940–49			
(1)	0.07	. . .	. . .
	(0.07)		
(2)	0.07	−0.55	−0.14
	(0.07)	(0.47)	(0.06)
1950–59			
(1)	0.09	. . .	. . .
	(0.11)		
(2)	0.06	−1.83	−0.20
	(0.96)	(0.82)	(0.07)

Table 7C-15. (Continued)

Birth cohort and model	Pupil-teacher ratio[b]	Teacher salary	Term length
	High school dropouts		
1930–39			
(1)	0.88	. . .	. . .
	(0.42)		
(2)	0.88	−4.87	−0.90
	(0.37)	(1.96)	(0.29)
1940–49			
(1)	1.59	. . .	. . .
	(0.58)		
(2)	1.63	−3.93	−1.27
	(0.55)	(3.61)	(0.47)
1950–59			
(1)	2.66	. . .	. . .
	(0.75)		
(2)	2.45	−10.89	−1.07
	(0.71)	(6.12)	(0.52)

Source: Authors' calculations. The dependent variable is the log of the proportion of people in each education category. The estimated coefficients give the percent change in the proportion of the state's population with a given education level for a 1 percent change in the quality measure.

a. $[\ln (N_{Ed.\ level}/\text{Population}) = a + \ln(Q_{bc})\beta_c]$. The numbers in parentheses are standard errors.

b. Attendance based.

c. Includes men with some college.

Appendix D: Rejoinder to David Card and Alan Krueger

The survey by Card and Krueger in this volume acknowledges developments inspired by their work and at the same time retreats from the basic position previously maintained in that work.[76] In summarizing our research, they now recognize that there are many different effects of schooling quality on earnings, in contrast to the one effect they focused on in their earlier paper. In fact, our paper identifies more than the four effects defined in the models they consider.[77] We distinguish various effects of quality on individual earnings, including the effect of increasing quality at a given level of education, the effect of quality on educational attainment, and the effect of quality and schooling aggregates on the pricing of both the quantity and the quality of schooling. These different effects answer different policy questions.

Retreating from the position in their 1992 paper, Card and Krueger in their survey no longer distinguish between "causal" effects of quality on earnings and correlations between quality and earnings.[78] What is missing in their interpretation of the evidence is any parameter that might usefully inform educational policy planning. None of the estimates in their tables 5-1 to 5-3 can be said to approximate, in any well-defined sense, the effect of mandated increases in schooling expenditure on earnings. None effectively counters the Coleman report's (1966) critique that measured schooling quality is only a proxy for family background and early community influences. Moreover, since much of the evidence they present is for models that we test and reject, even their associational evidence is not as clear as they make it out to be.

Our nonparametric test of stability in the ranks in earnings distributions across regions of residence for persons born in the same state is consistent with the Coleman report's analysis. So is our evidence of no correlation between the ranks in earnings and the ranks in schooling quality within a state of residence. The data support the notion that early environments affect earnings. They do not clearly separate the effects of schooling quality from the effects of family background.

It is important to reemphasize a major point made in our papers.[79]

76. Card and Krueger (1992b).
77. Heckman, Layne-Farrar, and Todd (1996).
78. Estimates from the econometric scheme introduced in that work are now placed side by side with OLS estimates that do not control for state-of-birth fixed effects that were a source of bias they sought to eliminate in their 1992 paper.
79. Heckman, Layne-Farrar, and Todd (1996).

Even granting Card and Krueger's functional form assumptions about linearity in education and about the absence of certain interactions, their fixed effect estimation method does not separate quality effects from early environmental effects. It only separates state-of-birth effects from state-of-residence effects in the intercept and slope of log wage–education equations. Their strategy for separating quality effects from family-background effects hinges on assumptions about which state-of-birth effects will be regressed on the aggregate measures of quality. The particular choice crucially affects their estimates. Table 7D-1, which summarizes estimates from our chapter in this volume, illustrates this point. Consider estimates of the effects of quality on the slope ("rate of return"), the parameter emphasized in the original Card and Krueger study. The sharp contrast in any row between the estimates in the columns labeled with state effects and without state effects demonstrates that the decision of which state-of-birth effects to relate to quality makes a great deal of difference. There is a substantial change in the size and sign of the estimated quality effect depending on whether returns are deviated from state means (with state fixed effects versus without state fixed effects). Why should quality be related only to the interaction between state of birth and cohort in the rate of return? Why exclude–or include–main effects? The decomposition of state-of-birth effects into "quality" and "other early environmental" effects is clearly very arbitrary and has substantial consequences for the estimated effect of quality on earnings. Nothing in the methodology of Card and Krueger resolves the fundamental problem of separating the effect of quality from the effects of other early environmental factors on earnings.

Linearity of the Earnings Equation in Education

The evidence in our papers, in Hungerford and Solon, and in Jaeger and Page clearly refutes linearity of the earnings function in terms of years of education.[80] Our papers demonstrate that relaxing linearity leads to different inferences about the quality-earnings relationship. The only evidence of any effect of quality on earnings is for college graduates. We also note that the differential effects of local labor-market shocks on the

---

80. Heckman, Layne-Farrar, and Todd (1996); Hungerford and Solon (1987); Jaeger and Page (1996).

rates of return to various educational classes eliminates linearity as a valid description of the earnings function.

Card and Krueger's response to the evidence that there is no measurable effect of quality for high school graduates is to invoke a form of the ability bias argument. They present conditions under which the only measured effect of schooling quality is on the earnings of highly educated workers. If ability bias is an important factor, all of the estimated earnings equations summarized in their tables are just correlations without any causal foundation. No causal parameter is being estimated and hence no policy prescription is possible using their evidence.

In light of our strong evidence against linearity, we are surprised that they choose to report only the results from our linear specification in their table 5-3. A better summary is presented by the nonlinear results in table 7D-1, which demonstrate the wide range of estimates of the effect of quality on earnings when linearity is relaxed.

Selective Migration and Comparative Advantage

Card and Krueger acknowledge a main finding of our paper: that there are statistically significant and numerically important state-of-birth–region-of-residence interactions in the rate of return to schooling. The presence of these interactions undermines the empirical strategy used by Card and Krueger in their earlier study to separate state-of-birth effects from region-of-residence effects. There is no longer a unique state-of-birth effect that can be identified separately from a region-of-residence effect. Such interactions could arise if migration is selective on earnings and if there are costs of migration that depend on distance.

Introducing interactions, as we do, demonstrates that there is a problem with Card and Krueger's identifying assumptions but does not solve the problem. A more general model of selective migration has to be estimated. (We are currently undertaking this task.) Accordingly, no special causal significance can be assigned to the summary of evidence reported in table 5-5 of Card and Krueger's survey. As shown by the regional interaction results in table 7D-1, when their identifying assumption is relaxed, the estimated effects of quality on earnings are statistically strong and perverse for the New England census region, weak for many other regions, and statistically significant and "of the right sign" only for a few regions.

Table 7D-1. Effect of Pupil-Teacher Ratio on Return to One Year of Schooling, Census Years 1970, 1980, 1990[a]

Model	1970		1980		1990	
	With state effects[b]	Without state effects[c]	With state effects[b]	Without state effects[c]	With state effects[b]	Without state effects[c]
Linear–α	-1.51 (0.26)	-0.36 (0.12)	-1.07 (0.25)	0.23 (0.09)	-1.81 (0.25)	0.26 (0.13)
Fixed effects–θ[d]	0.15 (0.02)	0.01 (0.02)	0.17 (0.02)	-0.06 (0.01)	0.23 (0.02)	-0.11 (0.01)
Nonlinear						
Linear base	0.39 (0.43)	0.06 (0.20)	-0.50 (0.32)	0.60 (0.12)	1.44 (0.79)	0.05 (0.30)
Marginal return to 1–3 years of college	-2.82 (2.25)	-0.33 (0.97)	-4.93 (2.14)	2.08 (0.64)	-0.27 (2.63)	8.88 (0.92)
Marginal return to 4 or more years of college	-9.30 (3.25)	1.42 (1.38)	-4.83 (2.78)	-0.77 (1.02)	-15.54 (4.04)	5.71 (1.75)
Regional interaction						
New England	0.46 (0.87)	...	1.29 (0.75)	...	-4.69 (1.16)	...
Middle Atlantic	-1.65 (0.64)	...	-1.23 (0.58)	...	-5.31 (1.43)	...

East North Central	−2.10 (0.60)	...	−1.16 (0.52)	...	−5.46 (1.02)	...
West North Central	−0.99 (0.68)	...	−0.88 (0.60)	...	−4.56 (1.21)	...
South Atlantic	−2.94 (0.62)	...	−1.58 (0.54)	...	−8.31 (0.98)	...
East South Central	−0.48 (0.84)	...	−1.05 (0.63)	...	−5.45 (1.05)	...
West South Central	−2.29 (0.66)	...	−0.47 (0.49)	...	−4.41 (0.95)	...
Mountain	−1.31 (0.69)	...	−0.42 (0.52)	...	−2.38 (1.37)	...
Pacific	−2.02 (0.62)	...	−0.92 (0.50)	...	−3.16 (0.88)	...

Source: Authors' calculations as presented in this chapter. Standard errors shown in parentheses. The results for the linear − α model are taken from tables 7-7, 7C-1, 7C-2; for the fixed effects − θ model, from tables 7-9, 7C-3, 7C-4; for the nonlinear models, from tables 7-11, 7C-5 through 7C-10; and for the regional interaction models, from tables 7-16, 7C-11. The latter results are based on the specification found in column 4 of these tables.

a. The change in the percentage return to one year of education for a 1 percent change in the pupil-teacher ratio. Because the pupil-teacher ratio declines with increasing quality, negative numbers indicate an increase in the return. Calculations assume seventeen students per class. See this chapter for details on these specifications and for notation.

b. With state effects refers to the specification including state-of-birth dummy variables. In this specification quality is modeled as $\alpha_{bc} = \varphi Q_{bc}$. In most tables this specification is presented in column 2.

c. Without state effects refers to the specification omitting state-of-birth dummy variables from the list of regressors. In this specification quality is modeled as $\alpha_b + \alpha_{bc} = \varphi Q_{bc}$. In most tables these results are presented in column 3.

d. For the specifications in this row, quality enters the wage equations through the intercept terms. For the specifications with state effects, the model is $\theta_{bc} = \varphi Q_{bc}$. For the specifications without state effects, the model is $\theta_b + \theta_{bc} = \varphi Q_{bc}$.

The Power of Nonparametric Tests

In our paper we use two nonparametric rank tests. One shows no relationship between quality ranks and earnings ranks. The other shows some stability in ranks across state-of-residence earnings distributions for persons born in a given state. Our rejection of the second hypothesis—that there are no stable state-of-birth effects across regions of residence in earnings distributions—but not the first hypothesis—that there is no correlation between the quality ranks and the earnings ranks across regions of residence—is consistent with the Coleman report's finding and is also consistent with our evidence of weak effects of quality on earnings. Moreover, the fact that the second test rejects but the first does not shows that no categorical statement can be made that our rank tests have "limited power." Note also that we perform these tests at two levels of education, for high school graduates and for college graduates, so our results are not only "for middle levels of education," as Card and Krueger claim.

Reduced Form Models

Reduced form models of quality on education answer one interesting question—what is the effect of quality inclusive of its effect on stimulation of educational attainment? But they suffer from some of the same defects as structural models. Use of reduced form models eliminates the ability bias problem. However, the problem of separating family environmental effects from schooling quality remains. So does the problem of endogeneity arising from factors of political economy that lead one state to spend more on schooling quality than another. For these issues, the aggregate strategy used by Card and Krueger in their earlier paper is no more likely to be successful in reduced form models than in the conditional (on education) models.

Aggregation

Card and Krueger use the argument advanced in our companion paper to explain the empirical regularity first detected by Julian Betts and by Eric Hanushek, Steven Rivkin, and Lori Taylor that estimated quality effects based on more aggregative quality measures are more positive.[81]

81. See Betts's chapter in this volume (chapter 6) and Hanushek, Rivkin, and Taylor (1995).

We note that if more able students receive more school resources, self-selection biases should make estimates based on disaggregated school or school district quality measures more positive than estimates based on state-aggregated quality measures, which average out individual ability components that are likely to be positively correlated with individual schooling quality. Averaging reduces the correlation between the individual level components of quality and ability. Of course, if at the individual level (district or school) less able people receive more resources than more able people, as Card and Krueger claim the literature finds, the estimated effect of quality on earnings would be *downward* biased and using state average measures would *raise* the estimated effect of quality on earnings. This could explain the evidence on aggregation rather nicely.

In our companion paper we go on to note that if states allocate more funds to districts with more able people, the estimated schooling quality effect based on aggregates would be larger than the effect based on individual district or school data measures. Egalitarian redistribution policies across districts would make estimates based on the more aggregative measures less positive. Since there are several levels of aggregation, it is possible that aggregation from the school to the district to the state could have nonmonotonic effects of educational quality on earnings as a function of the level of aggregation.

Even if school districts are egalitarian, states need not be. Moreover, even if states are neutral in terms of transferring resources across districts with students of different levels of ability, if voters in districts with more able children spend more money on schools, egalitarianism within a district could be offset by greater expenditure in districts that on average have more able children. As a result the use of more aggregated measures of schooling quality in individual earnings regressions might generate more positive estimated effects of schooling quality on earnings, despite intradistrict egalitarianism. Much more study of the political economy of school expenditure is required to understand the importance of this argument. One needs to decompose between district and within district spending-ability relationships before any definite conclusion on this matter can be reached.

Conclusion

Card and Krueger now agree with us that the jury is still out on the question whether there is a causal effect of schooling quality on earnings. Their evidence and our evidence reveal an association between quality and earnings for the college educated. Our nonparametric evidence reveals a stronger and more robust effect for state-of-birth effects on earnings than for quality effects on earnings. The relationship between earnings and state-of-birth could arise from family background, community effects, schooling quality, or other early environmental factors.

References

Behrman, Jere R., and Nancy Birdsall. 1983. "The Quality of Schooling: Quantity Alone Is Misleading." *American Economic Review* 73 (December): 928–46.

Blanchflower, Daniel, and Andrew Oswald. 1994. *The Wage Curve*. MIT Press.

Card, David, and Alan B. Krueger. 1992a. "School Quality and Black-White Relative Earnings: A Direct Assessment." *Quarterly Journal of Economics* 107 (February): 151–200.

———. 1992b. "Does School Quality Matter: Returns to Education and the Characteristics of Public Schools in the United States." *Journal of Political Economy* 100 (February): 1–40.

———. 1994. "The Economic Return to School Quality: A Partial Survey." Working paper. Princeton University.

Coleman, James S., and others. 1966. *Equality of Educational Opportunity*. Government Printing Office.

Hamilton, Horace. 1959–60. "Educational Selectivity of Net Migration from the South." *Social Forces* 38: 33–42.

Hanushek, Eric A. 1986. "The Economics of Schooling: Production and Efficiency in Public Schools." *Journal of Economic Literature* 24 (September): 1141–77.

———. 1989. "The Impact of Differential Expenditures on School Performance." *Educational Researcher* 18 (May): 45–51, 62.

———. 1991. "When School Finance 'Reform' May Not Be Good Policy." *Harvard Journal of Legislation* 28 (Summer): 423–56.

Hanushek, Eric A., Steven G. Rivkin, and Lori L. Taylor. 1994. "Aggregation, Omitted Variables and the Estimation of Educational Production Functions." University of Rochester.

———. 1995. "The Identification of School Resource Effects." University of Rochester.

Harbison, Ralph W., and Eric A. Hanushek. 1992. *Educational Performance of the Poor: Lessons from Rural Northeast Brazil*. Oxford University Press for the World Bank.

Heckman, James, Anne Layne-Farrar, and Petra Todd. 1996. "Human Capital Pricing Equations with an Application to Estimating the Effect of Schooling Quality on Earnings." *Review of Economics and Statistics* (forthcoming).

Heckman, James, and Derek Neal. 1996. "Coleman's Contribution to Education: An Intellectual Odyssey." In *James S. Coleman: Falmer Sociology Series.* London-New York-Philadelphia: Falmer Press.

Heckman, James, and Jose Scheinkman. 1987. "The Importance of Bundling in a Gorman-Lancaster Model of Earnings." *Review of Economic Studies* 54 (April): 243–55.

Hedges, Larry V., Richard D. Laine, and Rob Greenwald. 1994. "Does Money Matter? A Meta-Analysis of Studies of the Effects of Differential School Inputs on Student Outcomes." *Educational Researcher* 23 (April): 5–14.

Hungerford, Thomas, and Gary Solon. 1987. "Sheepskin Effects in the Returns to Education." *Review of Economics and Statistics* 69 (February): 175–77.

Jaeger, David, and Marianne Page. 1996. "Degrees Matter: New Evidence on Sheepskin Effects in Returns to Education." *Review of Economics and Statistics* (forthcoming).

Johnson, George E., and Frank P. Stafford. 1973. "Social Returns to Quantity and Quality of Schooling." *Journal of Human Resources* 8 (Spring): 139–55.

Mincer, Jacob. 1974. *Schooling, Experience and Earnings.* New York: National Bureau of Economic Research.

Rosen, Sherwin. 1983. "A Note on Aggregation of Skills and Labor Quality." *Journal of Human Resources* 18 (Summer): 425–31.

Sattinger, Michael. 1980. *Capital and the Distribution of Labor Earnings.* New York: North Holland.

Tinbergen, Jan. 1975. *Income Distribution: Analysis and Policies.* New York: American Elsevier.

Wachtel, Paul. 1976. "The Effect on Earnings of School and College Investment Expenditures." *Review of Economics and Statistics* 58 (August): 326–31.

Index